ou are now ent

he Magic Whistle

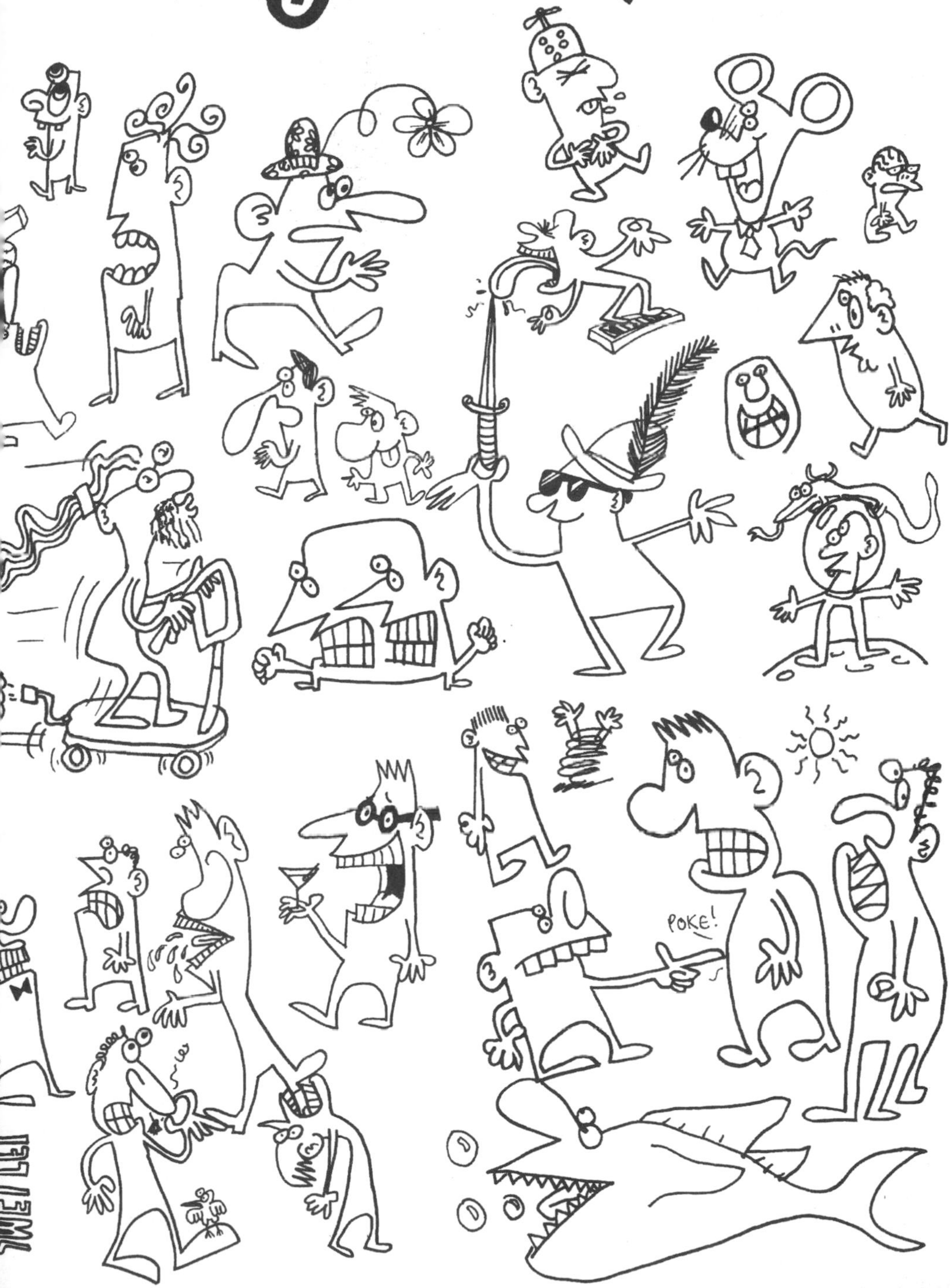
POKE!

Yeah, that's right. I'm saying what you're thinking.[1]

The short story: This is essentially an attempt to gain the legitimacy of "graphic novels"[2] while still keeping a foot in the ever self-marginalizing direct market. Instead of doing three "pamphlets"[3] a year[4], why not do one roughly annual volume? We'll see how this works.

This will probably cause a little more confusion. Long-time readers may see this and pass on it thinking it's reprints of earlier issues. New readers may buy this and pass on back issues thinking they're collected here[5]. To avoid this, here is a record of *Magic Whistle*'s publishing history so far.

MAGIC WHISTLE volume 1, numbers 1-10 (self-published, 1993-1997, out of print)
1-8-   @5 1/2" x 8 1/2" photocopied, 20 pages b/w including covers on color stock.
9-   5 1/2" x 8 1/2" photocopied, 36 pages b/w including covers on color stock.
10-   6" x 9" offset on newsprint, 32 pages b/w plus 2-color cover on slick paper.

MAGIC WHISTLE volume 2, numbers 1-9 (Alternative Comics, 1998-present)
1-8-   @6" x 9" on 50 lb. stock, 32 pages plus color covers on slick paper.
9-   You're reading it.

-v1#s1-8 were collected in *Humor Can Be Funny,* two versions of this exist: Dodecaphonic Books (1996, out of print) and 2004 (Alternative Comics)
-v1#s9 and 10, v2#s1-3 were collected in *The Magic Whistle Blows* (St. Martin's Griffin, 1999, try Amazon)
-v2#s4-8 have yet to be reprinted anywhere.

Both collections omit a few contents as well as add a few from other sources. There was also a collection called *Oh That Monroe* in 1995 that is long out of print and has no overlap with either of the aforementioned books[6].

Sorry to waste space for those who already know this stuff, but while I'm here, I'll waste some more space to answer the question I'm most tired of answering …

Are you the Spongebob guy?

I was *a* Spongebob guy during the last season of the show. I was one of six people with the title of storyboard director, there are a few gags that are unmistakably mine, I still keep in touch with some of the crew, and would gladly work with them again. It paid well and I lived off what I saved for a few months after I left. I'm grateful to have had such an opportunity when I had no prior experience in animation, and being nominated for an Emmy is a great addition to my resume. **But**, and I can't stress this enough—*especially to potential employers whom I've later found out were interested in contacting me but didn't bother because they assumed I was busy with Spongebob*— I have had nothing to do with the show since writing stopped production in November 2001.

And I don't, nor have I ever, had the authority to get free Spongebob merchandise for you.

I have a funny comic book[8] for you to read, though. I hope you like it. And if you're a Hollywood bigwig, hire me.

KA-BLOOM
NERDS!!
YOU THINK BECAUSE YOU'RE RICH AND FAMOUS, YOU CAN KICK GUYS LIKE ME AROUND! I THINK YOU'RE JEALOUS OF NEW TALENT.
HACK!
PICKLES
TEX DREW

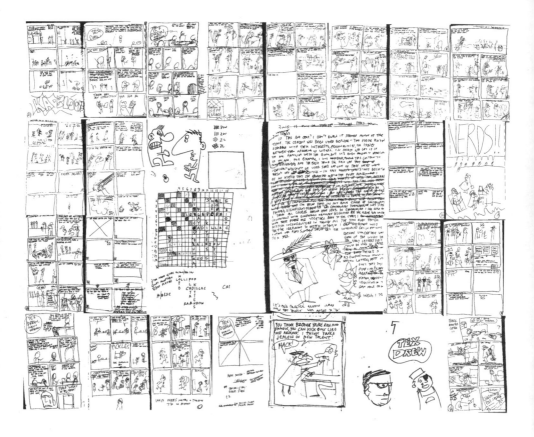

1. Though if you've already paid for this and are reading it at home, I guess these questions are moot.
2. A term I despise for the same reason I hate politically correct language in that it's one of those phrases that's coined with the intent to enforce tolerance of a particular culture or idea, but instead polarizes things further.
3. ibid.
4. More or less
5. See note 1.
6. Oops. OTM does reprint four pages from the first self-published MW.
7. Ironically, when I started at the show, nobody ever heard of it and a lot of people assumed I was making it up. Now that it's over, well… enough venting.
8. That's right, I said it. Comic book.

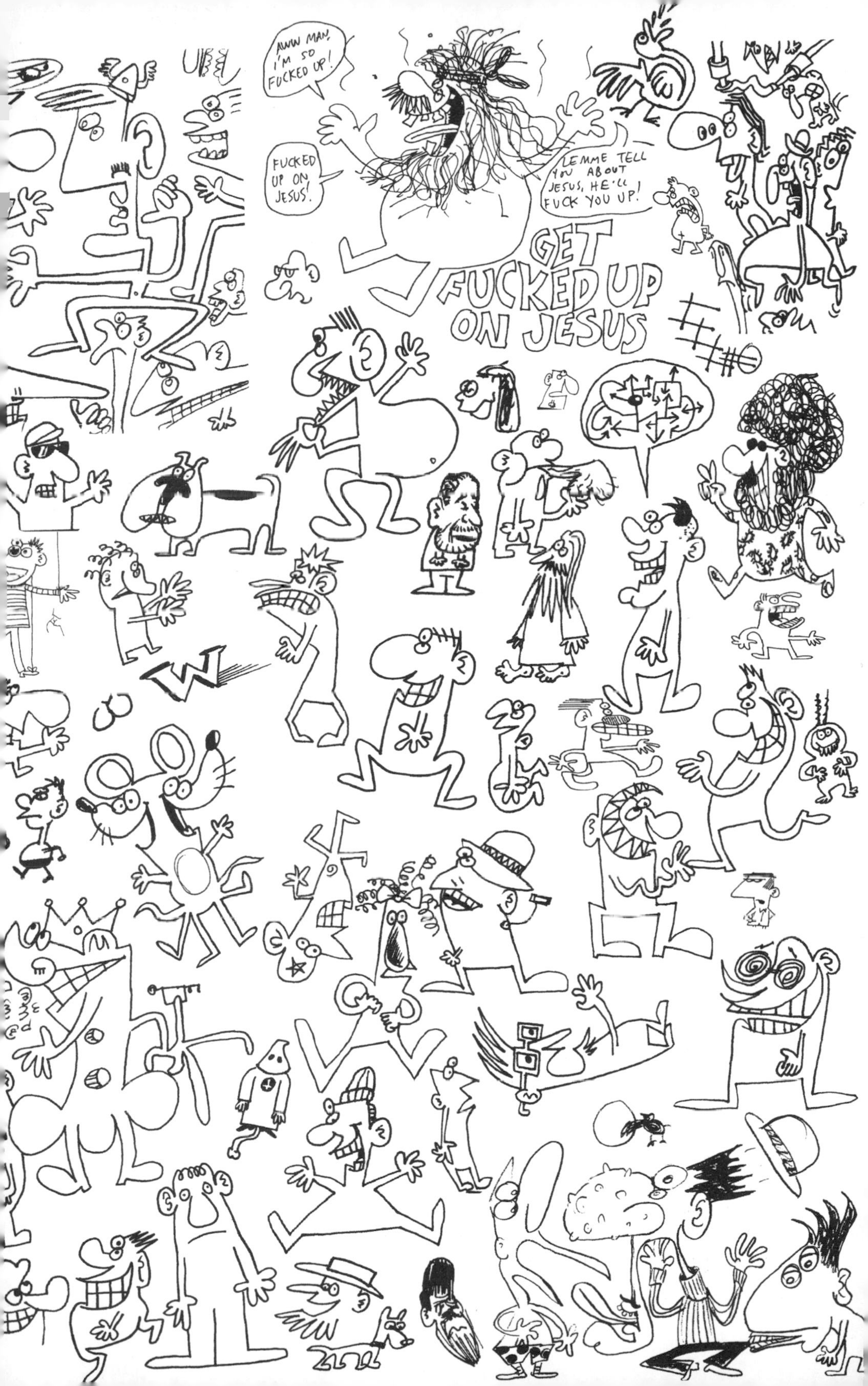
AWW MAN, I'M SO FUCKED UP!
FUCKED UP ON JESUS!
LEMME TELL YOU ABOUT JESUS, HE'LL FUCK YOU UP!
GET FUCKED UP ON JESUS

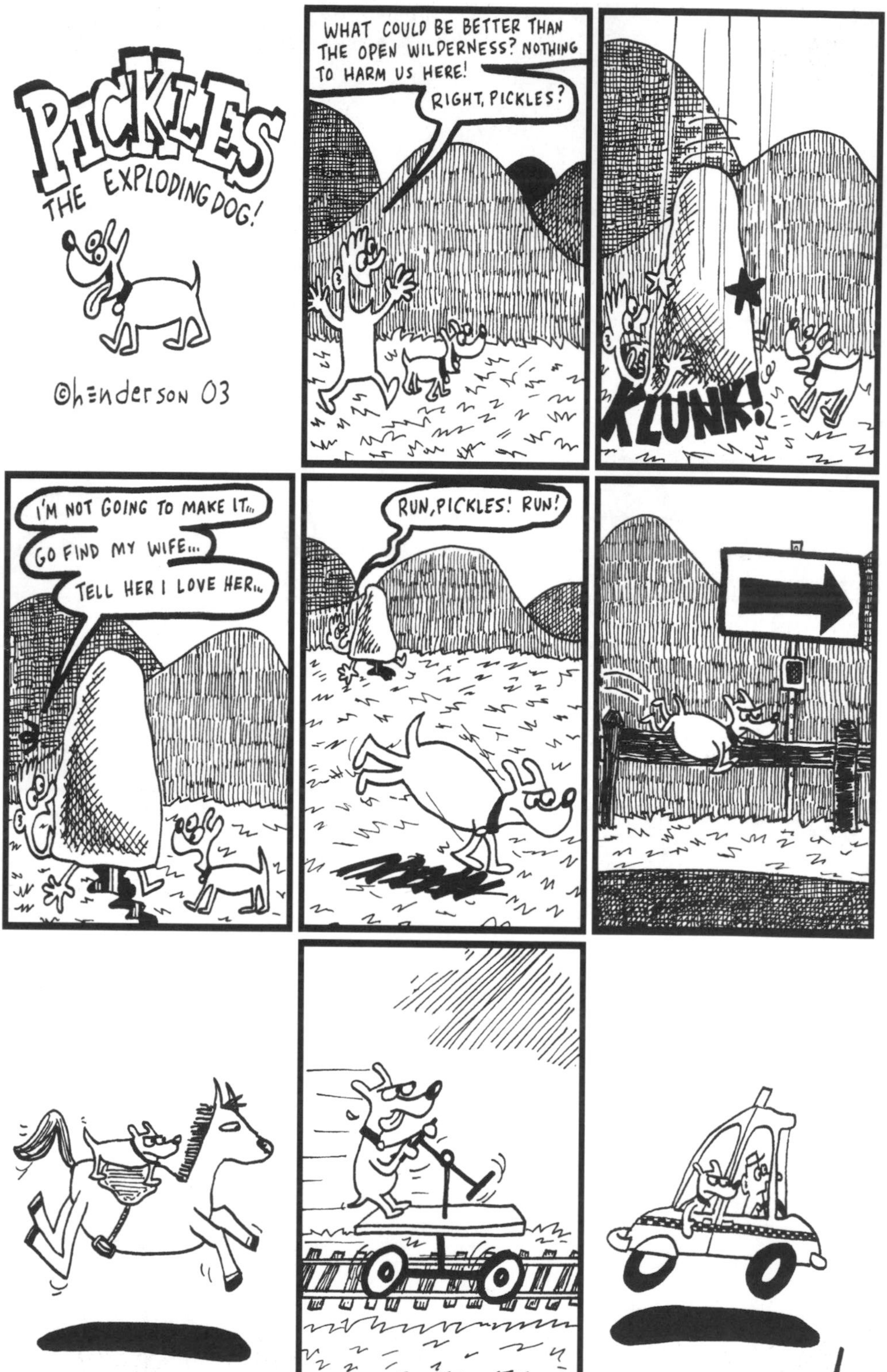
PICKLES
THE EXPLODING DOG!
©henderson 03
WHAT COULD BE BETTER THAN THE OPEN WILDERNESS? NOTHING TO HARM US HERE!
RIGHT, PICKLES?
KLUNK!
I'M NOT GOING TO MAKE IT...
GO FIND MY WIFE...
TELL HER I LOVE HER...
RUN, PICKLES! RUN!
1

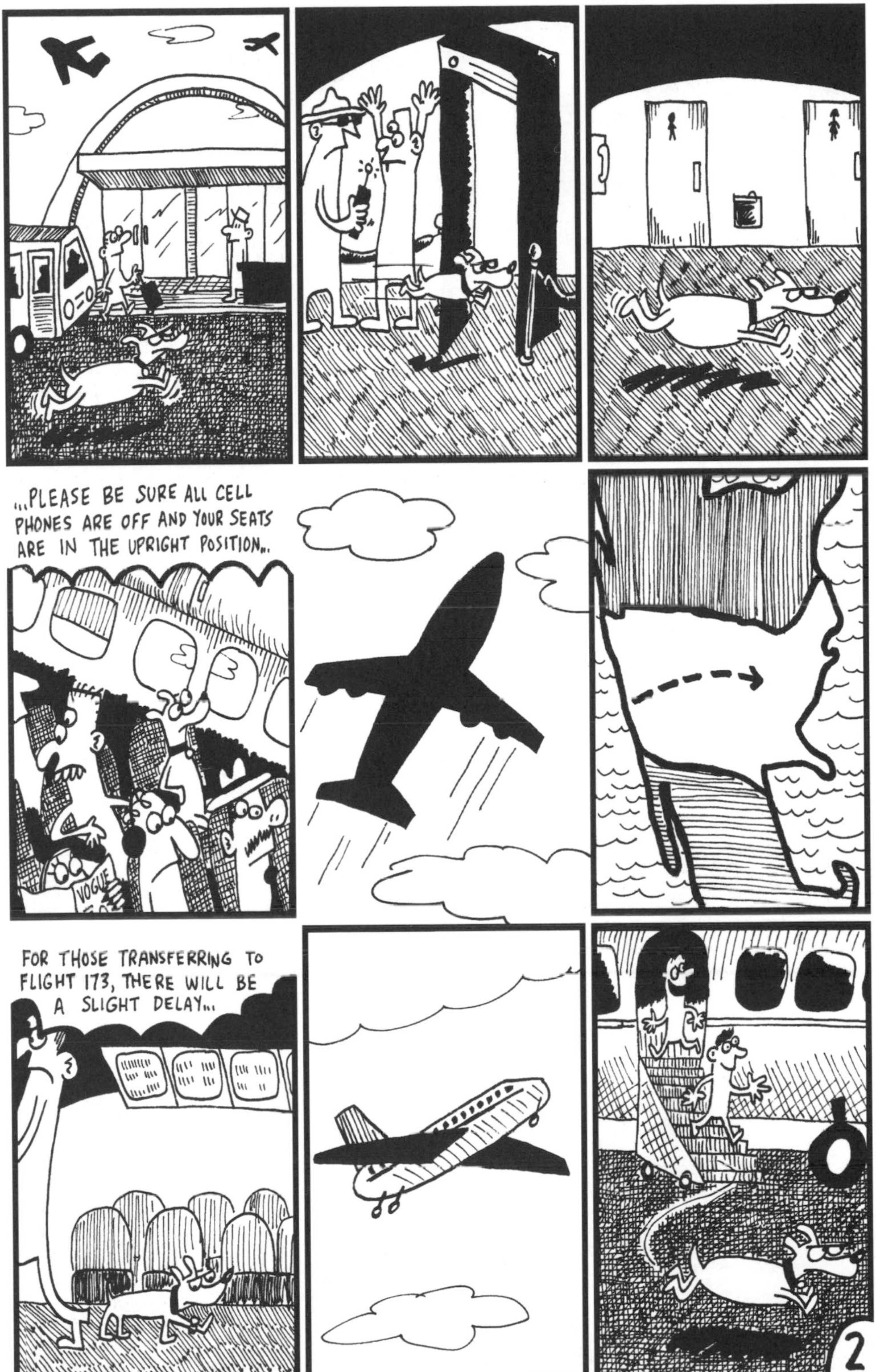
...PLEASE BE SURE ALL CELL PHONES ARE OFF AND YOUR SEATS ARE IN THE UPRIGHT POSITION...
VOGUE
FOR THOSE TRANSFERRING TO FLIGHT 173, THERE WILL BE A SLIGHT DELAY...
2

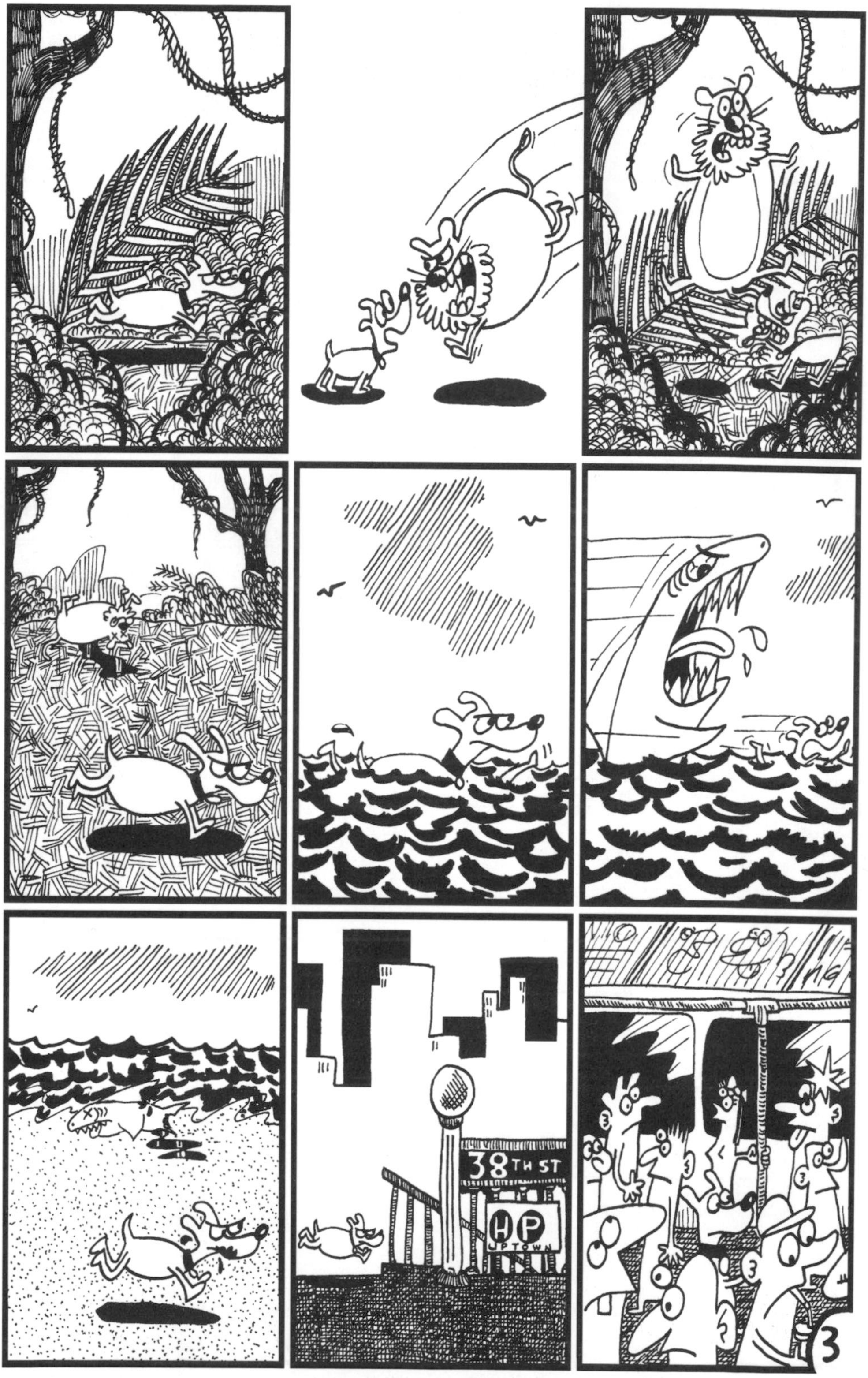
38TH ST
HP
UPTOWN
3

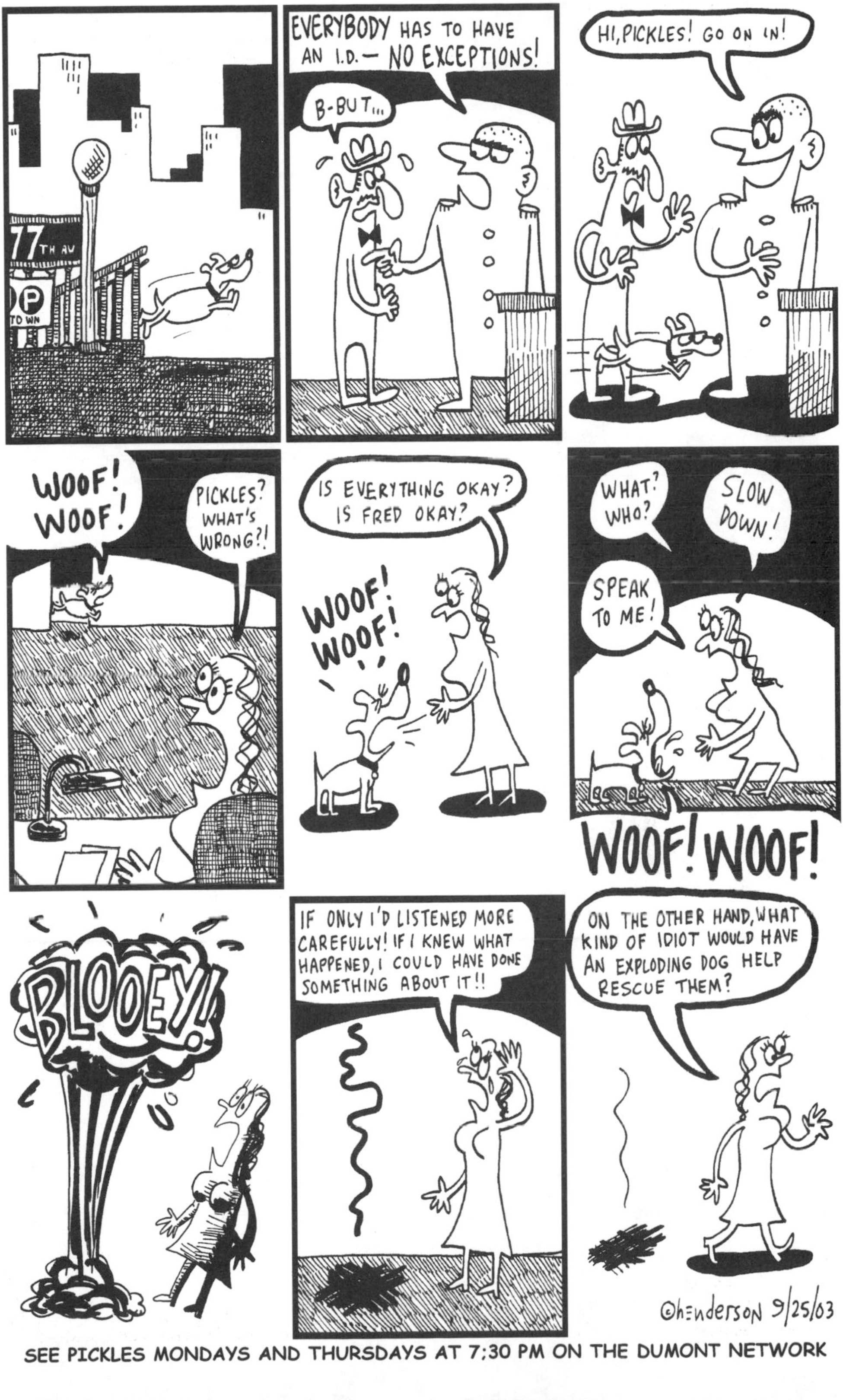
77TH AV
EVERYBODY HAS TO HAVE AN I.D.— NO EXCEPTIONS!
B-BUT...
HI, PICKLES! GO ON IN!
WOOF! WOOF!
PICKLES? WHAT'S WRONG?!
IS EVERYTHING OKAY? IS FRED OKAY?
WOOF! WOOF!
WHAT? WHO?
SLOW DOWN!
SPEAK TO ME!
WOOF! WOOF!
BLOOEY!
IF ONLY I'D LISTENED MORE CAREFULLY! IF I KNEW WHAT HAPPENED, I COULD HAVE DONE SOMETHING ABOUT IT!!
ON THE OTHER HAND, WHAT KIND OF IDIOT WOULD HAVE AN EXPLODING DOG HELP RESCUE THEM?
©henderson 9/25/03

SEE PICKLES MONDAYS AND THURSDAYS AT 7:30 PM ON THE DUMONT NETWORK

DON'T ASK!!!

STARRING OINKY, THE PIG-FACED CAT

MEOWY, THE CAT-FACED BIRD

SINGY, THE BIRD-FACED MOUSE

AND INTRODUCING FACEY, THE FACE-FACED FACE

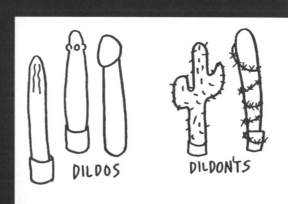

DILDOS

DILDON'TS

DON'T BE PLAYIN' ME LIKE THAT!

ME

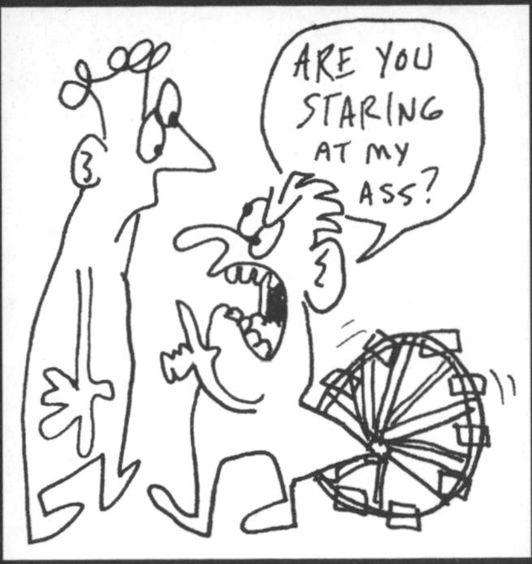
ARE YOU STARING AT MY ASS?

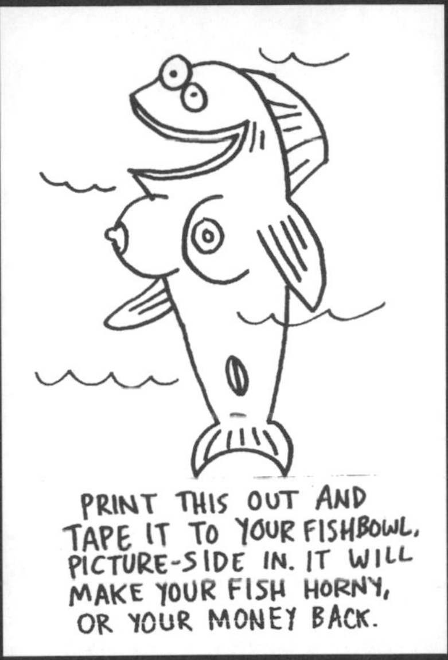
PRINT THIS OUT AND TAPE IT TO YOUR FISHBOWL, PICTURE-SIDE IN. IT WILL MAKE YOUR FISH HORNY, OR YOUR MONEY BACK.

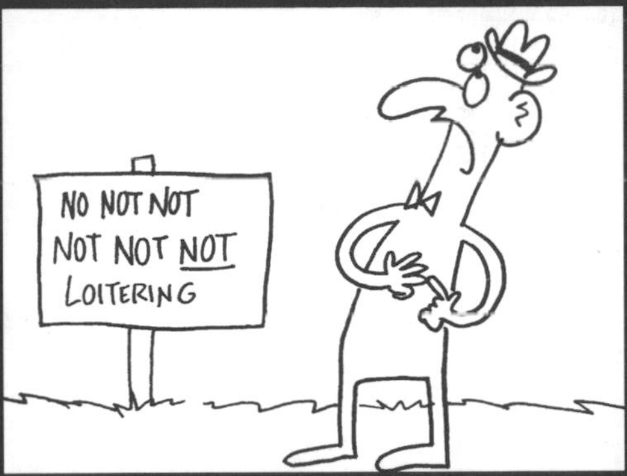
NO NOT NOT NOT NOT NOT LOITERING

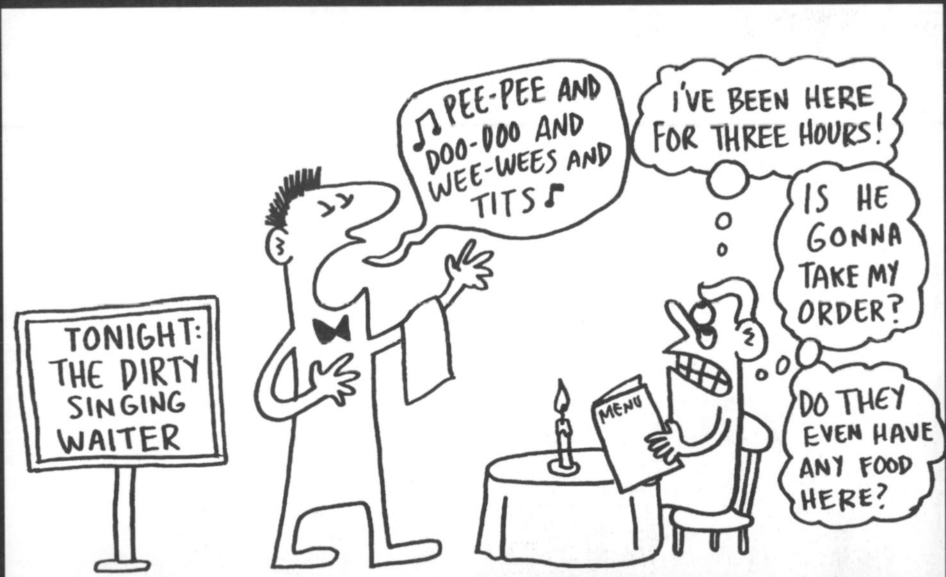
TONIGHT: THE DIRTY SINGING WAITER
♫ PEE-PEE AND DOO-DOO AND WEE-WEES AND TITS ♪
I'VE BEEN HERE FOR THREE HOURS!
IS HE GONNA TAKE MY ORDER?
DO THEY EVEN HAVE ANY FOOD HERE?
MENU

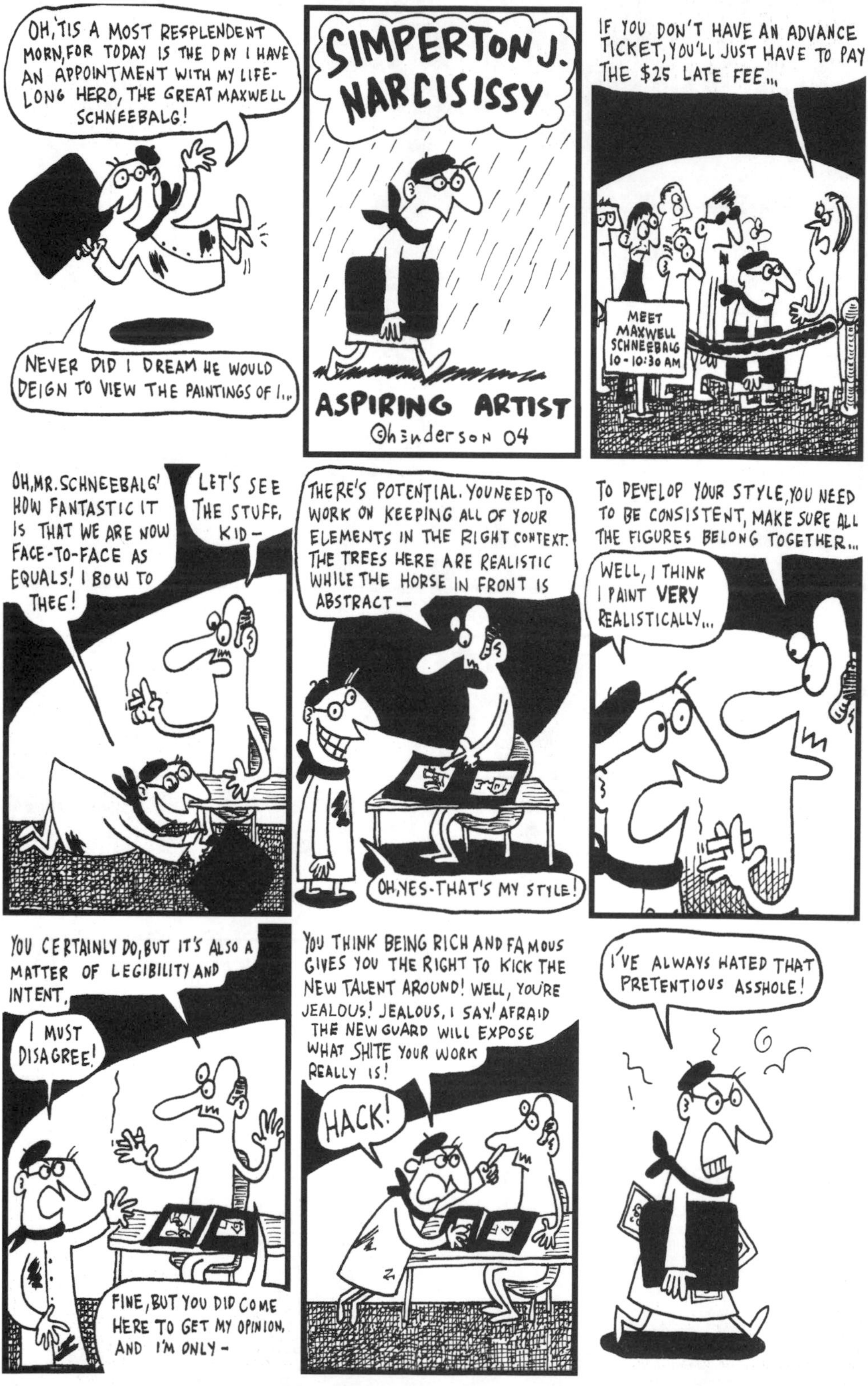
OH, 'TIS A MOST RESPLENDENT MORN, FOR TODAY IS THE DAY I HAVE AN APPOINTMENT WITH MY LIFE-LONG HERO, THE GREAT MAXWELL SCHNEEBALG!
NEVER DID I DREAM HE WOULD DEIGN TO VIEW THE PAINTINGS OF I...
SIMPERTON J. NARCISISSY
ASPIRING ARTIST
©henderson 04
IF YOU DON'T HAVE AN ADVANCE TICKET, YOU'LL JUST HAVE TO PAY THE $25 LATE FEE...
MEET MAXWELL SCHNEEBALG 10-10:30 AM
OH, MR. SCHNEEBALG! HOW FANTASTIC IT IS THAT WE ARE NOW FACE-TO-FACE AS EQUALS! I BOW TO THEE!
LET'S SEE THE STUFF, KID -
THERE'S POTENTIAL. YOU NEED TO WORK ON KEEPING ALL OF YOUR ELEMENTS IN THE RIGHT CONTEXT. THE TREES HERE ARE REALISTIC WHILE THE HORSE IN FRONT IS ABSTRACT -
OH, YES - THAT'S MY STYLE!
TO DEVELOP YOUR STYLE, YOU NEED TO BE CONSISTENT, MAKE SURE ALL THE FIGURES BELONG TOGETHER...
WELL, I THINK I PAINT VERY REALISTICALLY...
YOU CERTAINLY DO, BUT IT'S ALSO A MATTER OF LEGIBILITY AND INTENT,
I MUST DISAGREE!
FINE, BUT YOU DID COME HERE TO GET MY OPINION, AND I'M ONLY -
YOU THINK BEING RICH AND FAMOUS GIVES YOU THE RIGHT TO KICK THE NEW TALENT AROUND! WELL, YOU'RE JEALOUS! JEALOUS, I SAY! AFRAID THE NEW GUARD WILL EXPOSE WHAT SHITE YOUR WORK REALLY IS!
HACK!
I'VE ALWAYS HATED THAT PRETENTIOUS ASSHOLE!

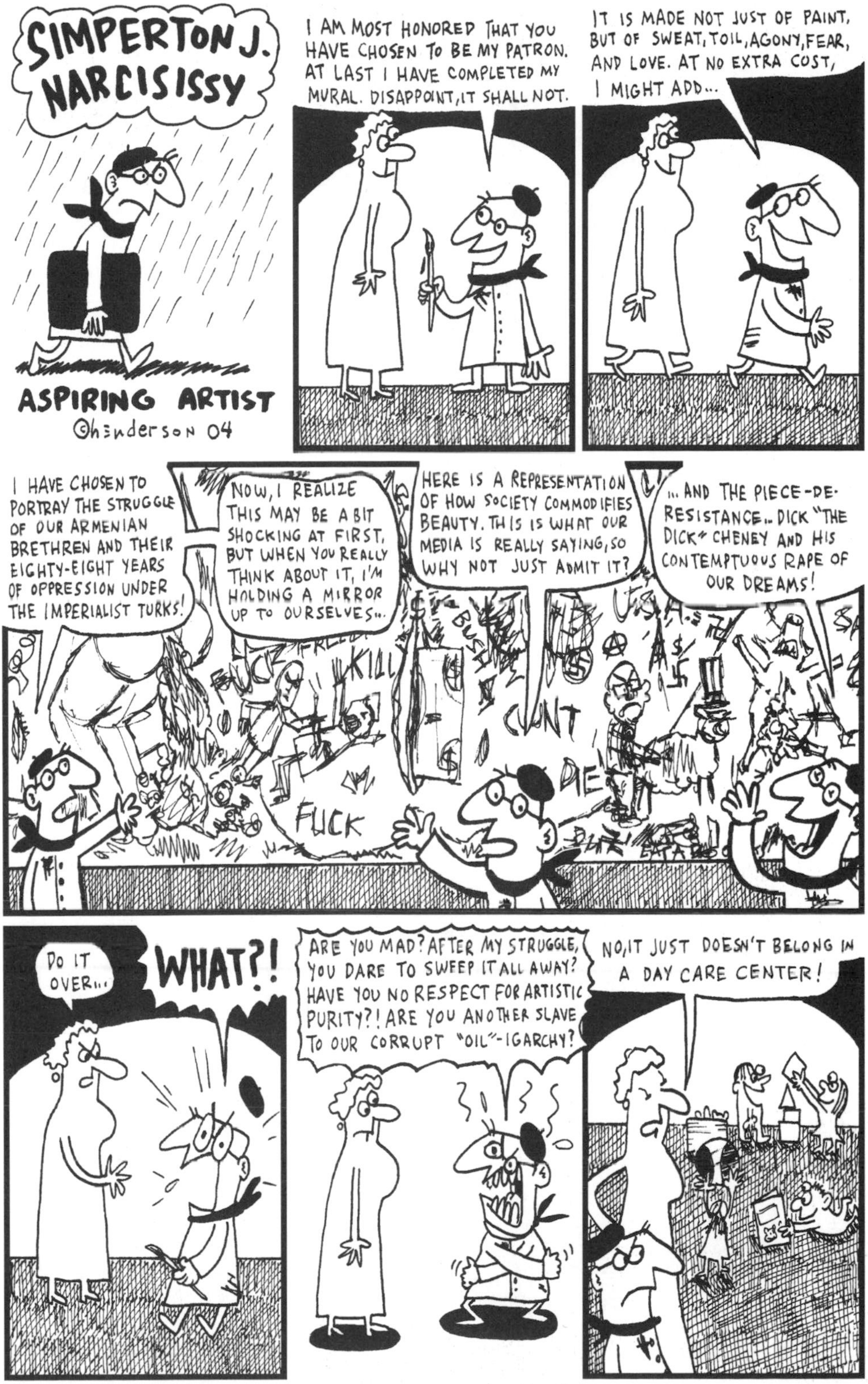
SIMPERTON J. NARCISISSY
ASPIRING ARTIST
©henderson 04
I AM MOST HONORED THAT YOU HAVE CHOSEN TO BE MY PATRON. AT LAST I HAVE COMPLETED MY MURAL. DISAPPOINT, IT SHALL NOT.
IT IS MADE NOT JUST OF PAINT, BUT OF SWEAT, TOIL, AGONY, FEAR, AND LOVE. AT NO EXTRA COST, I MIGHT ADD...
I HAVE CHOSEN TO PORTRAY THE STRUGGLE OF OUR ARMENIAN BRETHREN AND THEIR EIGHTY-EIGHT YEARS OF OPPRESSION UNDER THE IMPERIALIST TURKS!
NOW, I REALIZE THIS MAY BE A BIT SHOCKING AT FIRST, BUT WHEN YOU REALLY THINK ABOUT IT, I'M HOLDING A MIRROR UP TO OURSELVES...
HERE IS A REPRESENTATION OF HOW SOCIETY COMMODIFIES BEAUTY. THIS IS WHAT OUR MEDIA IS REALLY SAYING, SO WHY NOT JUST ADMIT IT?
... AND THE PIECE-DE-RESISTANCE... DICK "THE DICK" CHENEY AND HIS CONTEMPTUOUS RAPE OF OUR DREAMS!
FUCK
KILL
BUSH
CUNT
DIE
FUCK
DO IT OVER...
WHAT?!
ARE YOU MAD? AFTER MY STRUGGLE, YOU DARE TO SWEEP IT ALL AWAY? HAVE YOU NO RESPECT FOR ARTISTIC PURITY?! ARE YOU ANOTHER SLAVE TO OUR CORRUPT "OIL"-IGARCHY?
NO, IT JUST DOESN'T BELONG IN A DAY CARE CENTER!

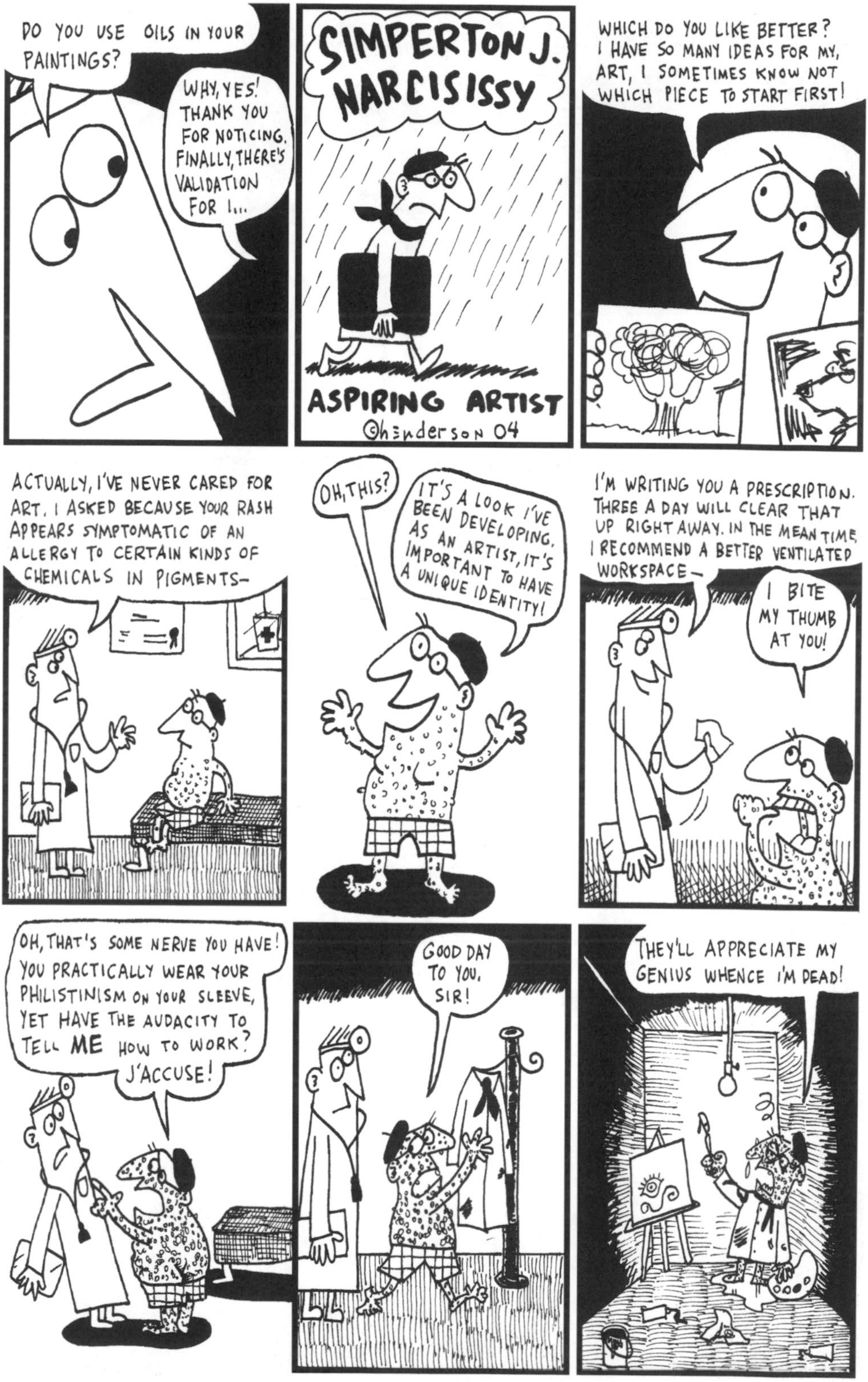
DO YOU USE OILS IN YOUR PAINTINGS?
WHY, YES! THANK YOU FOR NOTICING. FINALLY, THERE'S VALIDATION FOR I...
SIMPERTON J. NARCISISSY
ASPIRING ARTIST
©henderson 04
WHICH DO YOU LIKE BETTER? I HAVE SO MANY IDEAS FOR MY, ART, I SOMETIMES KNOW NOT WHICH PIECE TO START FIRST!
ACTUALLY, I'VE NEVER CARED FOR ART. I ASKED BECAUSE YOUR RASH APPEARS SYMPTOMATIC OF AN ALLERGY TO CERTAIN KINDS OF CHEMICALS IN PIGMENTS–
OH, THIS?
IT'S A LOOK I'VE BEEN DEVELOPING. AS AN ARTIST, IT'S IMPORTANT TO HAVE A UNIQUE IDENTITY!
I'M WRITING YOU A PRESCRIPTION. THREE A DAY WILL CLEAR THAT UP RIGHT AWAY. IN THE MEAN TIME, I RECOMMEND A BETTER VENTILATED WORKSPACE–
I BITE MY THUMB AT YOU!
OH, THAT'S SOME NERVE YOU HAVE! YOU PRACTICALLY WEAR YOUR PHILISTINISM ON YOUR SLEEVE, YET HAVE THE AUDACITY TO TELL ME HOW TO WORK?
J'ACCUSE!
GOOD DAY TO YOU, SIR!
THEY'LL APPRECIATE MY GENIUS WHENCE I'M DEAD!

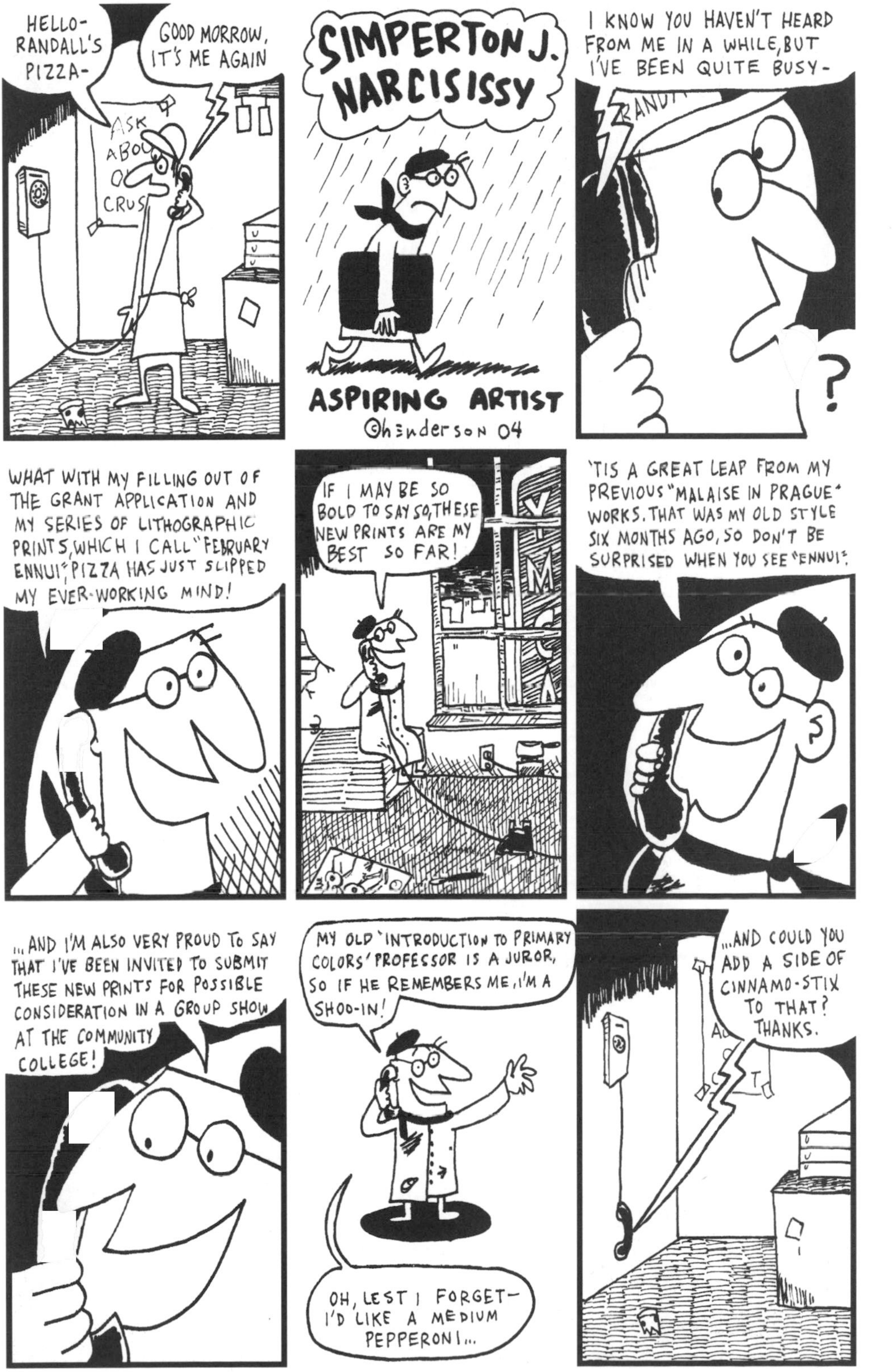
HELLO-RANDALL'S PIZZA-
GOOD MORROW, IT'S ME AGAIN
SIMPERTON J. NARCISISSY
ASPIRING ARTIST
©henderson 04
I KNOW YOU HAVEN'T HEARD FROM ME IN A WHILE, BUT I'VE BEEN QUITE BUSY-
?
WHAT WITH MY FILLING OUT OF THE GRANT APPLICATION AND MY SERIES OF LITHOGRAPHIC PRINTS, WHICH I CALL "FEBRUARY ENNUI", PIZZA HAS JUST SLIPPED MY EVER-WORKING MIND!
IF I MAY BE SO BOLD TO SAY SO, THESE NEW PRINTS ARE MY BEST SO FAR!
'TIS A GREAT LEAP FROM MY PREVIOUS "MALAISE IN PRAGUE" WORKS. THAT WAS MY OLD STYLE SIX MONTHS AGO, SO DON'T BE SURPRISED WHEN YOU SEE "ENNUI".
...AND I'M ALSO VERY PROUD TO SAY THAT I'VE BEEN INVITED TO SUBMIT THESE NEW PRINTS FOR POSSIBLE CONSIDERATION IN A GROUP SHOW AT THE COMMUNITY COLLEGE!
MY OLD 'INTRODUCTION TO PRIMARY COLORS' PROFESSOR IS A JUROR, SO IF HE REMEMBERS ME, I'M A SHOO-IN!
OH, LEST I FORGET- I'D LIKE A MEDIUM PEPPERONI...
...AND COULD YOU ADD A SIDE OF CINNAMO-STIX TO THAT? THANKS.

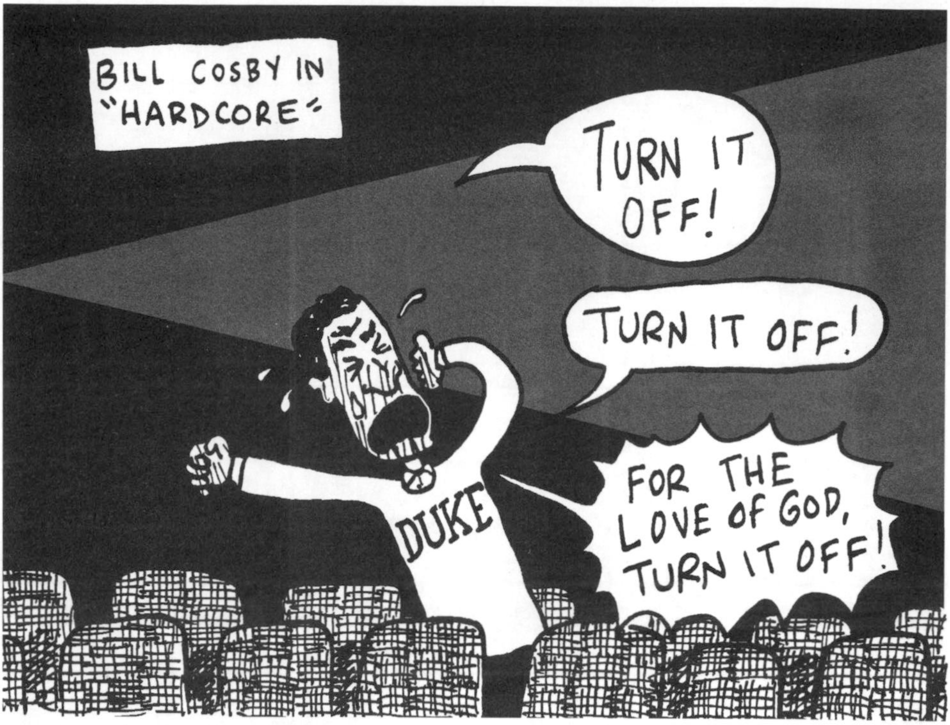
BILL COSBY IN "HARDCORE"
TURN IT OFF!
TURN IT OFF!
FOR THE LOVE OF GOD, TURN IT OFF!
DUKE

BELIEVE IT OR NOT, I'VE BEEN SITTING ON THIS ONE FOR TWO DECADES, AND IT REQUIRES FAMILIARITY WITH THE MOVIE 'HARDCORE'. FOR THOSE WHO ARE UNFAMILIAR WITH THIS 1979 PAUL SCHRADER FILM, IT IS ABOUT A RELIGIOUS FATHER (GEORGE C. SCOTT) WHOSE TEENAGE DAUGHTER RUNS AWAY AND BECOMES A PORN STAR. OR IS KIDNAPPED, I DON'T REMEMBER. THAT'S NOT IMPORTANT, THOUGH. AT THE END, HE GETS TO SEE ONE OF HER MOVIES AND STARTS SOBBING THAT HE CAN'T WATCH IT ANYMORE.

A FEW YEARS LATER, IN REAL LIFE, COMEDIAN BILL COSBY WAS THE STAR OF THE MOST POPULAR SHOW ON TELEVISION. THE YOUNG WOMAN WHO PLAYED HER DAUGHTER, LISA BONET, WAS CAST IN THE MOVIE 'ANGEL HEART'. AT THE TIME, IT WAS A BIG SCANDAL IN ENTERTAINMENT NEWS THAT THIS ACTRESS FROM THE WHOLESOME SITCOM HAD A SEX SCENE IN THIS R-RATED MOVIE. IF I REMEMBER CORRECTLY, IT GOT HER FIRED FROM THE SHOW.

I THINK I HAD JUST SEEN 'HARDCORE' ON CABLE WHEN THIS STORY BROKE, AND I IMMEDIATELY PUT THESE THINGS TOGETHER. LIKE MANY OF MY ABORTED GAGS, IT REQUIRES TO ELABORATE A SETUP TO BE FULLY UNDERSTOOD, YET NO LONGER FUNNY AFTER EXPLAINED. EVEN HAVING THE PROPER FRAME OF REFERENCE IN ADVANCE, IT FALLS FLAT ON PAPER. IT HAS TO HAVE SOUND AND MOTION AND NEEDS THE PRONOUNCED "FLABBITY-FLURBITY-ZOOP" CADENCE ASSOCIATED WITH THE BILL COSBY IMPERSONATIONS THAT IT'S FASHIONABLE TO DO THESE DAYS.

OH WELL... LIVE AND LEARN.

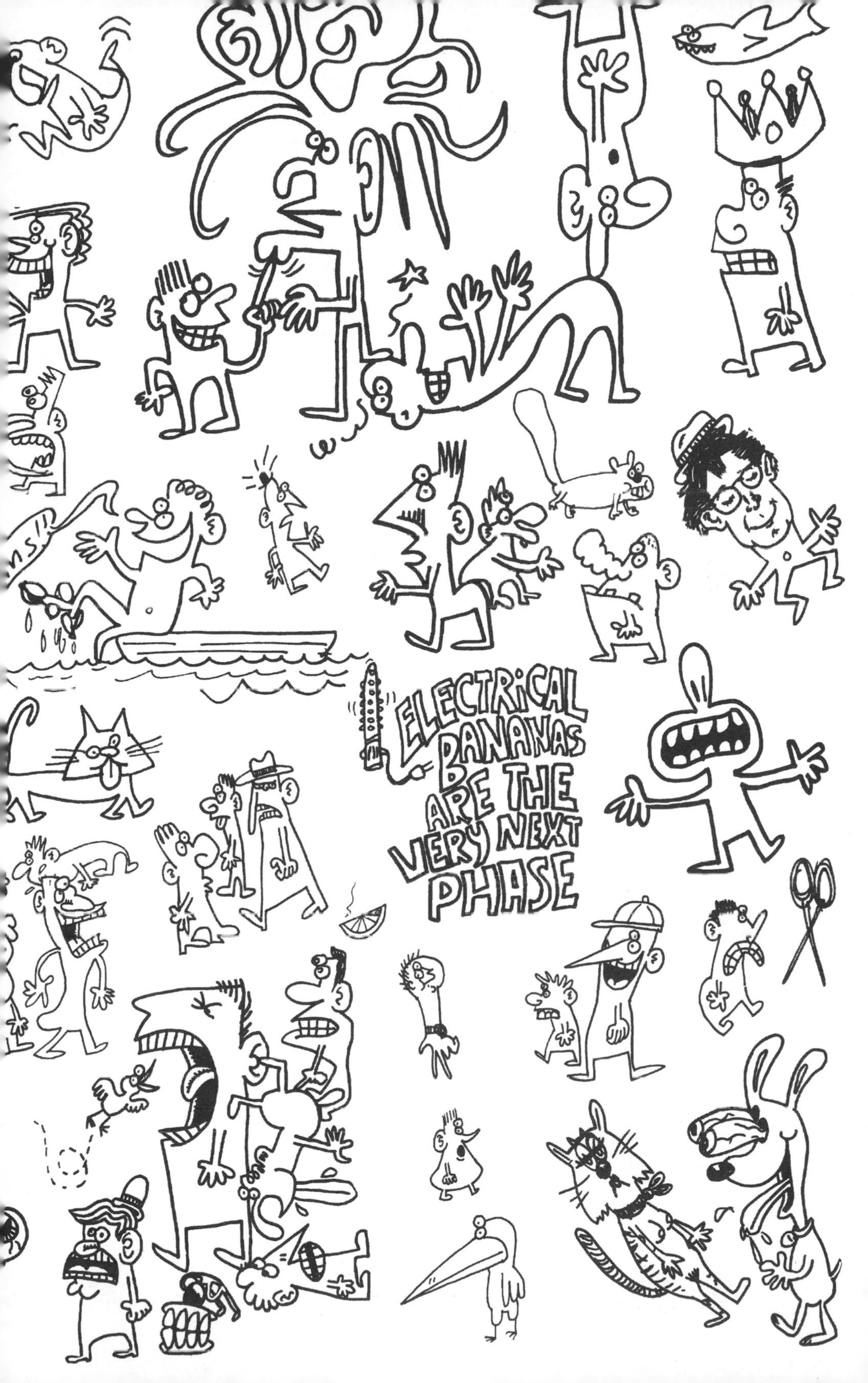
ELECTRICAL BANANAS ARE THE VERY NEXT PHASE

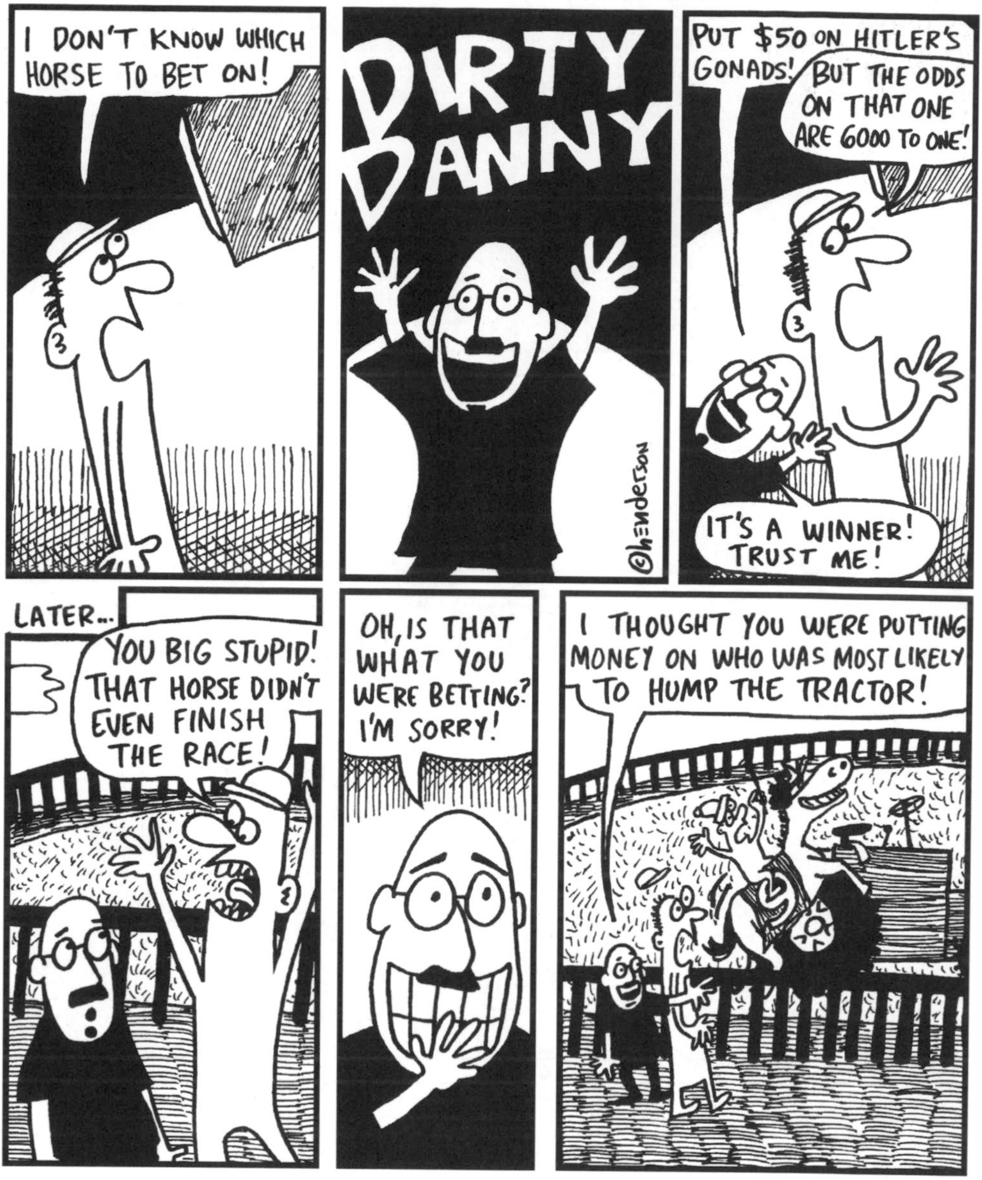
I DON'T KNOW WHICH HORSE TO BET ON!
DIRTY DANNY
PUT $50 ON HITLER'S GONADS!
BUT THE ODDS ON THAT ONE ARE 6000 TO ONE!
IT'S A WINNER! TRUST ME!
LATER...
YOU BIG STUPID! THAT HORSE DIDN'T EVEN FINISH THE RACE!
OH, IS THAT WHAT YOU WERE BETTING? I'M SORRY!
I THOUGHT YOU WERE PUTTING MONEY ON WHO WAS MOST LIKELY TO HUMP THE TRACTOR!
©henderson

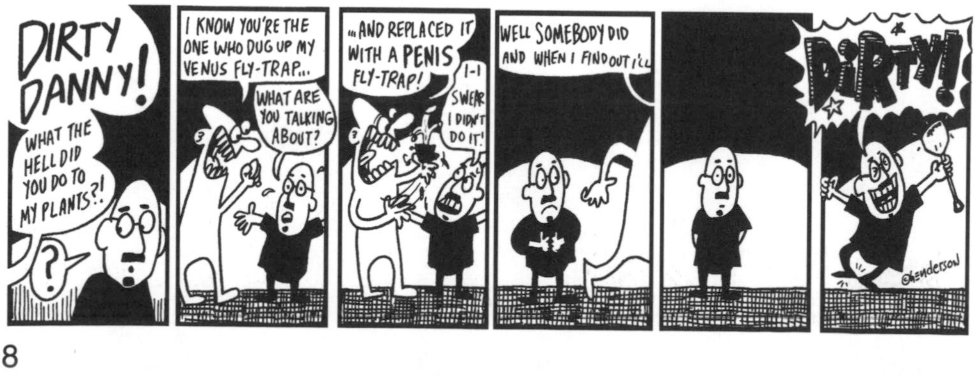
DIRTY DANNY!
WHAT THE HELL DID YOU DO TO MY PLANTS?!
?
I KNOW YOU'RE THE ONE WHO DUG UP MY VENUS FLY-TRAP...
WHAT ARE YOU TALKING ABOUT?
...AND REPLACED IT WITH A PENIS FLY-TRAP!
I-I SWEAR I DIDN'T DO IT!
WELL SOMEBODY DID AND WHEN I FIND OUT I'LL
DIRTY!
©henderson

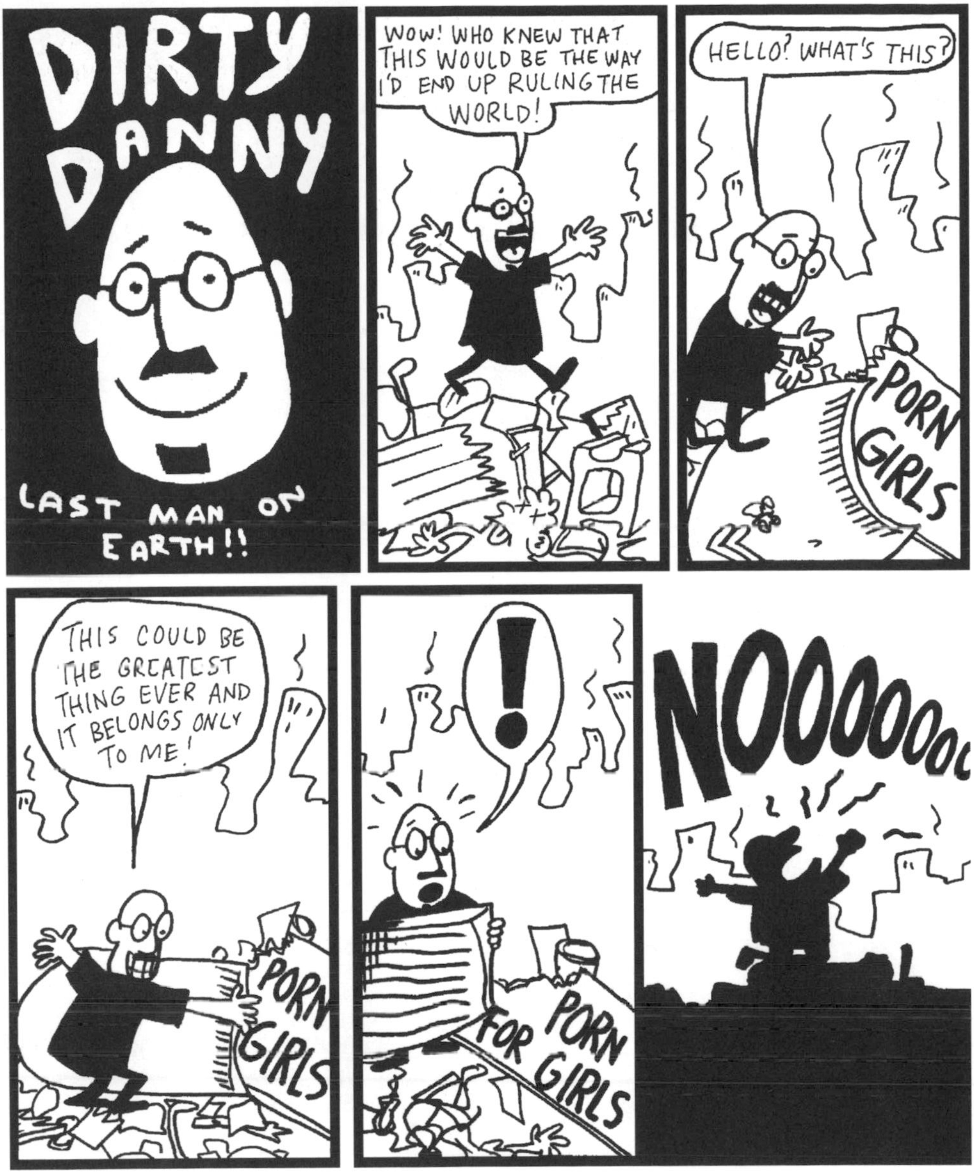
DIRTY DANNY
LAST MAN ON EARTH!!
WOW! WHO KNEW THAT THIS WOULD BE THE WAY I'D END UP RULING THE WORLD!
HELLO? WHAT'S THIS?
PORN GIRLS
THIS COULD BE THE GREATEST THING EVER AND IT BELONGS ONLY TO ME!
PORN GIRLS
!
PORN FOR GIRLS
NOOOOOOO

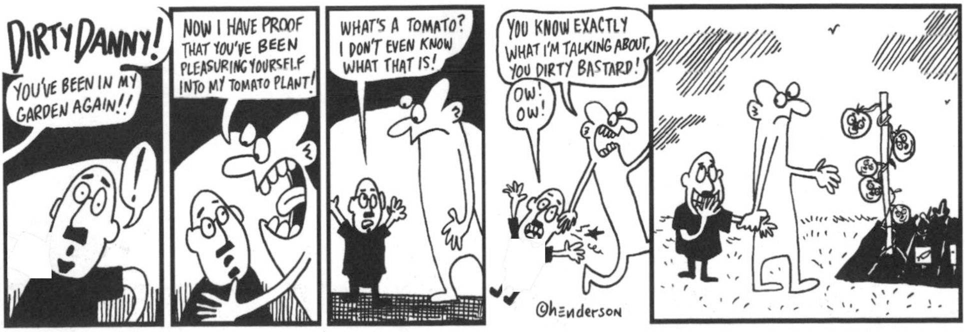
DIRTY DANNY!
YOU'VE BEEN IN MY GARDEN AGAIN!!
!
NOW I HAVE PROOF THAT YOU'VE BEEN PLEASURING YOURSELF INTO MY TOMATO PLANT!
WHAT'S A TOMATO? I DON'T EVEN KNOW WHAT THAT IS!
YOU KNOW EXACTLY WHAT I'M TALKING ABOUT, YOU DIRTY BASTARD!
OW! OW!
©henderson

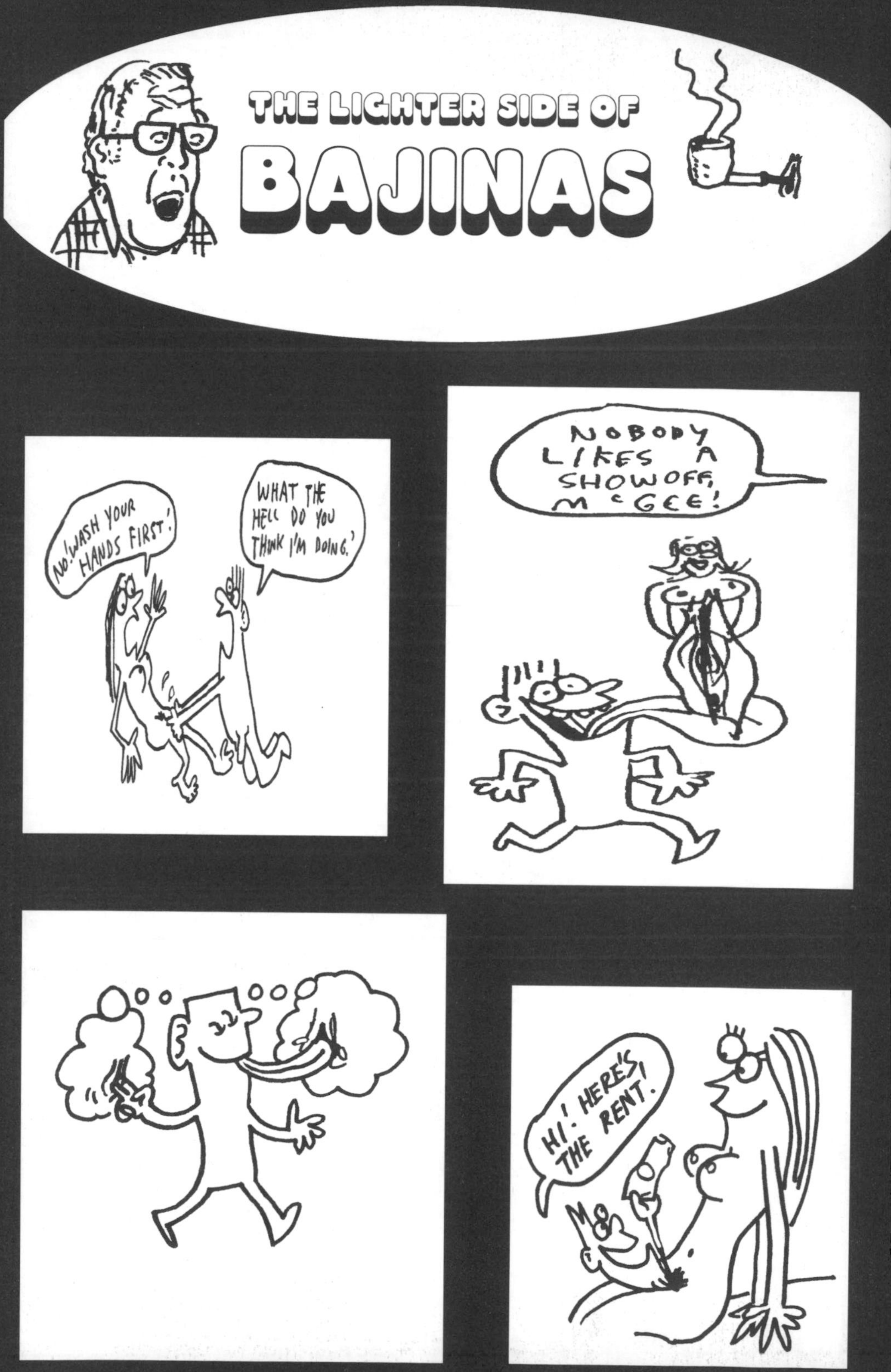
THE LIGHTER SIDE OF
BAJINAS
NO! WASH YOUR HANDS FIRST!
WHAT THE HELL DO YOU THINK I'M DOING?
NOBODY LIKES A SHOWOFF, McGEE!
HI! HERE'S THE RENT!

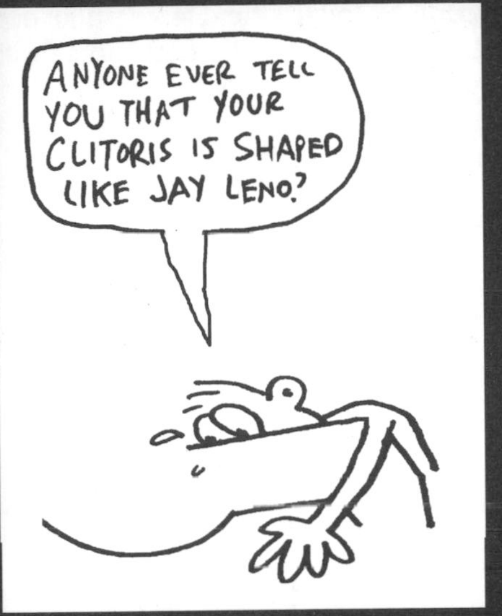
ANYONE EVER TELL YOU THAT YOUR CLITORIS IS SHAPED LIKE JAY LENO?

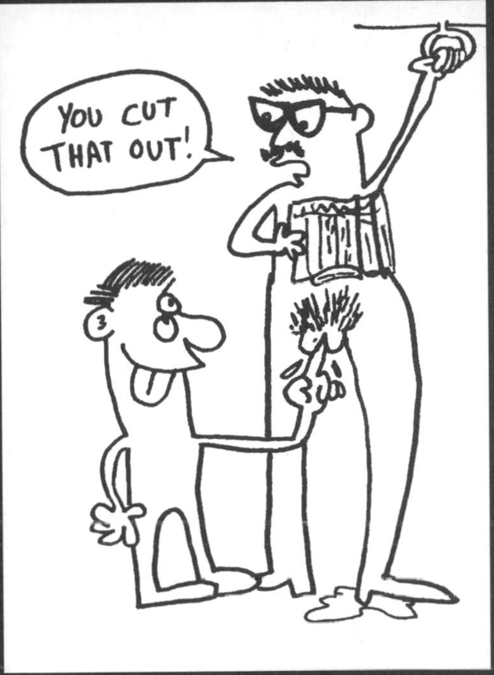
YOU CUT THAT OUT!

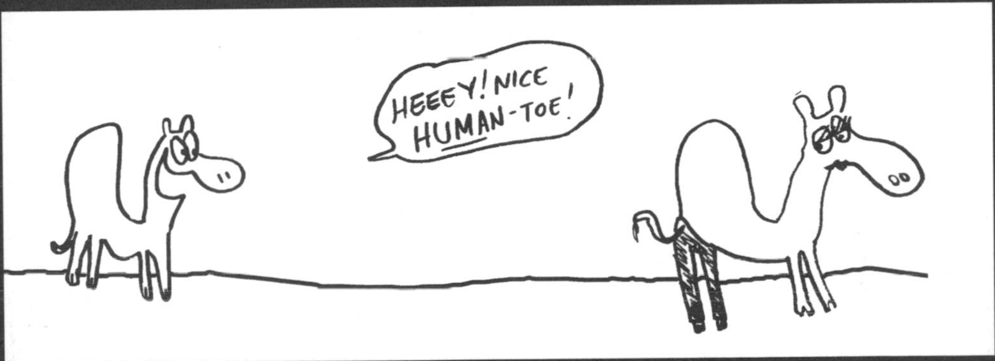
HEEEY! NICE HUMAN-TOE!

special bonus lost "HE AIMS TO PLEASE"

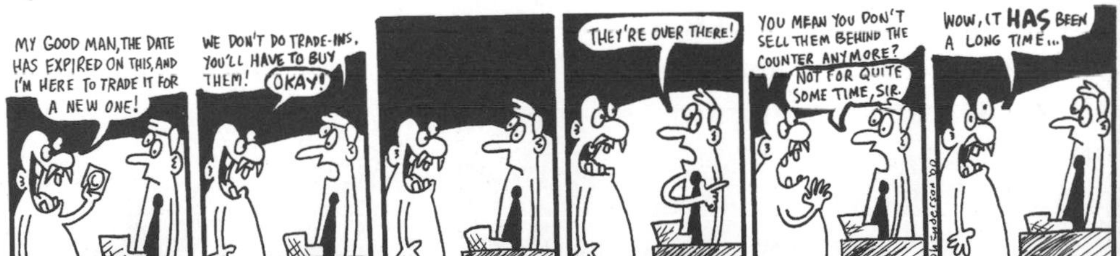
MY GOOD MAN, THE DATE HAS EXPIRED ON THIS, AND I'M HERE TO TRADE IT FOR A NEW ONE!
WE DON'T DO TRADE-INS. YOU'LL HAVE TO BUY THEM!
OKAY!
THEY'RE OVER THERE!
YOU MEAN YOU DON'T SELL THEM BEHIND THE COUNTER ANYMORE?
NOT FOR QUITE SOME TIME, SIR.
WOW, IT HAS BEEN A LONG TIME...

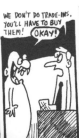

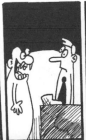

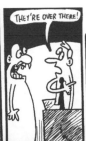

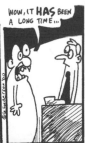

THE DELEGATE RORSCHACH TEST

In the summer of 2000, *modernhumorist.com* attended the Democratic and Republican conventions in Philadelphia and L.A. They approached delegates with these four drawings and asked politely, "These political cartoons lost their captions. Can you help us?"

REPUBLICANS

"Why don't we name that bird Al?"
—Marty, Ohio

"Gee whiz, you just killed freedom by taxing the Internet."
—Susan, Oregon

Larry King (in glasses) to Ted Turner: *"I've just fried another conservative with my interview."*
—Scott, Oregon

DEMOCRATS

"Republicans choked this chicken to the horror of we pacifist Democrats."
—Tom, Maryland

"Let me explain compassionate conservatism to you."
—Manny, Arizona

REPUBLICANS   DEMOCRATS

"There goes another tax dollar"!
—Name Withheld

"What I'm thinking is not very nice."
—Sharon, New Jersey

"That's Clinton: Down and out."
—Julie, Texas

"Could be special interest politics. Mmm. That's hard."
—Ray, New Hampshire

"George rises above them all."
—Ryan, Georgia

"Dancing on the backs of the poor downtrodden people to the tune of the Wall Street guy with the bucks. Yep."
—Tom, Maryland

"Did you know that one-third of the delegates in Philadelphia were millionaires? Call this one, "I believe in compassionate millionaires."
—Manny, Arizona

"The man on stilts is obviously Bush. And that guy [on the ground] is Cheney just pushing George along. The other fellow is handing him another buck so he can do his thing. Oh, well."
—Carolyn, Kansas

23

DEMOCRATS  REPUBLICANS

Man behind tree: *"I'm trying to understand GOP diversity in action."*
—Manny, Arizona

"The banana is Bush. The banana is strutting because he's arrogant."
—Carolyn, Kansas

Man behind tree: *"Throw in a tomato and you'd have Reagan!"* You know, a vegetable?
—Greg, California

Gore is the pear and Bradley is the banana since he's a tall, lean, fightin' machine. Clinton is looking on, going, *"You're beating each other up."*
—Phillip and Patty, Arizona

Bush is behind the tree: *"Drop your peel—let 'im fall and slip on it."*
—John, Rhode Island

"Wonder which one has stronger appeal?"
—Dave, Alabama

"Get out of here, you fighting fruits!"
—Dave, Wisconsin (alternate)

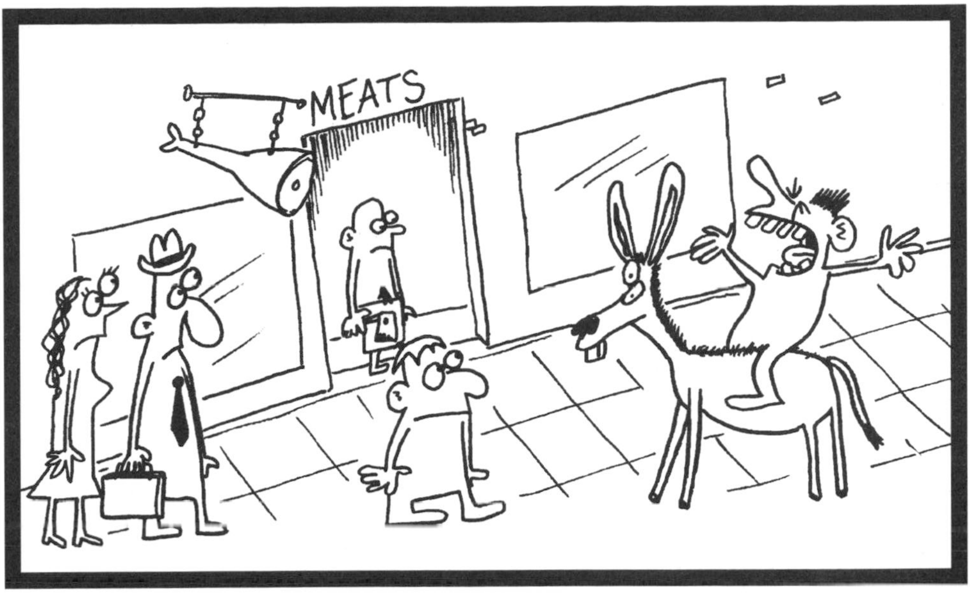
MEATS

DEMOCRATS

"Look at the donkey with two assholes." You heard me. I'll make fun of both parties. I don't care.
—Tom, Maryland

"I come to praise Lieberman, not to bury him!"
—Manny, Arizona

REPUBLICANS

That's Al Gore on the donkey yelling *"Heeelp!"*
—Bob, Rhode Island

"Viand of the road."
—Paul, California (alternate)

"That would have been good for the* New Yorker.*"
Tom, Paul's friend and fellow alternate

"I tell you, I've already been circumcised."
—Freddie, Alaska

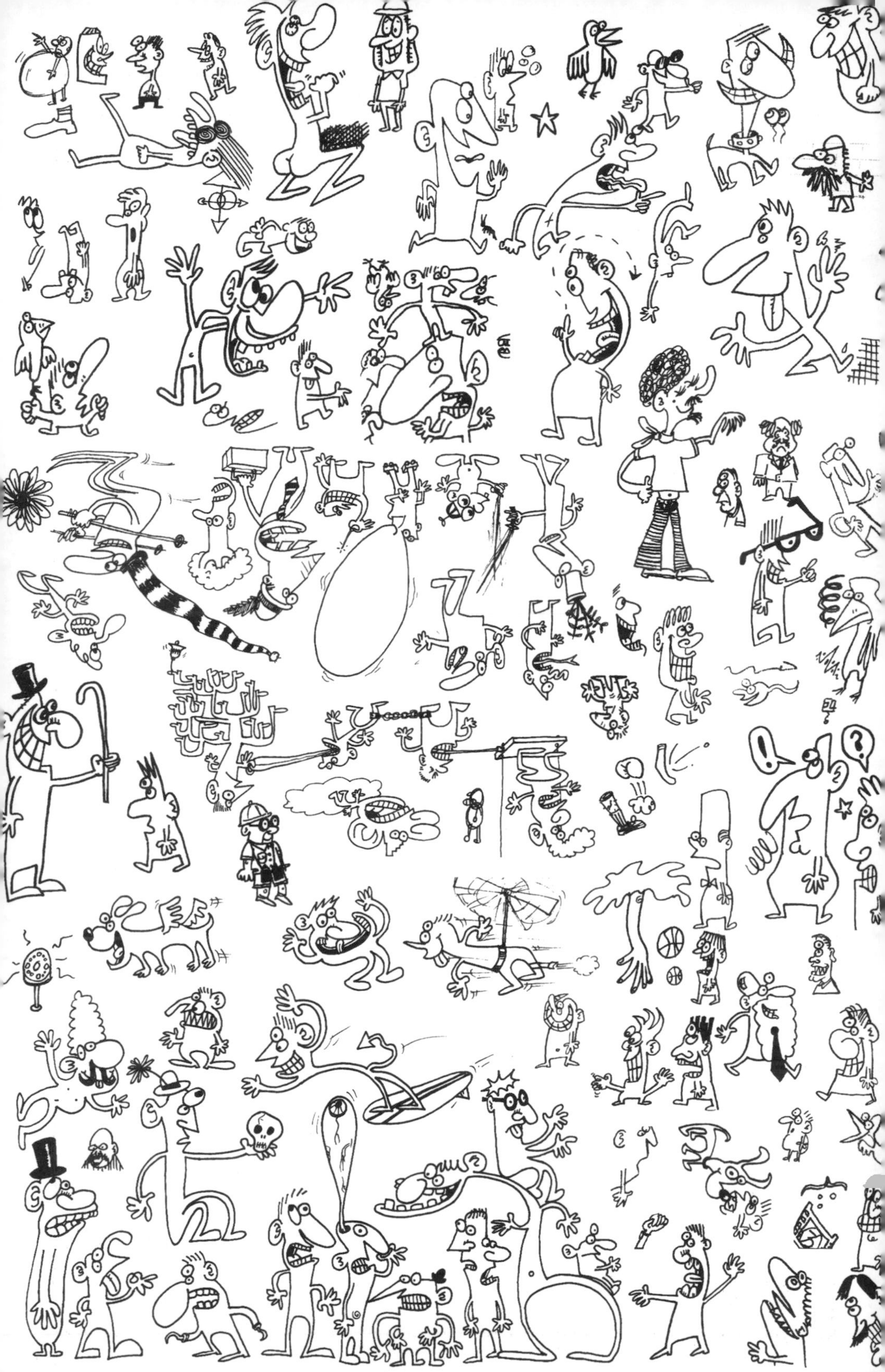

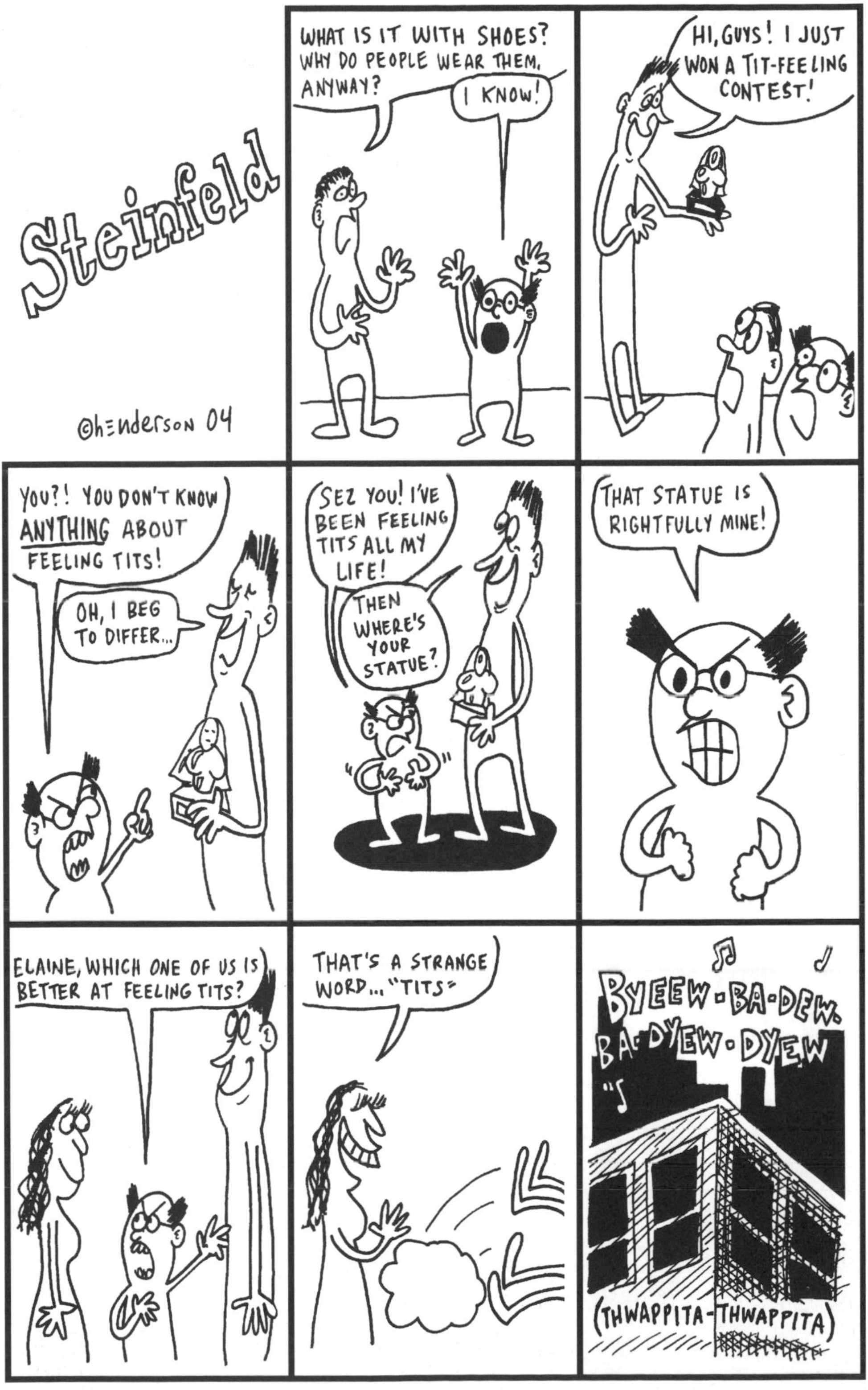
Steinfeld
©henderson 04
WHAT IS IT WITH SHOES? WHY DO PEOPLE WEAR THEM, ANYWAY?
I KNOW!
HI, GUYS! I JUST WON A TIT-FEELING CONTEST!
YOU?! YOU DON'T KNOW ANYTHING ABOUT FEELING TITS!
OH, I BEG TO DIFFER...
SEZ YOU! I'VE BEEN FEELING TITS ALL MY LIFE!
THEN WHERE'S YOUR STATUE?
THAT STATUE IS RIGHTFULLY MINE!
ELAINE, WHICH ONE OF US IS BETTER AT FEELING TITS?
THAT'S A STRANGE WORD... "TITS"
BYEEW-BA-DEW-BA-DYEW-DYEW
(THWAPPITA-THWAPPITA)

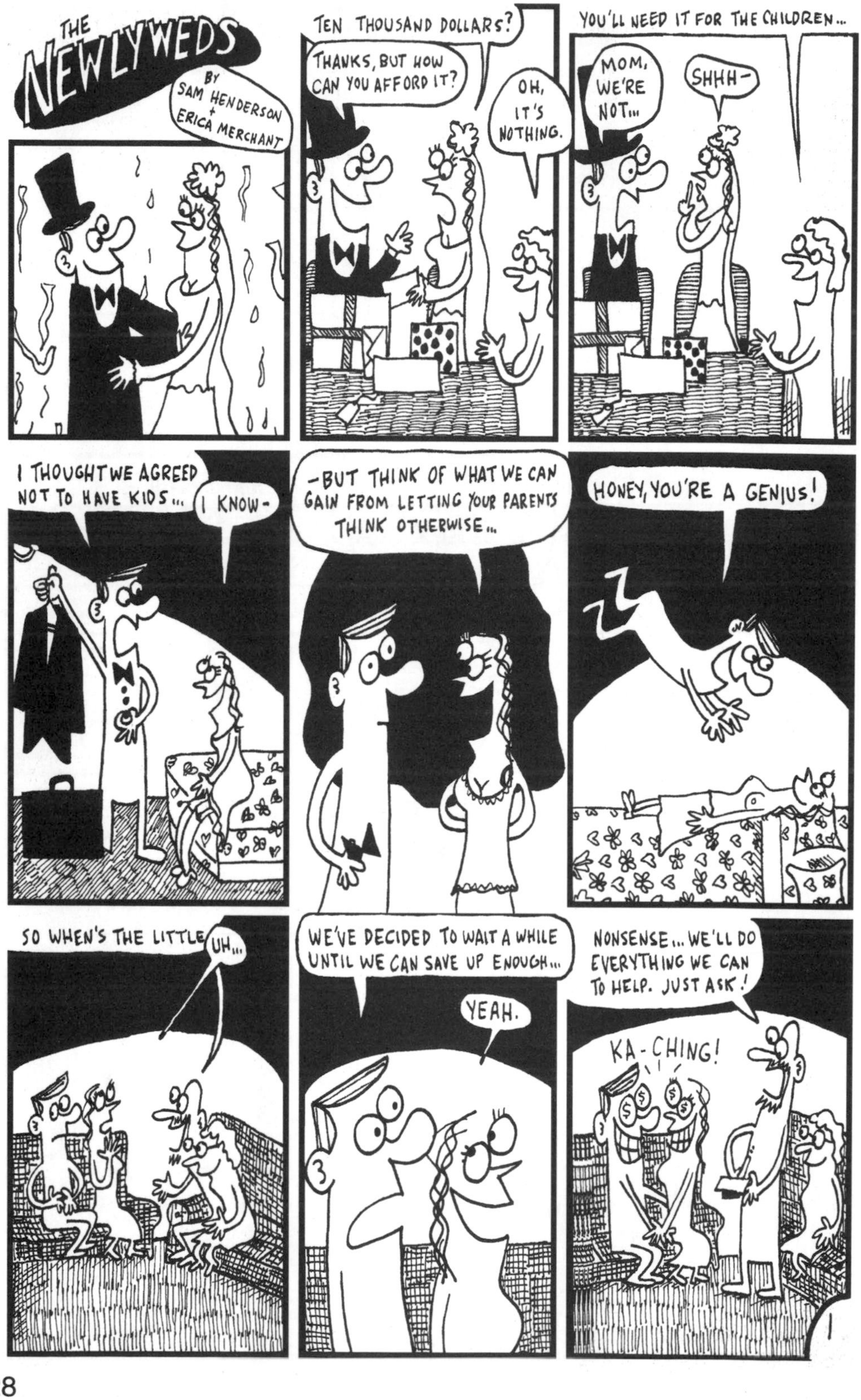
THE NEWLYWEDS
BY SAM HENDERSON + ERICA MERCHANT
TEN THOUSAND DOLLARS?
THANKS, BUT HOW CAN YOU AFFORD IT?
OH, IT'S NOTHING.
YOU'LL NEED IT FOR THE CHILDREN...
MOM, WE'RE NOT...
SHHH-
I THOUGHT WE AGREED NOT TO HAVE KIDS...
I KNOW-
-BUT THINK OF WHAT WE CAN GAIN FROM LETTING YOUR PARENTS THINK OTHERWISE...
HONEY, YOU'RE A GENIUS!
SO WHEN'S THE LITTLE
UH...
WE'VE DECIDED TO WAIT A WHILE UNTIL WE CAN SAVE UP ENOUGH...
YEAH.
NONSENSE... WE'LL DO EVERYTHING WE CAN TO HELP. JUST ASK!
KA-CHING!

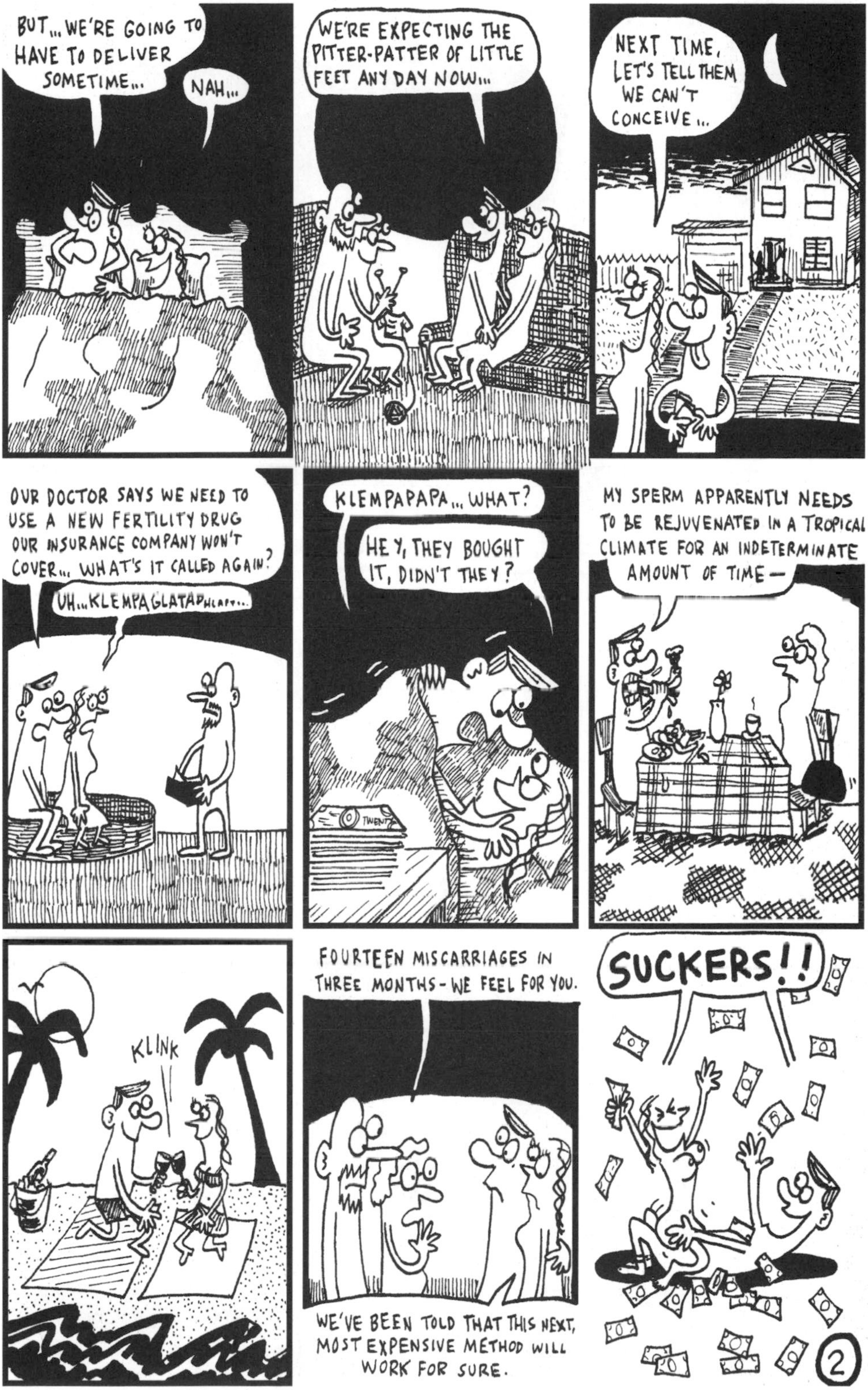
BUT... WE'RE GOING TO HAVE TO DELIVER SOMETIME...
NAH...
WE'RE EXPECTING THE PITTER-PATTER OF LITTLE FEET ANY DAY NOW...
NEXT TIME, LET'S TELL THEM WE CAN'T CONCEIVE...
OUR DOCTOR SAYS WE NEED TO USE A NEW FERTILITY DRUG OUR INSURANCE COMPANY WON'T COVER... WHAT'S IT CALLED AGAIN?
UH... KLEMPAGLATAPHLAPT...
KLEMPAPAPA... WHAT?
HEY, THEY BOUGHT IT, DIDN'T THEY?
MY SPERM APPARENTLY NEEDS TO BE REJUVENATED IN A TROPICAL CLIMATE FOR AN INDETERMINATE AMOUNT OF TIME—
KLINK
FOURTEEN MISCARRIAGES IN THREE MONTHS - WE FEEL FOR YOU.
WE'VE BEEN TOLD THAT THIS NEXT, MOST EXPENSIVE METHOD WILL WORK FOR SURE.
SUCKERS!!
2

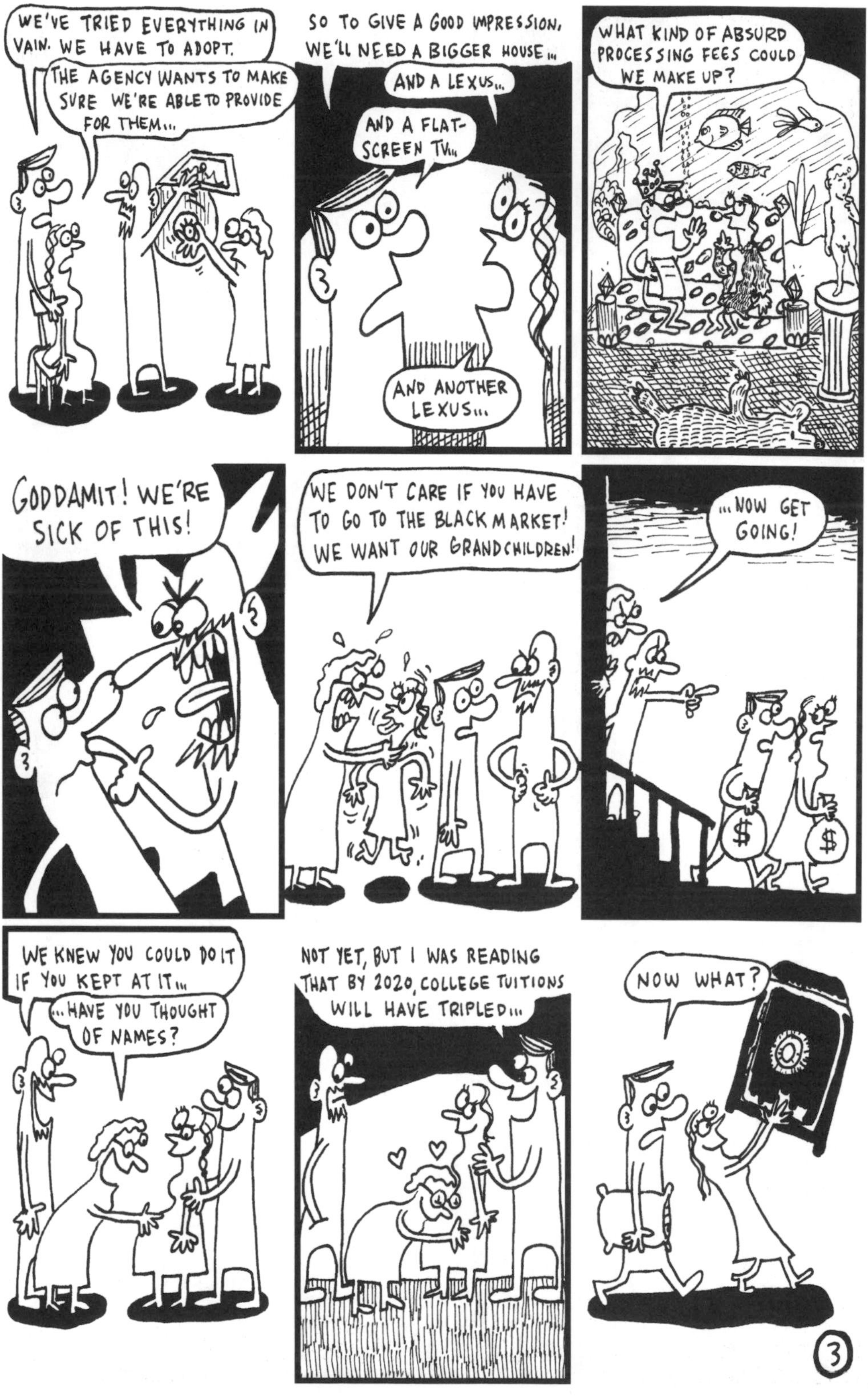
WE'VE TRIED EVERYTHING IN VAIN. WE HAVE TO ADOPT.
THE AGENCY WANTS TO MAKE SURE WE'RE ABLE TO PROVIDE FOR THEM...
SO TO GIVE A GOOD IMPRESSION, WE'LL NEED A BIGGER HOUSE...
AND A LEXUS...
AND A FLAT-SCREEN TV...
AND ANOTHER LEXUS...
WHAT KIND OF ABSURD PROCESSING FEES COULD WE MAKE UP?
GODDAMIT! WE'RE SICK OF THIS!
WE DON'T CARE IF YOU HAVE TO GO TO THE BLACK MARKET! WE WANT OUR GRANDCHILDREN!
...NOW GET GOING!
WE KNEW YOU COULD DO IT IF YOU KEPT AT IT...
...HAVE YOU THOUGHT OF NAMES?
NOT YET, BUT I WAS READING THAT BY 2020, COLLEGE TUITIONS WILL HAVE TRIPLED...
NOW WHAT?
3

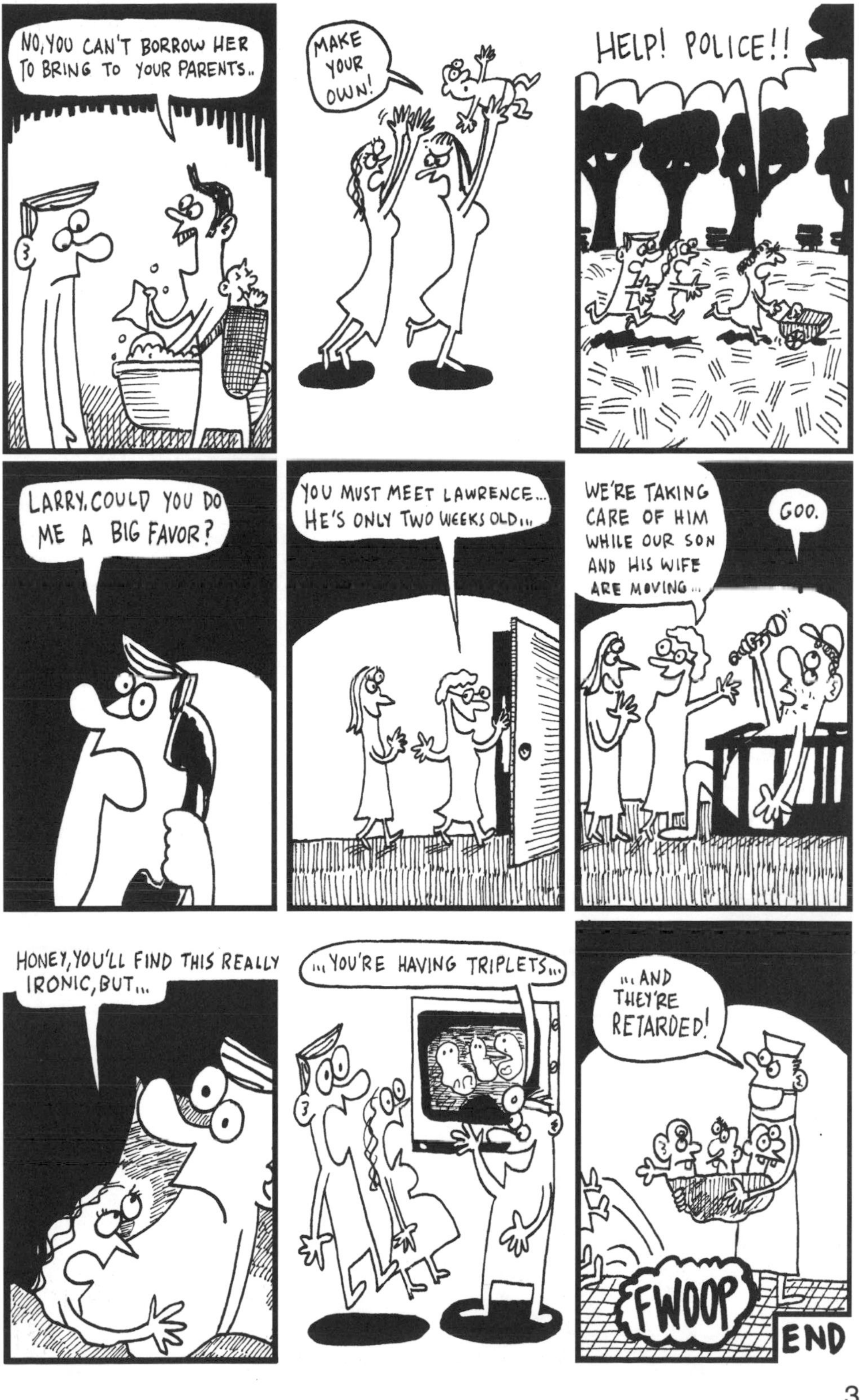
NO, YOU CAN'T BORROW HER TO BRING TO YOUR PARENTS..
MAKE YOUR OWN!
HELP! POLICE!!
LARRY, COULD YOU DO ME A BIG FAVOR?
YOU MUST MEET LAWRENCE... HE'S ONLY TWO WEEKS OLD...
WE'RE TAKING CARE OF HIM WHILE OUR SON AND HIS WIFE ARE MOVING...
GOO.
HONEY, YOU'LL FIND THIS REALLY IRONIC, BUT...
...YOU'RE HAVING TRIPLETS...
...AND THEY'RE RETARDED!
FWOOP
END

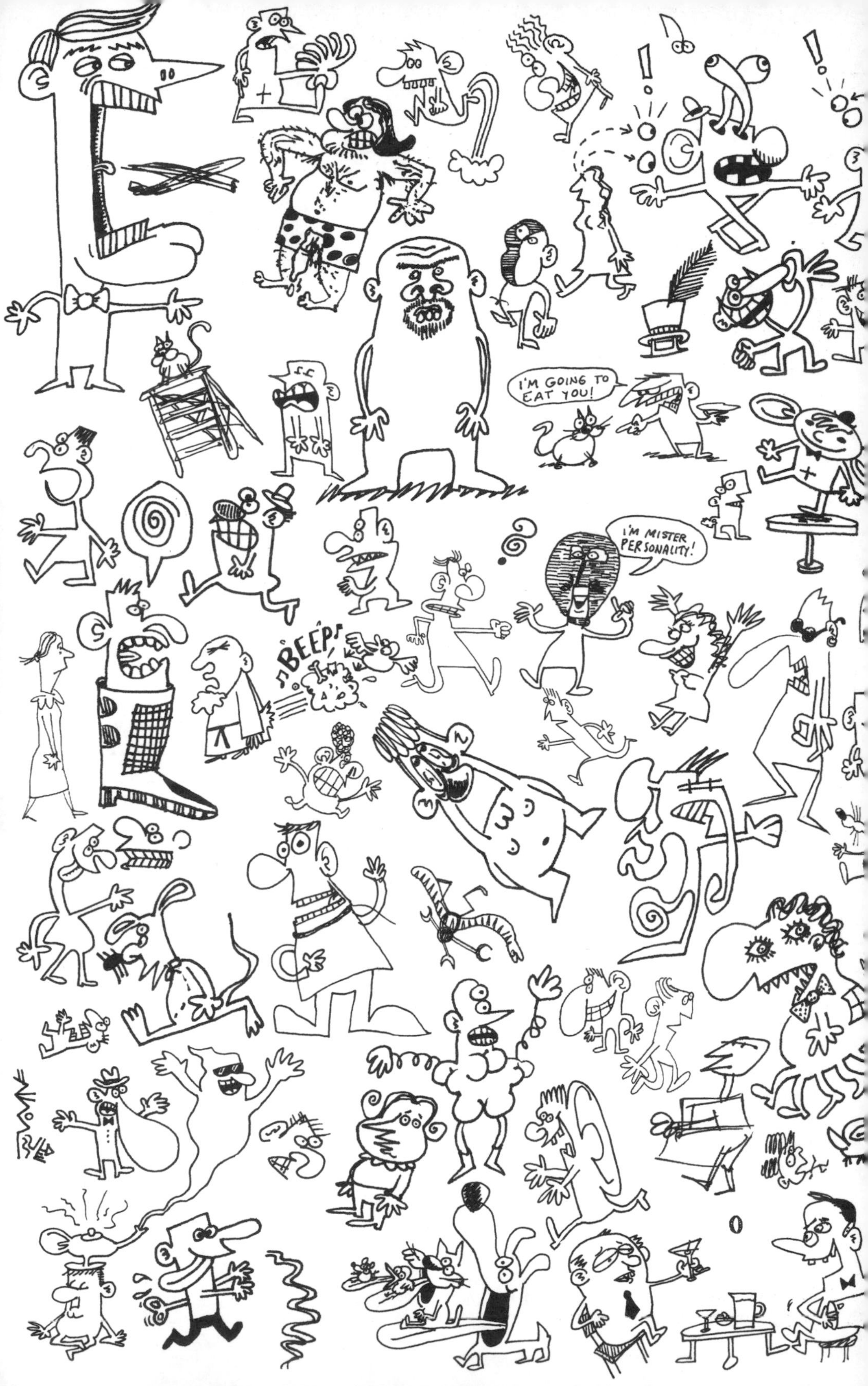
I'M GOING TO EAT YOU!
BEEP
I'M MISTER PERSONALITY!

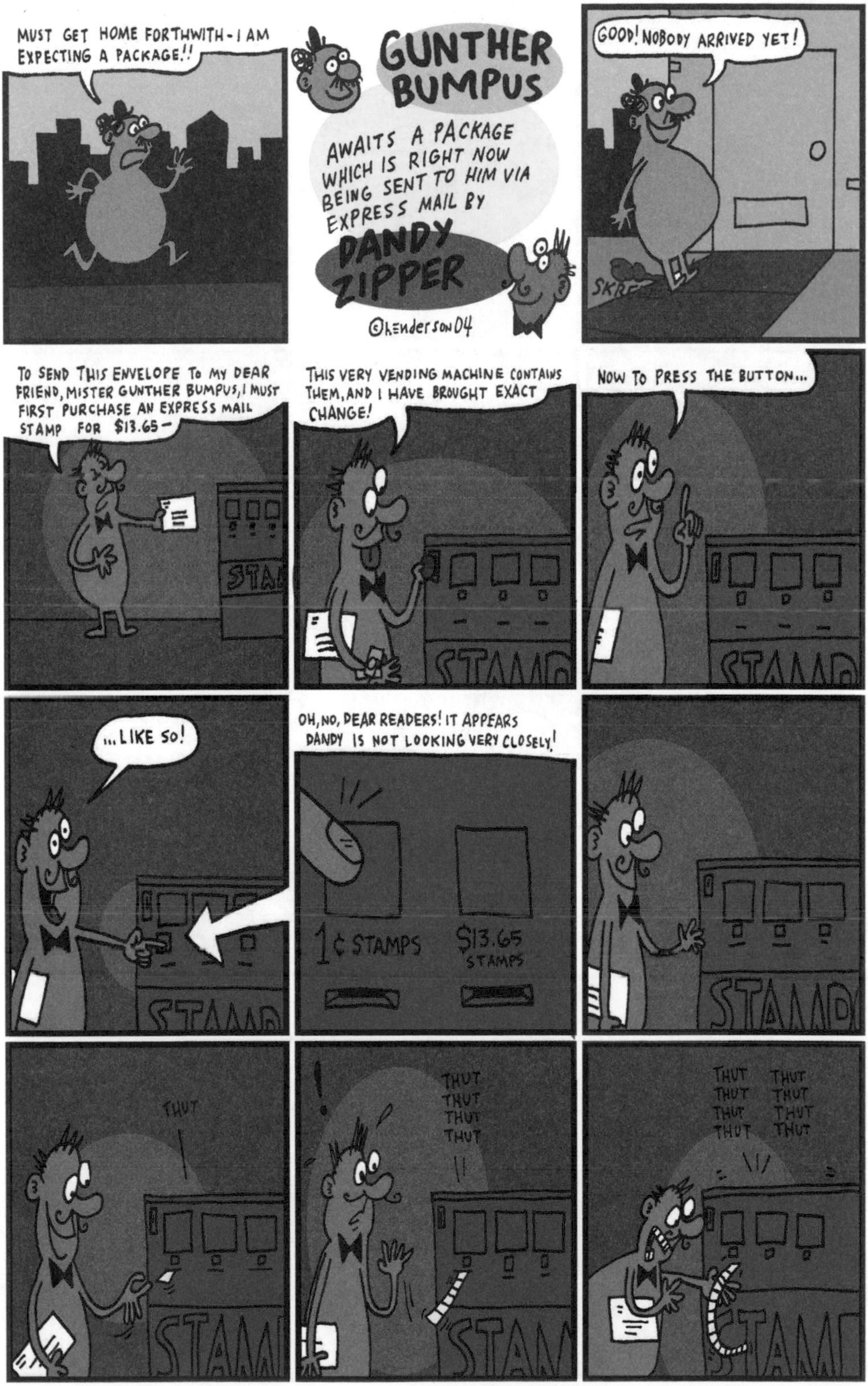
MUST GET HOME FORTHWITH - I AM EXPECTING A PACKAGE!!
GUNTHER BUMPUS
AWAITS A PACKAGE WHICH IS RIGHT NOW BEING SENT TO HIM VIA EXPRESS MAIL BY
DANDY ZIPPER
©henderson04
GOOD! NOBODY ARRIVED YET!
TO SEND THIS ENVELOPE TO MY DEAR FRIEND, MISTER GUNTHER BUMPUS, I MUST FIRST PURCHASE AN EXPRESS MAIL STAMP FOR $13.65 -
THIS VERY VENDING MACHINE CONTAINS THEM, AND I HAVE BROUGHT EXACT CHANGE!
NOW TO PRESS THE BUTTON...
...LIKE SO!
OH, NO, DEAR READERS! IT APPEARS DANDY IS NOT LOOKING VERY CLOSELY!
1¢ STAMPS
$13.65 STAMPS
THUT
!
THUT THUT THUT THUT
THUT THUT THUT THUT THUT THUT THUT THUT

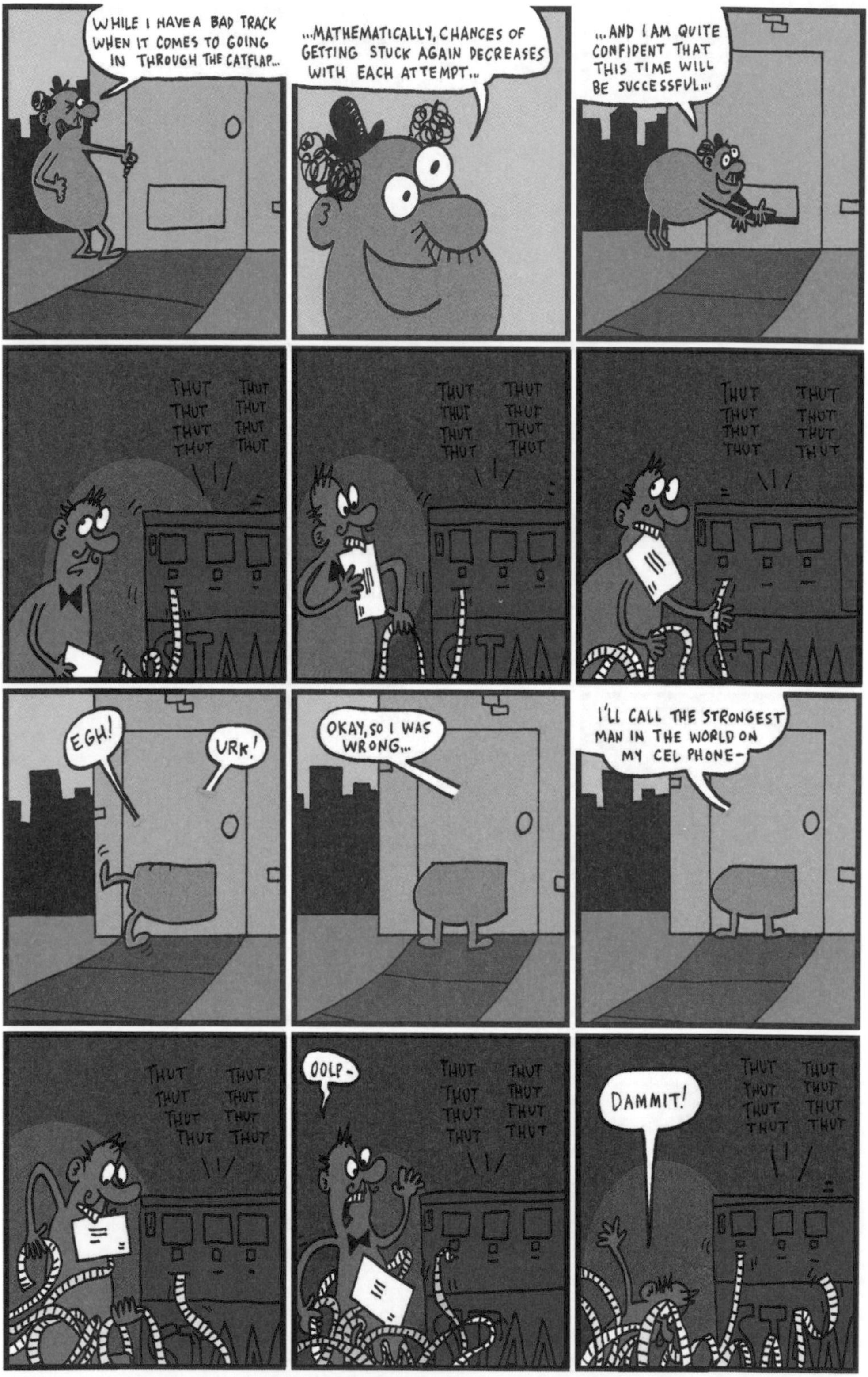

WHILE I HAVE A BAD TRACK WHEN IT COMES TO GOING IN THROUGH THE CATFLAP...
...MATHEMATICALLY, CHANCES OF GETTING STUCK AGAIN DECREASES WITH EACH ATTEMPT...
...AND I AM QUITE CONFIDENT THAT THIS TIME WILL BE SUCCESSFUL...
THUT THUT THUT THUT THUT THUT THUT THUT
THUT THUT THUT THUT THUT THUT THUT THUT
THUT THUT THUT THUT THUT THUT THUT THUT
EGH!
URK!
OKAY, SO I WAS WRONG...
I'LL CALL THE STRONGEST MAN IN THE WORLD ON MY CEL PHONE-
THUT THUT THUT THUT THUT THUT THUT THUT
OOLP-
THUT THUT THUT THUT THUT THUT THUT THUT
DAMMIT!
THUT THUT THUT THUT THUT THUT THUT THUT

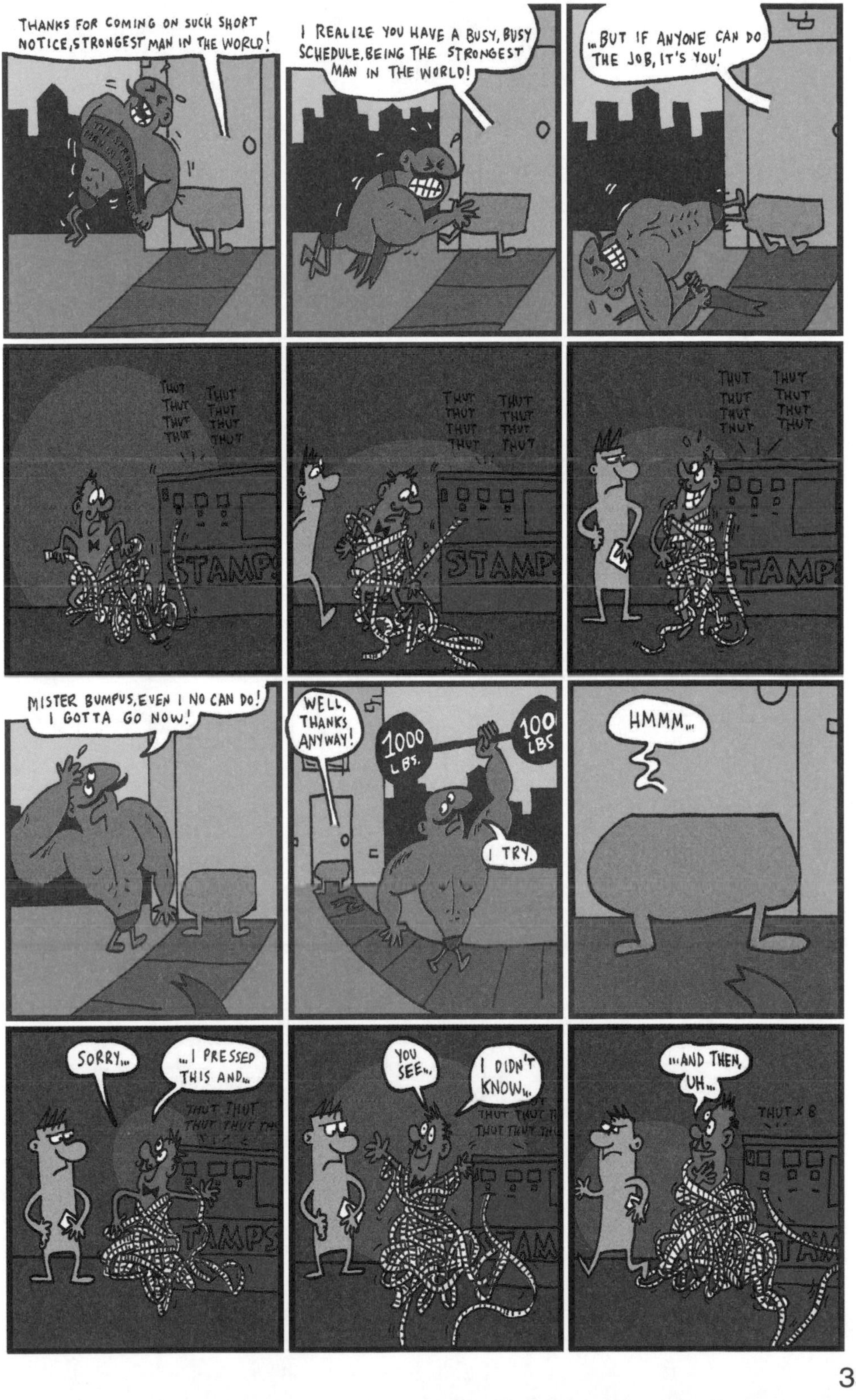
THANKS FOR COMING ON SUCH SHORT NOTICE, STRONGEST MAN IN THE WORLD!
I REALIZE YOU HAVE A BUSY, BUSY SCHEDULE, BEING THE STRONGEST MAN IN THE WORLD!
...BUT IF ANYONE CAN DO THE JOB, IT'S YOU!
THUT THUT THUT THUT THUT THUT THUT THUT
THUT THUT THUT THUT THUT THUT THUT THUT
STAMPS
THUT THUT THUT THUT THUT THUT THUT THUT
STAMPS
THUT THUT THUT THUT THUT THUT THUT THUT
STAMPS
MISTER BUMPUS, EVEN I NO CAN DO! I GOTTA GO NOW!
WELL, THANKS ANYWAY!
1000 LBS.
1000 LBS
I TRY.
HMMM...
SORRY...
...I PRESSED THIS AND...
YOU SEE...
I DIDN'T KNOW...
...AND THEN, UH...
THUT × 8

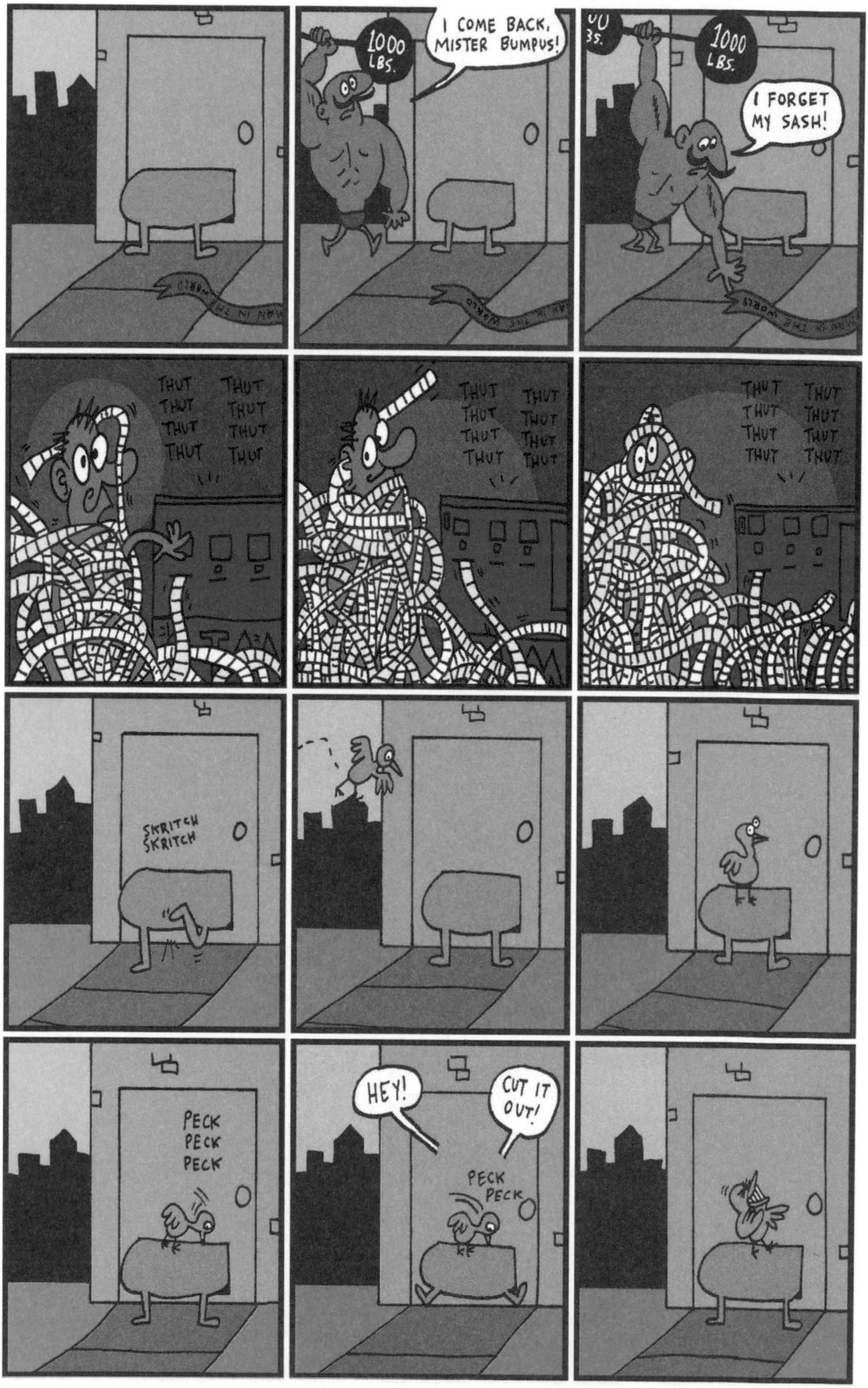
1000 LBS.
I COME BACK, MISTER BUMPUS!
1000 LBS.
I FORGET MY SASH!
THUT THUT THUT THUT THUT THUT THUT THUT
THUT THUT THUT THUT THUT THUT THUT THUT
THUT THUT THUT THUT THUT THUT THUT THUT
SKRITCH SKRITCH
PECK PECK PECK
HEY!
CUT IT OUT!
PECK PECK

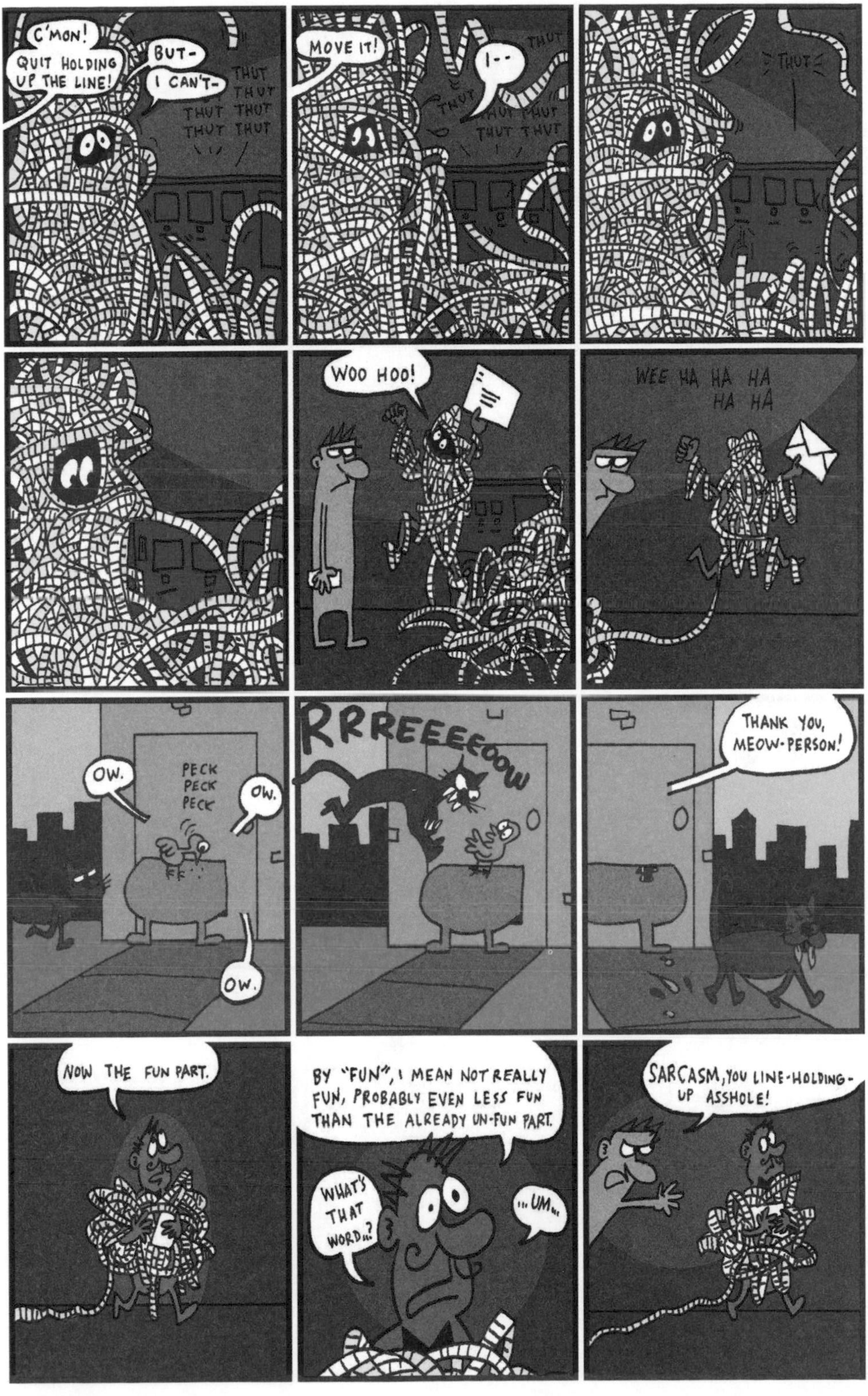
C'MON!
QUIT HOLDING UP THE LINE!
BUT-
I CAN'T-
THUT THUT THUT THUT THUT THUT THUT
MOVE IT!
I--
THUT THUT THUT THUT THUT THUT
THUT
WOO HOO!
WEE HA HA HA HA HA
OW.
PECK PECK PECK
OW.
OW.
RRREEEEEOOOW
THANK YOU, MEOW-PERSON!
NOW THE FUN PART.
BY "FUN", I MEAN NOT REALLY FUN, PROBABLY EVEN LESS FUN THAN THE ALREADY UN-FUN PART.
WHAT'S THAT WORD..?
...UM...
SARCASM, YOU LINE-HOLDING-UP ASSHOLE!

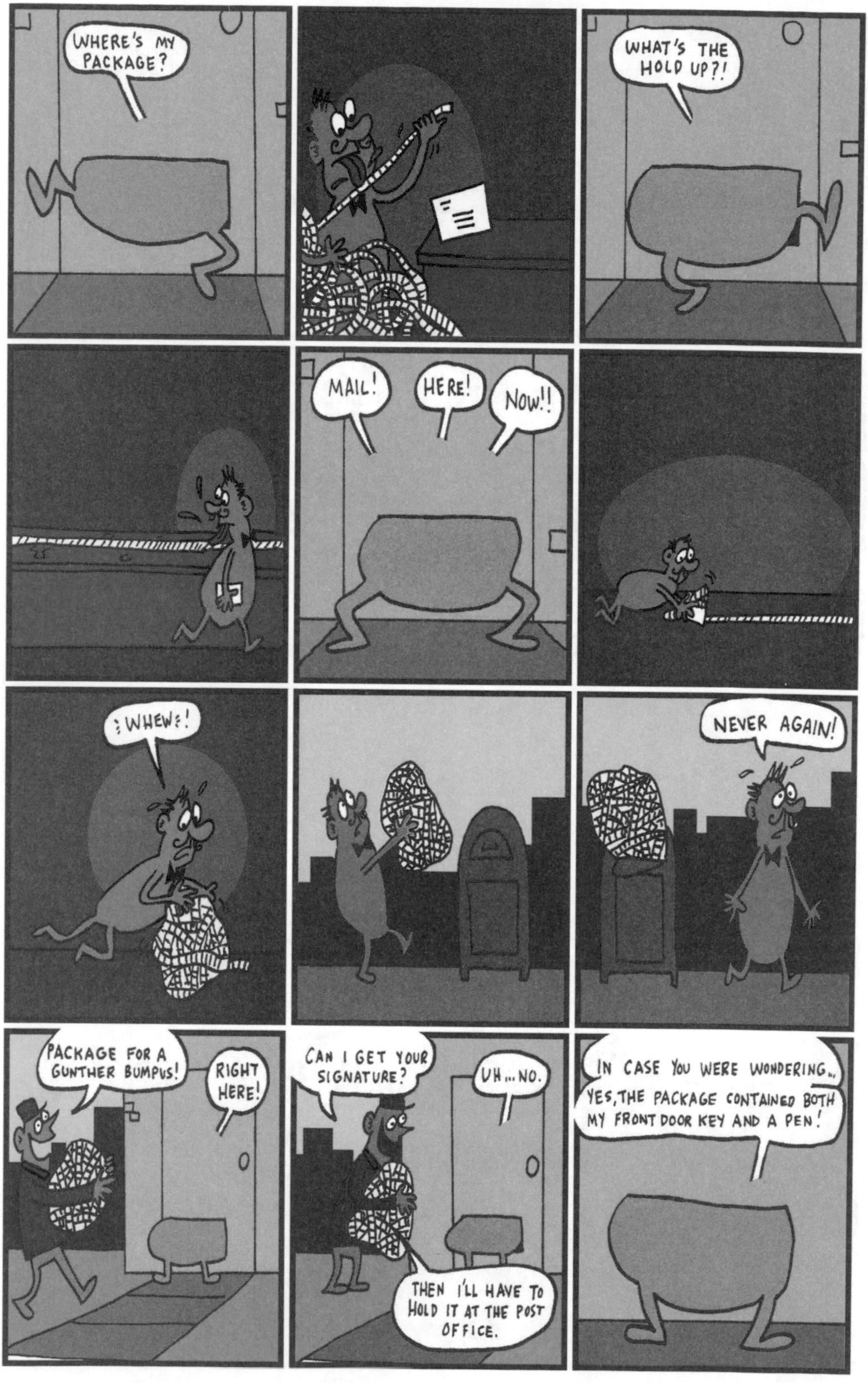
WHERE'S MY PACKAGE?
WHAT'S THE HOLD UP?!
MAIL!
HERE!
NOW!!
WHEW!
NEVER AGAIN!
PACKAGE FOR A GUNTHER BUMPUS!
RIGHT HERE!
CAN I GET YOUR SIGNATURE?
UH... NO.
THEN I'LL HAVE TO HOLD IT AT THE POST OFFICE.
IN CASE YOU WERE WONDERING..
YES, THE PACKAGE CONTAINED BOTH MY FRONT DOOR KEY AND A PEN!

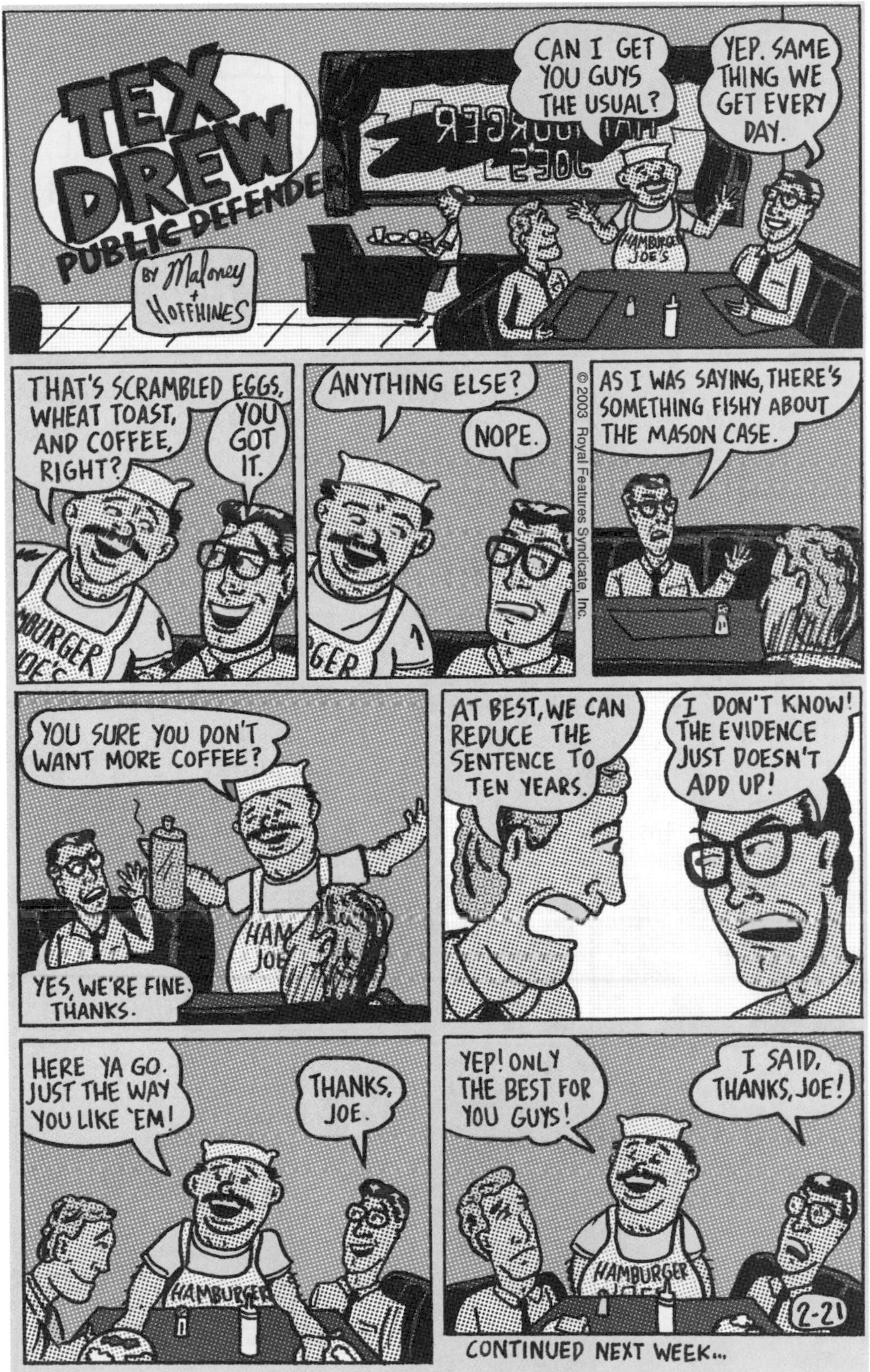
TEX DREW
PUBLIC DEFENDER
BY Maloney + HOFFHINES
CAN I GET YOU GUYS THE USUAL?
YEP. SAME THING WE GET EVERY DAY.
HAMBURGER JOE'S
THAT'S SCRAMBLED EGGS, WHEAT TOAST, AND COFFEE, RIGHT?
YOU GOT IT.
ANYTHING ELSE?
NOPE.
© 2003 Royal Features Syndicate, Inc.
AS I WAS SAYING, THERE'S SOMETHING FISHY ABOUT THE MASON CASE.
YOU SURE YOU DON'T WANT MORE COFFEE?
YES, WE'RE FINE. THANKS.
AT BEST, WE CAN REDUCE THE SENTENCE TO TEN YEARS.
I DON'T KNOW! THE EVIDENCE JUST DOESN'T ADD UP!
HERE YA GO. JUST THE WAY YOU LIKE 'EM!
THANKS, JOE.
YEP! ONLY THE BEST FOR YOU GUYS!
I SAID, THANKS, JOE!
2-21
CONTINUED NEXT WEEK...

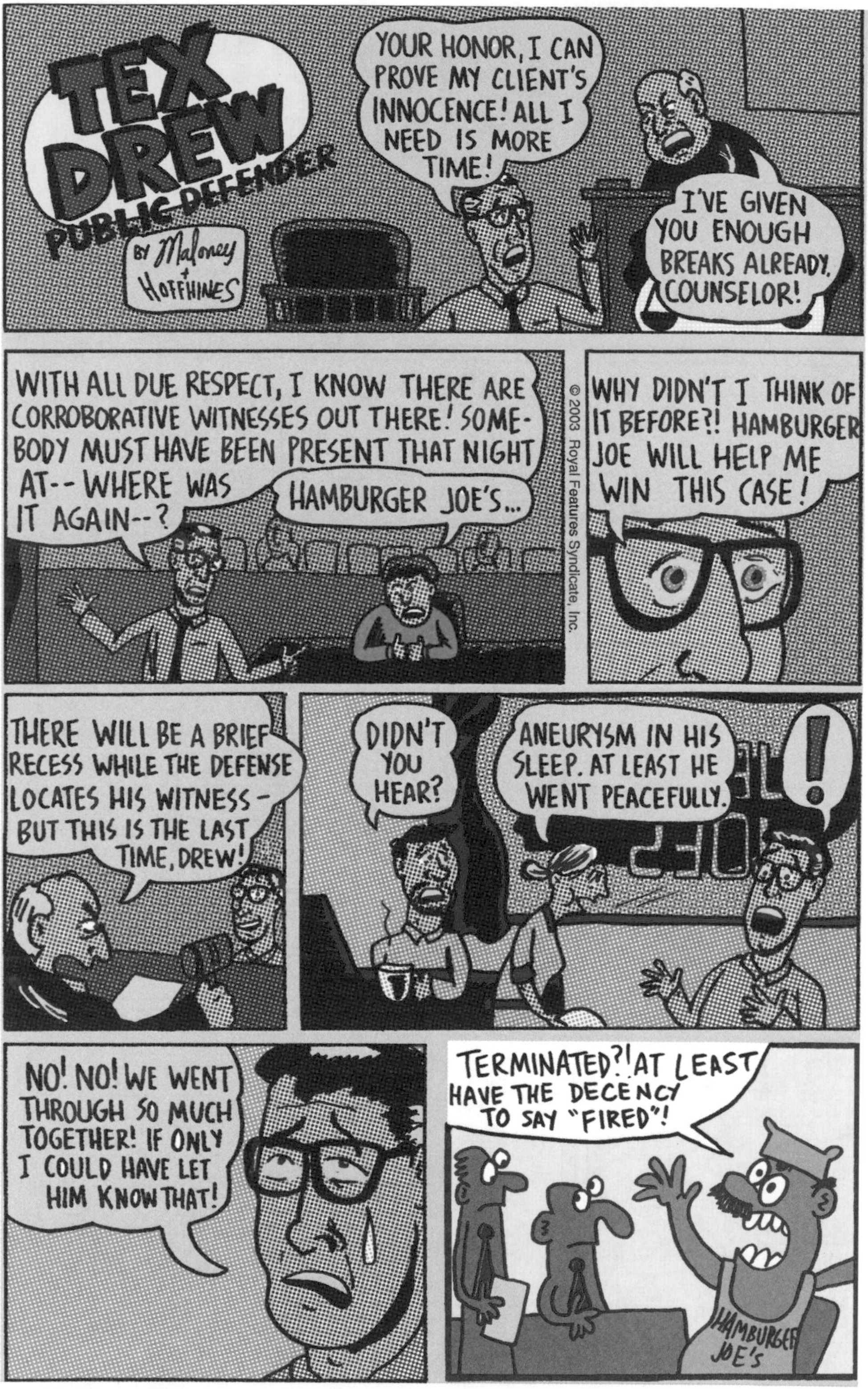
TEX DREW
PUBLIC DEFENDER
BY Maloney + HOFFHINES
YOUR HONOR, I CAN PROVE MY CLIENT'S INNOCENCE! ALL I NEED IS MORE TIME!
I'VE GIVEN YOU ENOUGH BREAKS ALREADY, COUNSELOR!
WITH ALL DUE RESPECT, I KNOW THERE ARE CORROBORATIVE WITNESSES OUT THERE! SOMEBODY MUST HAVE BEEN PRESENT THAT NIGHT AT-- WHERE WAS IT AGAIN--?
HAMBURGER JOE'S...
© 2003 Royal Features Syndicate, Inc.
WHY DIDN'T I THINK OF IT BEFORE?! HAMBURGER JOE WILL HELP ME WIN THIS CASE!
THERE WILL BE A BRIEF RECESS WHILE THE DEFENSE LOCATES HIS WITNESS - BUT THIS IS THE LAST TIME, DREW!
DIDN'T YOU HEAR?
ANEURYSM IN HIS SLEEP. AT LEAST HE WENT PEACEFULLY.
!
NO! NO! WE WENT THROUGH SO MUCH TOGETHER! IF ONLY I COULD HAVE LET HIM KNOW THAT!
TERMINATED?! AT LEAST HAVE THE DECENCY TO SAY "FIRED"!
HAMBURGER JOE'S

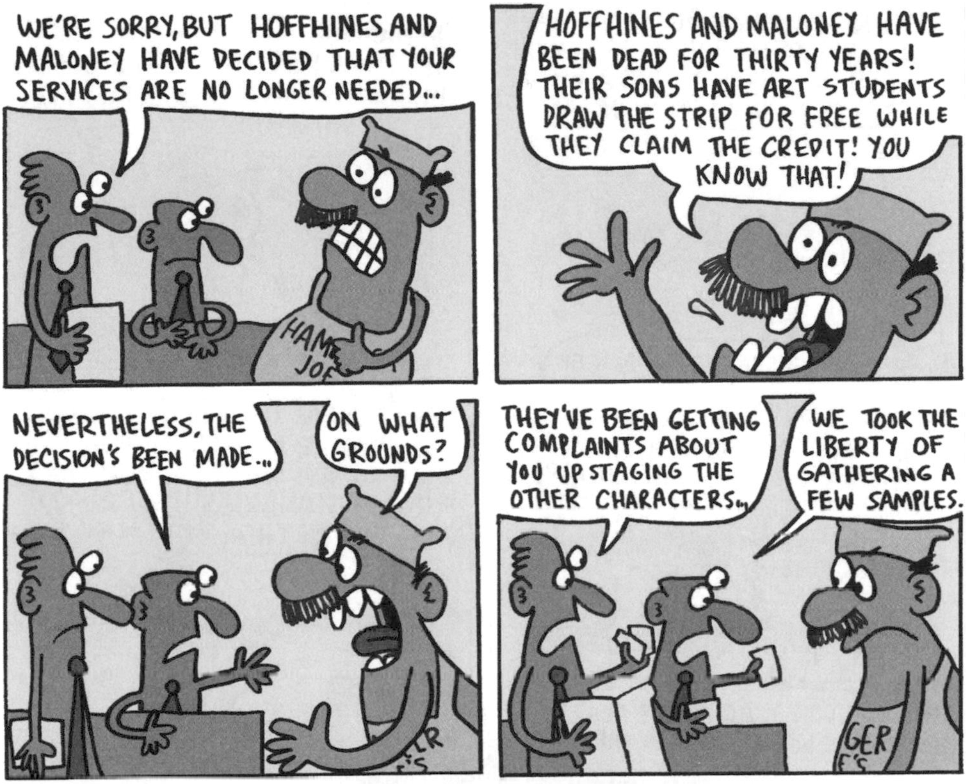
WE'RE SORRY, BUT HOFFHINES AND MALONEY HAVE DECIDED THAT YOUR SERVICES ARE NO LONGER NEEDED...
HOFFHINES AND MALONEY HAVE BEEN DEAD FOR THIRTY YEARS! THEIR SONS HAVE ART STUDENTS DRAW THE STRIP FOR FREE WHILE THEY CLAIM THE CREDIT! YOU KNOW THAT!
NEVERTHELESS, THE DECISION'S BEEN MADE...
ON WHAT GROUNDS?
THEY'VE BEEN GETTING COMPLAINTS ABOUT YOU UPSTAGING THE OTHER CHARACTERS...
WE TOOK THE LIBERTY OF GATHERING A FEW SAMPLES.

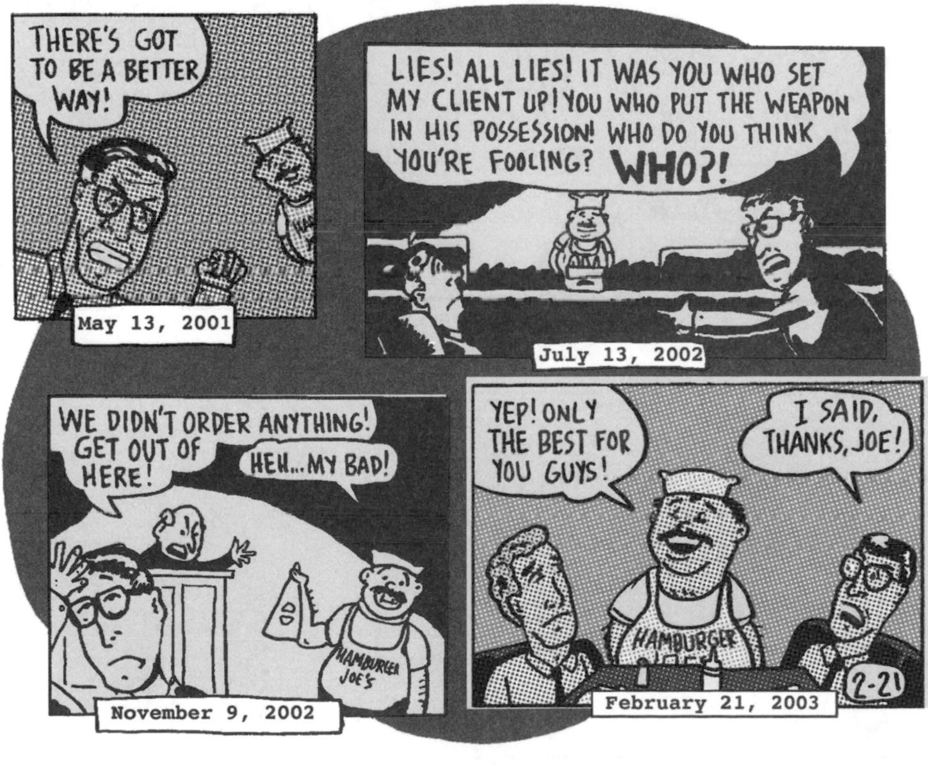
THERE'S GOT TO BE A BETTER WAY!
May 13, 2001
LIES! ALL LIES! IT WAS YOU WHO SET MY CLIENT UP! YOU WHO PUT THE WEAPON IN HIS POSSESSION! WHO DO YOU THINK YOU'RE FOOLING? WHO?!
July 13, 2002
WE DIDN'T ORDER ANYTHING! GET OUT OF HERE!
HEH... MY BAD!
HAMBURGER JOE'S
November 9, 2002
YEP! ONLY THE BEST FOR YOU GUYS!
I SAID, THANKS, JOE!
HAMBURGER
2-21
February 21, 2003

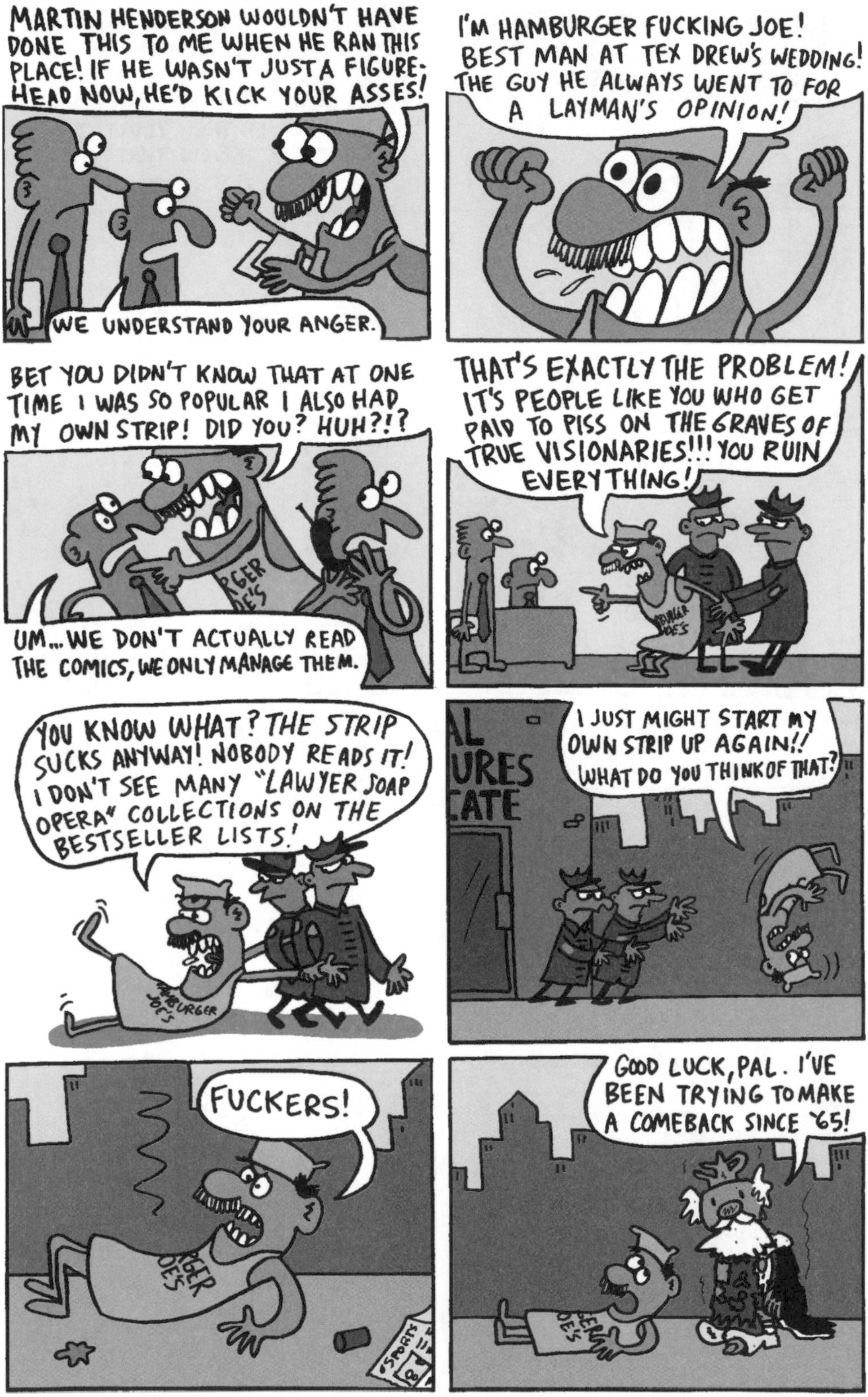
MARTIN HENDERSON WOULDN'T HAVE DONE THIS TO ME WHEN HE RAN THIS PLACE! IF HE WASN'T JUST A FIGURE-HEAD NOW, HE'D KICK YOUR ASSES!
WE UNDERSTAND YOUR ANGER.
I'M HAMBURGER FUCKING JOE! BEST MAN AT TEX DREW'S WEDDING! THE GUY HE ALWAYS WENT TO FOR A LAYMAN'S OPINION!
BET YOU DIDN'T KNOW THAT AT ONE TIME I WAS SO POPULAR I ALSO HAD MY OWN STRIP! DID YOU? HUH?!?
UM... WE DON'T ACTUALLY READ THE COMICS, WE ONLY MANAGE THEM.
THAT'S EXACTLY THE PROBLEM! IT'S PEOPLE LIKE YOU WHO GET PAID TO PISS ON THE GRAVES OF TRUE VISIONARIES!!! YOU RUIN EVERYTHING!
YOU KNOW WHAT? THE STRIP SUCKS ANYWAY! NOBODY READS IT! I DON'T SEE MANY "LAWYER SOAP OPERA" COLLECTIONS ON THE BESTSELLER LISTS!
HAMBURGER JOE'S
I JUST MIGHT START MY OWN STRIP UP AGAIN!! WHAT DO YOU THINK OF THAT?
FUCKERS!
SPORTS
GOOD LUCK, PAL. I'VE BEEN TRYING TO MAKE A COMEBACK SINCE '65!

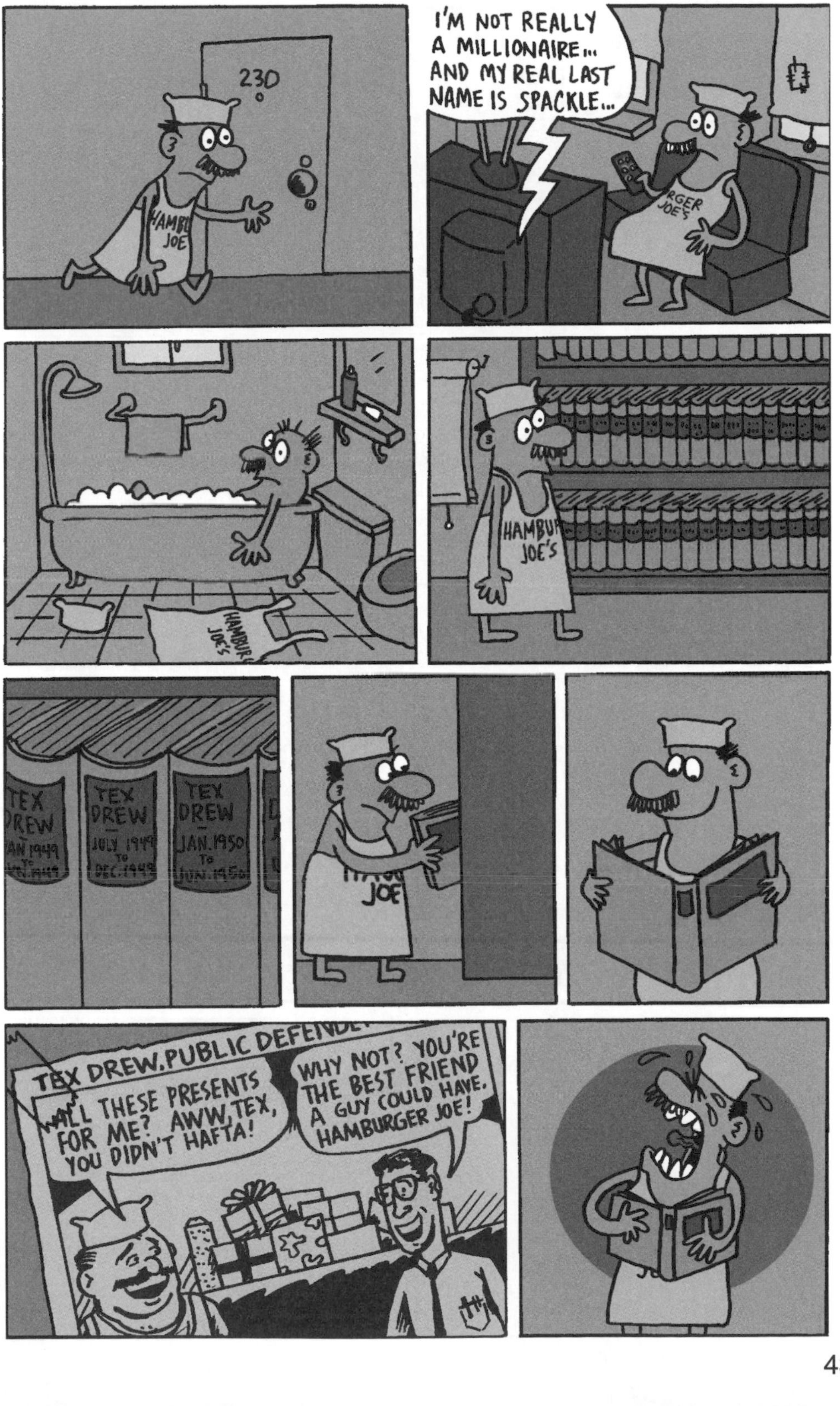
230
I'M NOT REALLY A MILLIONAIRE... AND MY REAL LAST NAME IS SPACKLE...
TEX DREW JAN 1949
TEX DREW JULY 1949 TO DEC. 1949
TEX DREW JAN. 1950
TEX DREW, PUBLIC DEFENDER
ALL THESE PRESENTS FOR ME? AWW, TEX, YOU DIDN'T HAFTA!
WHY NOT? YOU'RE THE BEST FRIEND A GUY COULD HAVE, HAMBURGER JOE!

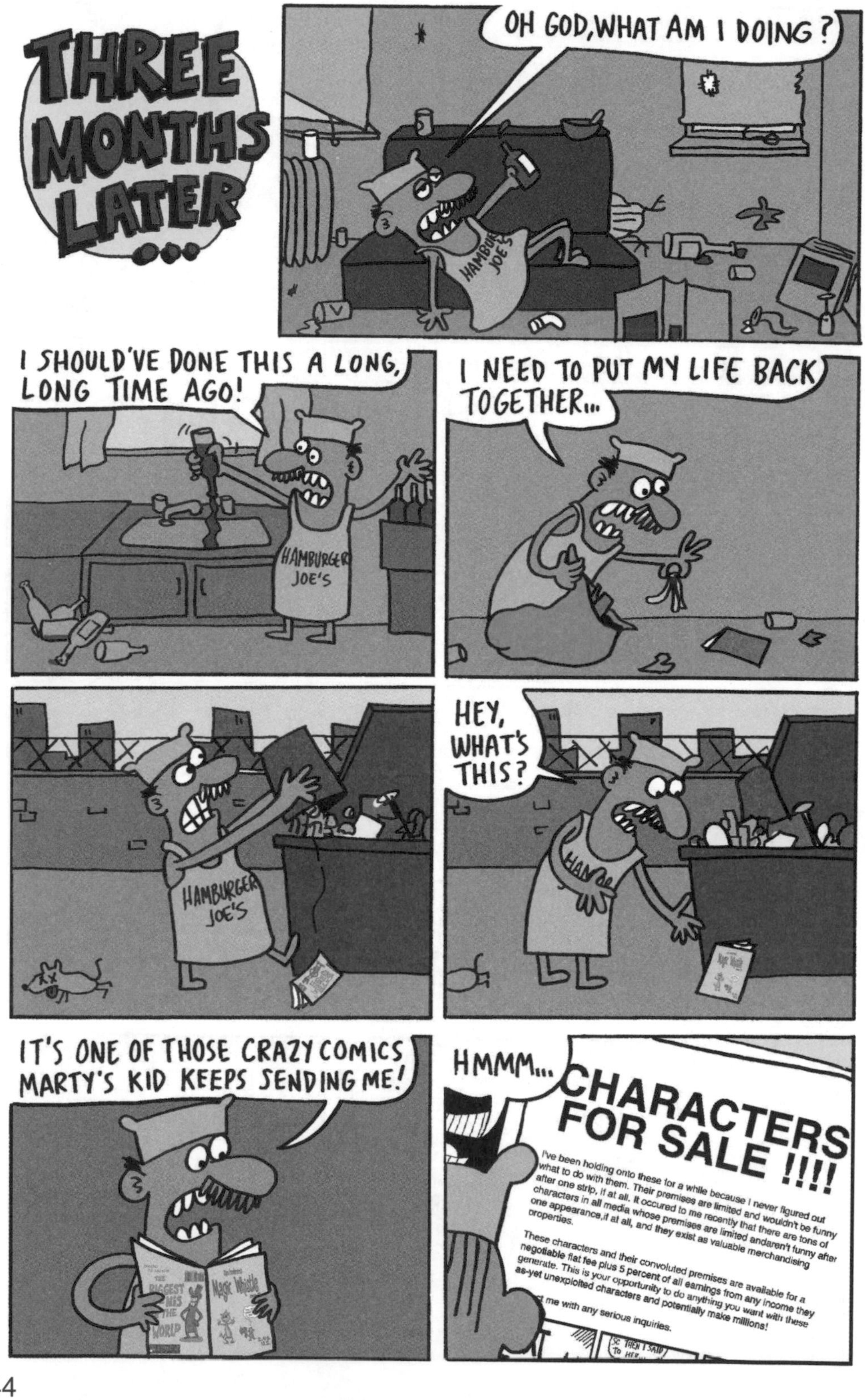
THREE MONTHS LATER...
OH GOD, WHAT AM I DOING?
HAMBURGER JOE'S
I SHOULD'VE DONE THIS A LONG, LONG TIME AGO!
HAMBURGER JOE'S
I NEED TO PUT MY LIFE BACK TOGETHER...
HAMBURGER JOE'S
HEY, WHAT'S THIS?
IT'S ONE OF THOSE CRAZY COMICS MARTY'S KID KEEPS SENDING ME!
THE BIGGEST NIS THE WORLD
Magic Whistle
HMMM...
CHARACTERS FOR SALE !!!!
I've been holding onto these for a while because I never figured out what to do with them. Their premises are limited and wouldn't be funny after one strip, if at all. It occured to me recently that there are tons of characters in all media whose premises are limited andaren't funny after one appearance,if at all, and they exist as valuable merchandising properties.
These characters and their convoluted premises are available for a negotiable flat fee plus 5 percent of all earnings from any income they generate. This is your opportunity to do anything you want with these as-yet unexploited characters and potentially make millions!
me with any serious inquiries.
THEN I SAID TO HER...

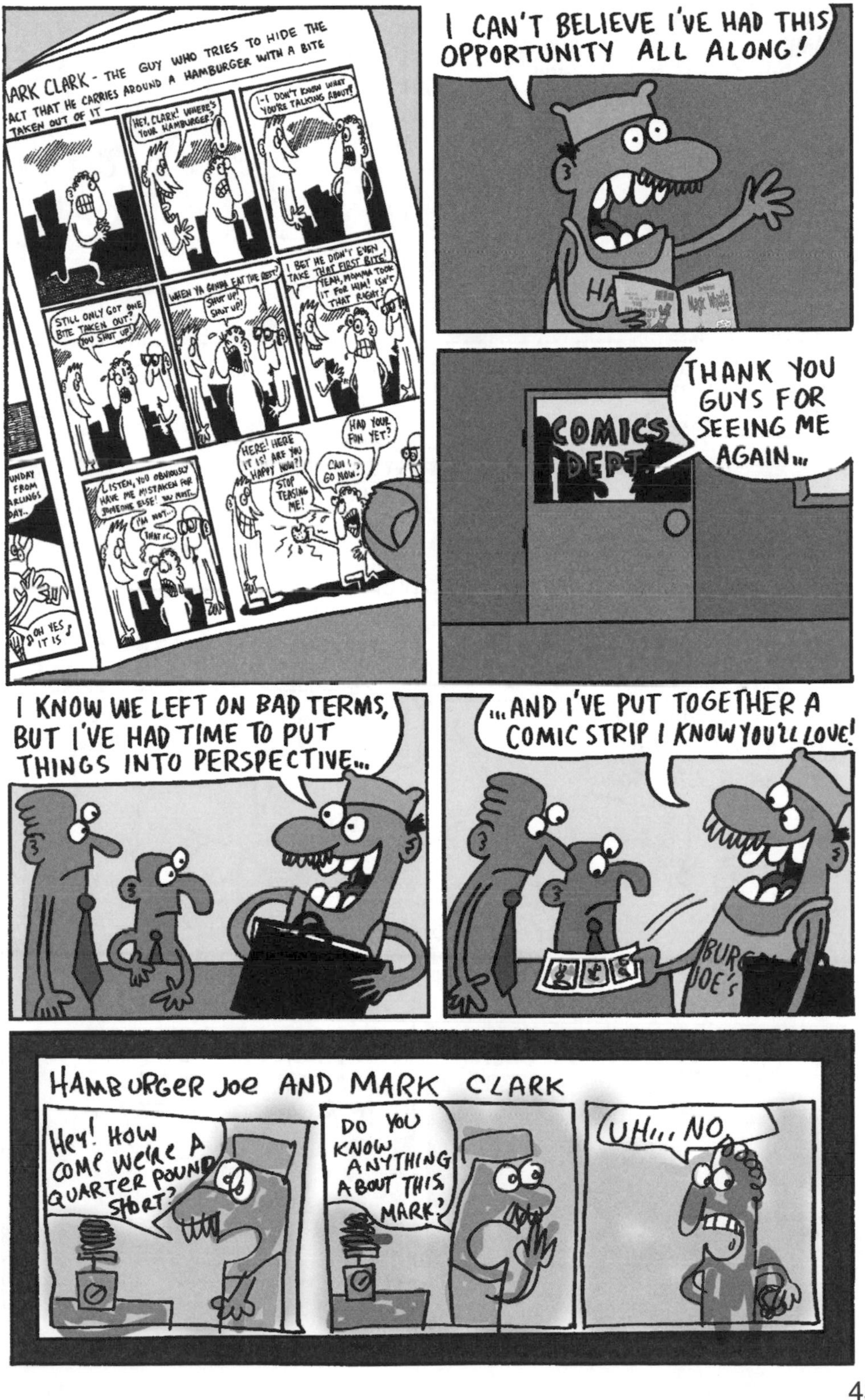
ARK CLARK - THE GUY WHO TRIES TO HIDE THE ACT THAT HE CARRIES AROUND A HAMBURGER WITH A BITE TAKEN OUT OF IT
HEY, CLARK! WHERE'S YOUR HAMBURGER?
!
I-I DON'T KNOW WHAT YOU'RE TALKING ABOUT!
STILL ONLY GOT ONE BITE TAKEN OUT?
YOU SHUT UP!
WHEN YA GONNA EAT THE REST?
SHUT UP! SHUT UP!
I BET HE DIDN'T EVEN TAKE THAT FIRST BITE!
YEAH, MOMMA TOOK IT FOR HIM! ISN'T THAT RIGHT?
OH YES IT IS
LISTEN, YOU OBVIOUSLY HAVE ME MISTAKEN FOR SOMEONE ELSE! YOU MUST...
I'M NOT...
THAT IC...
HERE! HERE IT IS! ARE YOU HAPPY NOW?!
STOP TEASING ME!
CAN I GO NOW?
HAD YOUR FUN YET?
I CAN'T BELIEVE I'VE HAD THIS OPPORTUNITY ALL ALONG!
Magic Whistle
COMICS DEPT.
THANK YOU GUYS FOR SEEING ME AGAIN...
I KNOW WE LEFT ON BAD TERMS, BUT I'VE HAD TIME TO PUT THINGS INTO PERSPECTIVE...
...AND I'VE PUT TOGETHER A COMIC STRIP I KNOW YOU'LL LOVE!
BURG JOE'S
HAMBURGER JOE AND MARK CLARK
Hey! HOW COME WE'RE A QUARTER POUND SHORT?
DO YOU KNOW ANYTHING ABOUT THIS, MARK?
UH... NO.

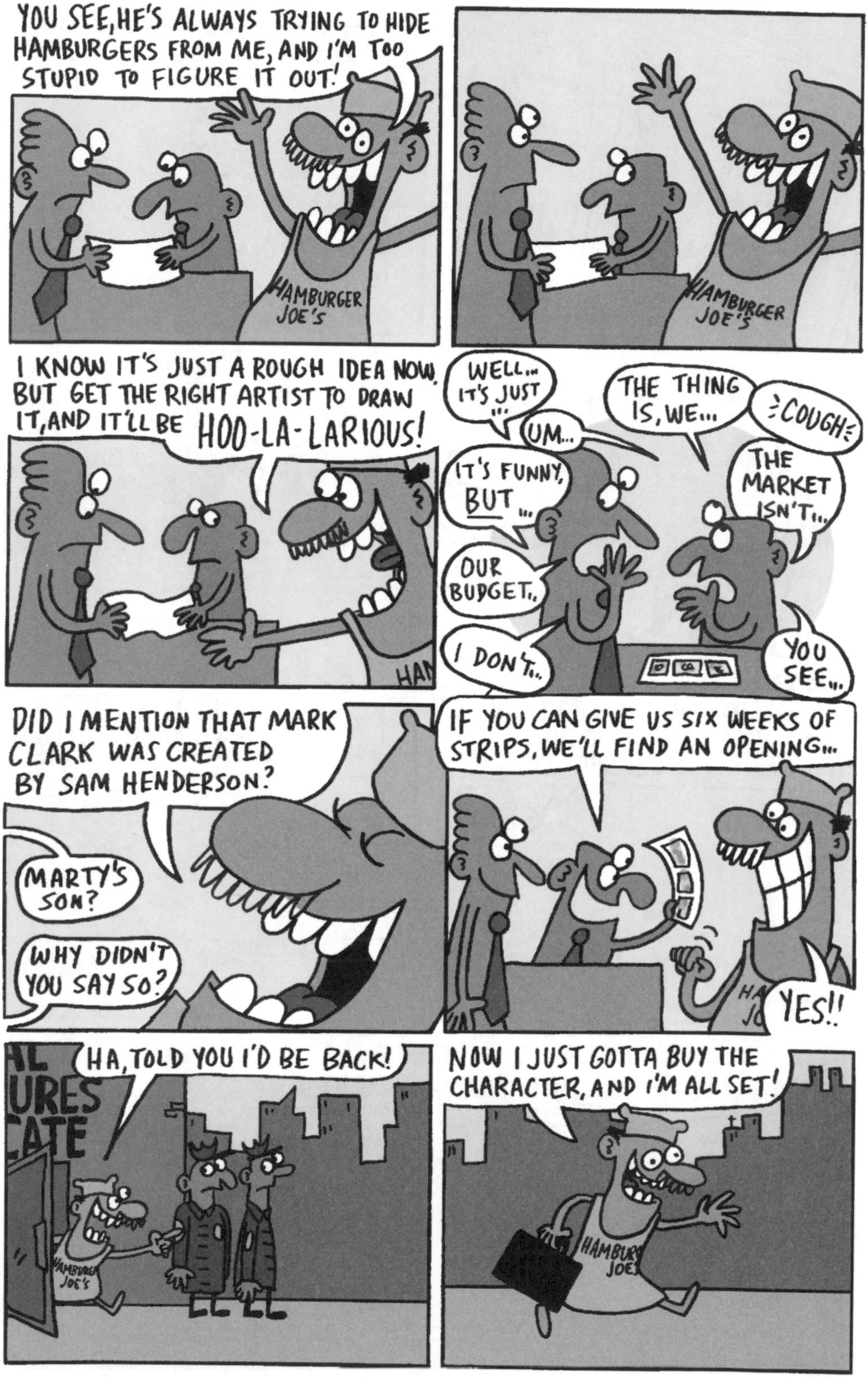
YOU SEE, HE'S ALWAYS TRYING TO HIDE HAMBURGERS FROM ME, AND I'M TOO STUPID TO FIGURE IT OUT!
HAMBURGER JOE'S
HAMBURGER JOE'S
I KNOW IT'S JUST A ROUGH IDEA NOW, BUT GET THE RIGHT ARTIST TO DRAW IT, AND IT'LL BE HOO-LA-LARIOUS!
HAM
WELL... IT'S JUST ...
UM...
THE THING IS, WE...
COUGH
IT'S FUNNY, BUT ...
THE MARKET ISN'T...
OUR BUDGET..
I DON'T...
YOU SEE...
DID I MENTION THAT MARK CLARK WAS CREATED BY SAM HENDERSON?
MARTY'S SON?
WHY DIDN'T YOU SAY SO?
IF YOU CAN GIVE US SIX WEEKS OF STRIPS, WE'LL FIND AN OPENING...
YES!!
HA, TOLD YOU I'D BE BACK!
HAMBURGER JOE'S
NOW I JUST GOTTA BUY THE CHARACTER, AND I'M ALL SET!
HAMBURG JOE'S

LOOK AT YOU! YOUR OWN STUDIO, AND YOU'RE GROWING A BEARD!

SAM HENDERSON STUDIOS

YEAH, AND I'M ONLY THIRTY-THREE!

YOU KNOW, THEY LOVE YOU AT THE SYNDICATE. HOW COME YOU DON'T WORK THERE?

I DON'T KNOW. THE DAILY NEWSPAPER STRIP'S NOT REALLY FOR ME.

THIS "CHARACTERS FOR SALE" GIMMICK DIDN'T TAKE OFF LIKE I THOUGHT. I'VE ONLY SOLD ONE SO FAR...

...SO WHICH ONE DO YOU LIKE?

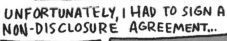

MARK CLARK, THE GUY WHO TRIES TO HIDE THE FACT THAT HE CARRIES AROUND A HAMBURGER WITH A BITE TAKEN OUT!

OH.

THAT'S...UH...THAT'S THE ONE I SOLD.

TO WHO? I'LL BUY IT FROM THEM!

UNFORTUNATELY, I HAD TO SIGN A NON-DISCLOSURE AGREEMENT...

BUT I'VE GOT OTHERS. FRIENDS OF FAMILY DISCOUNT...

THANKS ANYWAY...

NOOOOOO!!

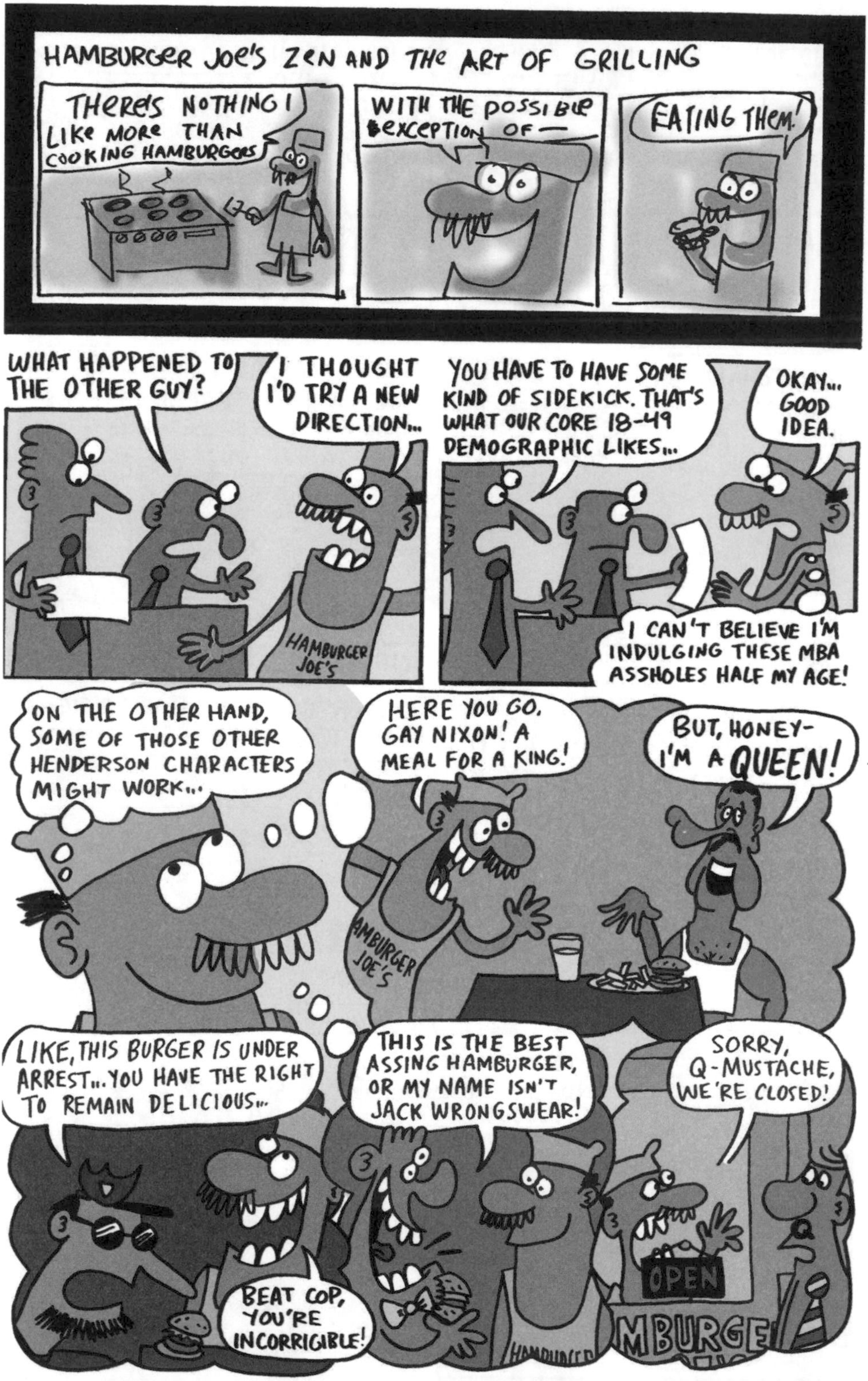
HAMBURGER JOE'S ZEN AND THE ART OF GRILLING
THERE'S NOTHING I LIKE MORE THAN COOKING HAMBURGERS
WITH THE POSSIBLE EXCEPTION OF—
EATING THEM!
WHAT HAPPENED TO THE OTHER GUY?
I THOUGHT I'D TRY A NEW DIRECTION...
HAMBURGER JOE'S
YOU HAVE TO HAVE SOME KIND OF SIDEKICK. THAT'S WHAT OUR CORE 18-49 DEMOGRAPHIC LIKES...
OKAY... GOOD IDEA.
I CAN'T BELIEVE I'M INDULGING THESE MBA ASSHOLES HALF MY AGE!
ON THE OTHER HAND, SOME OF THOSE OTHER HENDERSON CHARACTERS MIGHT WORK...
HERE YOU GO, GAY NIXON! A MEAL FOR A KING!
BUT, HONEY- I'M A QUEEN!
HAMBURGER JOE'S
LIKE, THIS BURGER IS UNDER ARREST... YOU HAVE THE RIGHT TO REMAIN DELICIOUS...
THIS IS THE BEST ASSING HAMBURGER, OR MY NAME ISN'T JACK WRONGSWEAR!
SORRY, Q-MUSTACHE, WE'RE CLOSED!
BEAT COP, YOU'RE INCORRIGIBLE!
OPEN
MBURGE

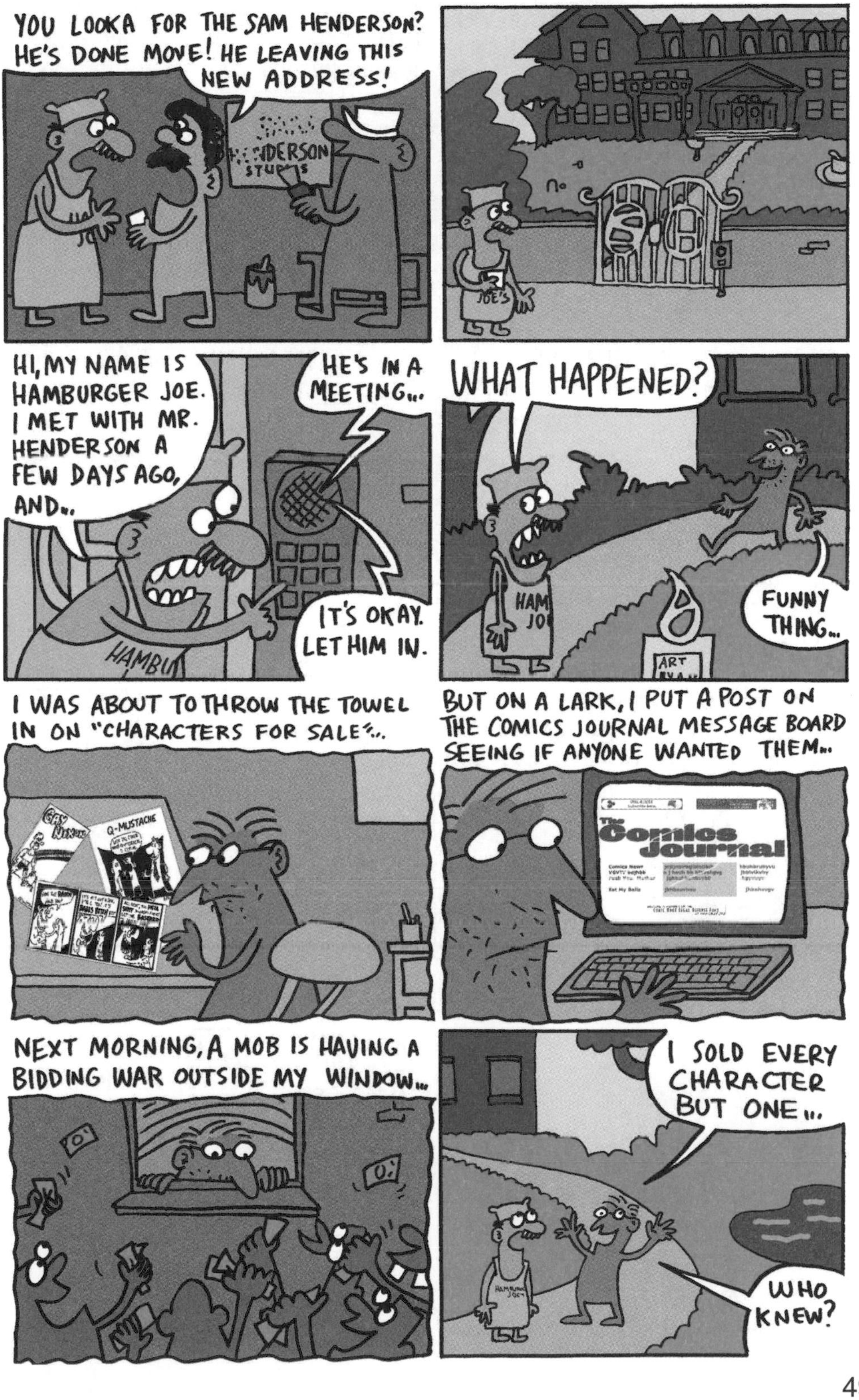

YOU LOOKA FOR THE SAM HENDERSON? HE'S DONE MOVE! HE LEAVING THIS NEW ADDRESS!
JOE'S
HI, MY NAME IS HAMBURGER JOE. I MET WITH MR. HENDERSON A FEW DAYS AGO, AND..
HE'S IN A MEETING...
IT'S OKAY. LET HIM IN.
WHAT HAPPENED?
FUNNY THING...
ART
I WAS ABOUT TO THROW THE TOWEL IN ON "CHARACTERS FOR SALE"..
Q-MUSTACHE
BUT ON A LARK, I PUT A POST ON THE COMICS JOURNAL MESSAGE BOARD SEEING IF ANYONE WANTED THEM..
The Comics Journal
NEXT MORNING, A MOB IS HAVING A BIDDING WAR OUTSIDE MY WINDOW...
I SOLD EVERY CHARACTER BUT ONE...
WHO KNEW?

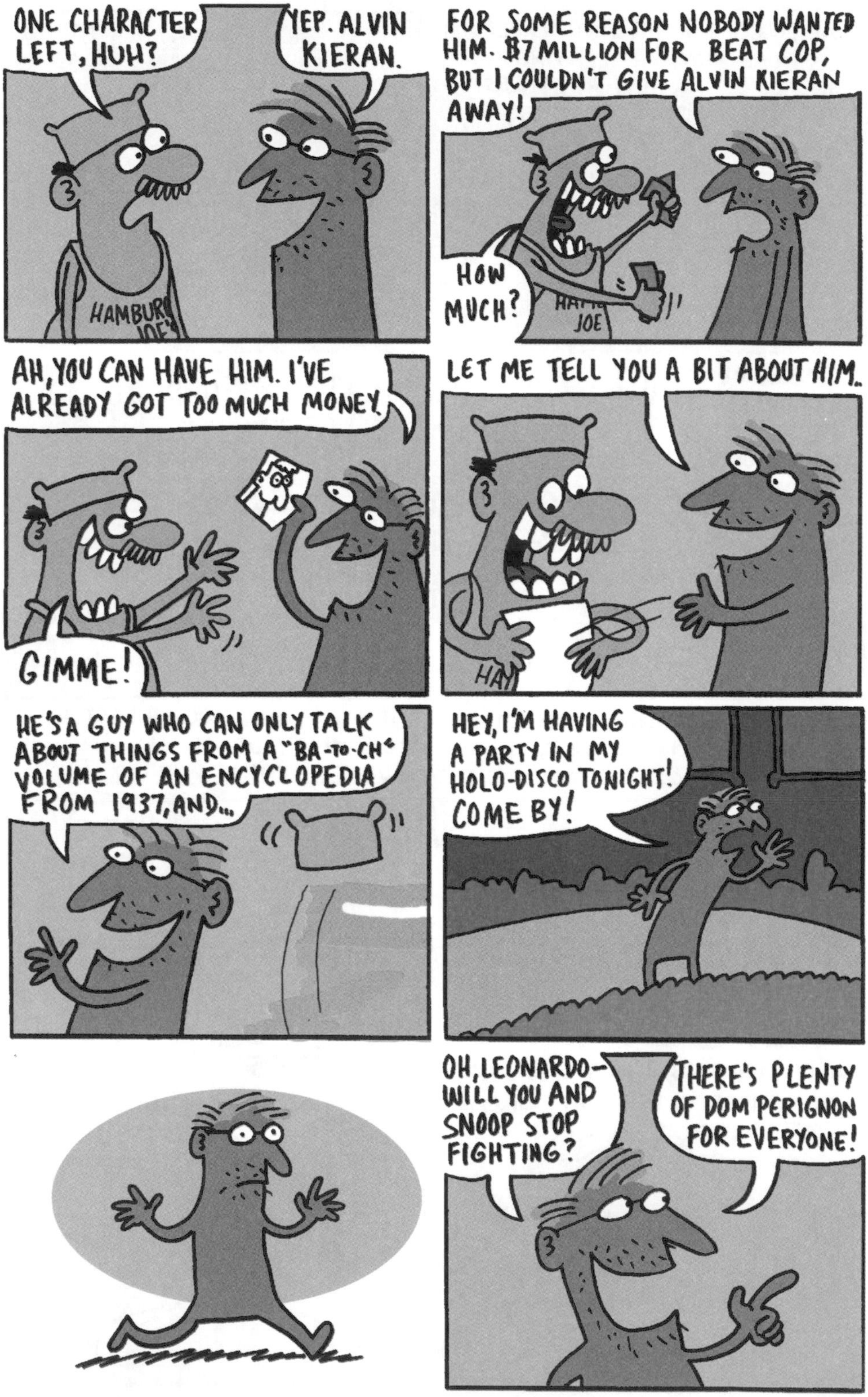
ONE CHARACTER LEFT, HUH?
YEP. ALVIN KIERAN.
HAMBURG JOE'S
FOR SOME REASON NOBODY WANTED HIM. $7 MILLION FOR BEAT COP, BUT I COULDN'T GIVE ALVIN KIERAN AWAY!
HOW MUCH?
JOE
AH, YOU CAN HAVE HIM. I'VE ALREADY GOT TOO MUCH MONEY.
GIMME!
LET ME TELL YOU A BIT ABOUT HIM..
HE'S A GUY WHO CAN ONLY TALK ABOUT THINGS FROM A "BA-TO-CH" VOLUME OF AN ENCYCLOPEDIA FROM 1937, AND...
HEY, I'M HAVING A PARTY IN MY HOLO-DISCO TONIGHT! COME BY!
OH, LEONARDO- WILL YOU AND SNOOP STOP FIGHTING?
THERE'S PLENTY OF DOM PERIGNON FOR EVERYONE!

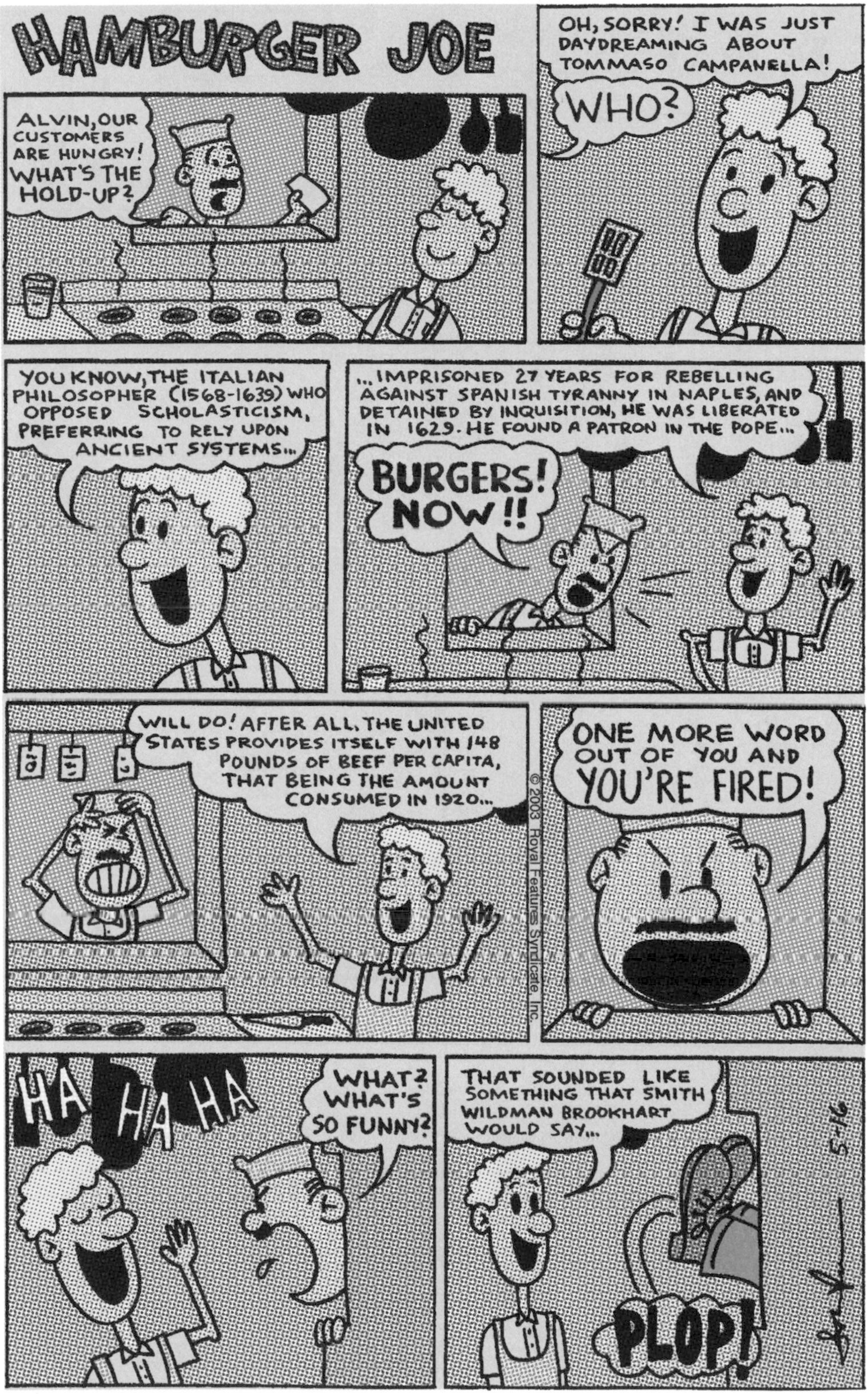
HAMBURGER JOE
ALVIN, OUR CUSTOMERS ARE HUNGRY! WHAT'S THE HOLD-UP?
OH, SORRY! I WAS JUST DAYDREAMING ABOUT TOMMASO CAMPANELLA!
WHO?
YOU KNOW, THE ITALIAN PHILOSOPHER (1568-1639) WHO OPPOSED SCHOLASTICISM, PREFERRING TO RELY UPON ANCIENT SYSTEMS...
...IMPRISONED 27 YEARS FOR REBELLING AGAINST SPANISH TYRANNY IN NAPLES, AND DETAINED BY INQUISITION, HE WAS LIBERATED IN 1629. HE FOUND A PATRON IN THE POPE...
BURGERS! NOW!!
WILL DO! AFTER ALL, THE UNITED STATES PROVIDES ITSELF WITH 148 POUNDS OF BEEF PER CAPITA, THAT BEING THE AMOUNT CONSUMED IN 1920...
© 2003 Royal Features Syndicate, Inc.
ONE MORE WORD OUT OF YOU AND YOU'RE FIRED!
HA HA HA HA
WHAT? WHAT'S SO FUNNY?
THAT SOUNDED LIKE SOMETHING THAT SMITH WILDMAN BROOKHART WOULD SAY...
PLOP!
5-16

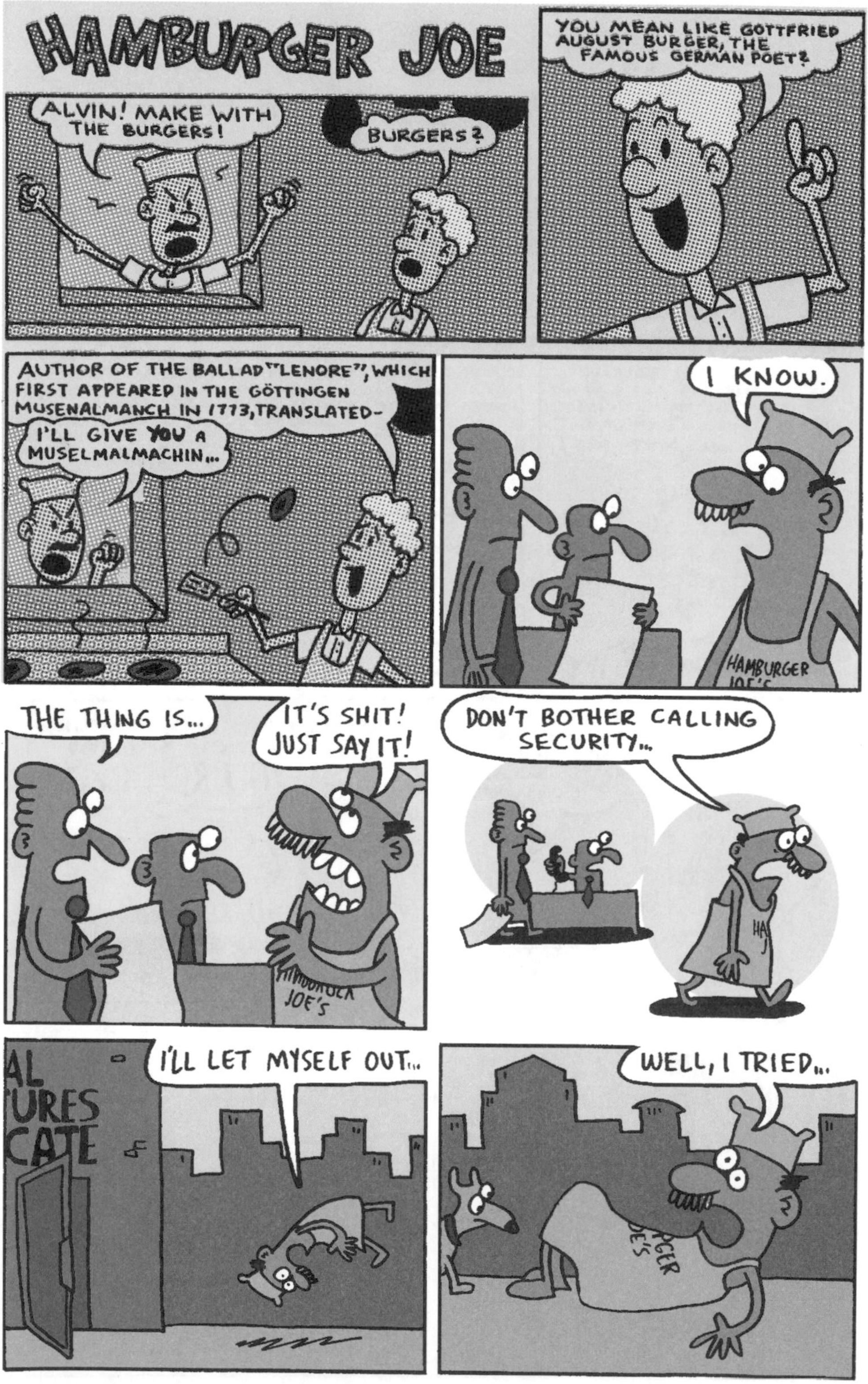
HAMBURGER JOE
ALVIN! MAKE WITH THE BURGERS!
BURGERS?
YOU MEAN LIKE GOTTFRIED AUGUST BURGER, THE FAMOUS GERMAN POET?
AUTHOR OF THE BALLAD "LENORE", WHICH FIRST APPEARED IN THE GÖTTINGEN MUSENALMANCH IN 1773, TRANSLATED-
I'LL GIVE YOU A MUSELMALMACHIN...
I KNOW.
HAMBURGER JOE'S
THE THING IS...
IT'S SHIT! JUST SAY IT!
JOE'S
DON'T BOTHER CALLING SECURITY...
I'LL LET MYSELF OUT...
WELL, I TRIED...

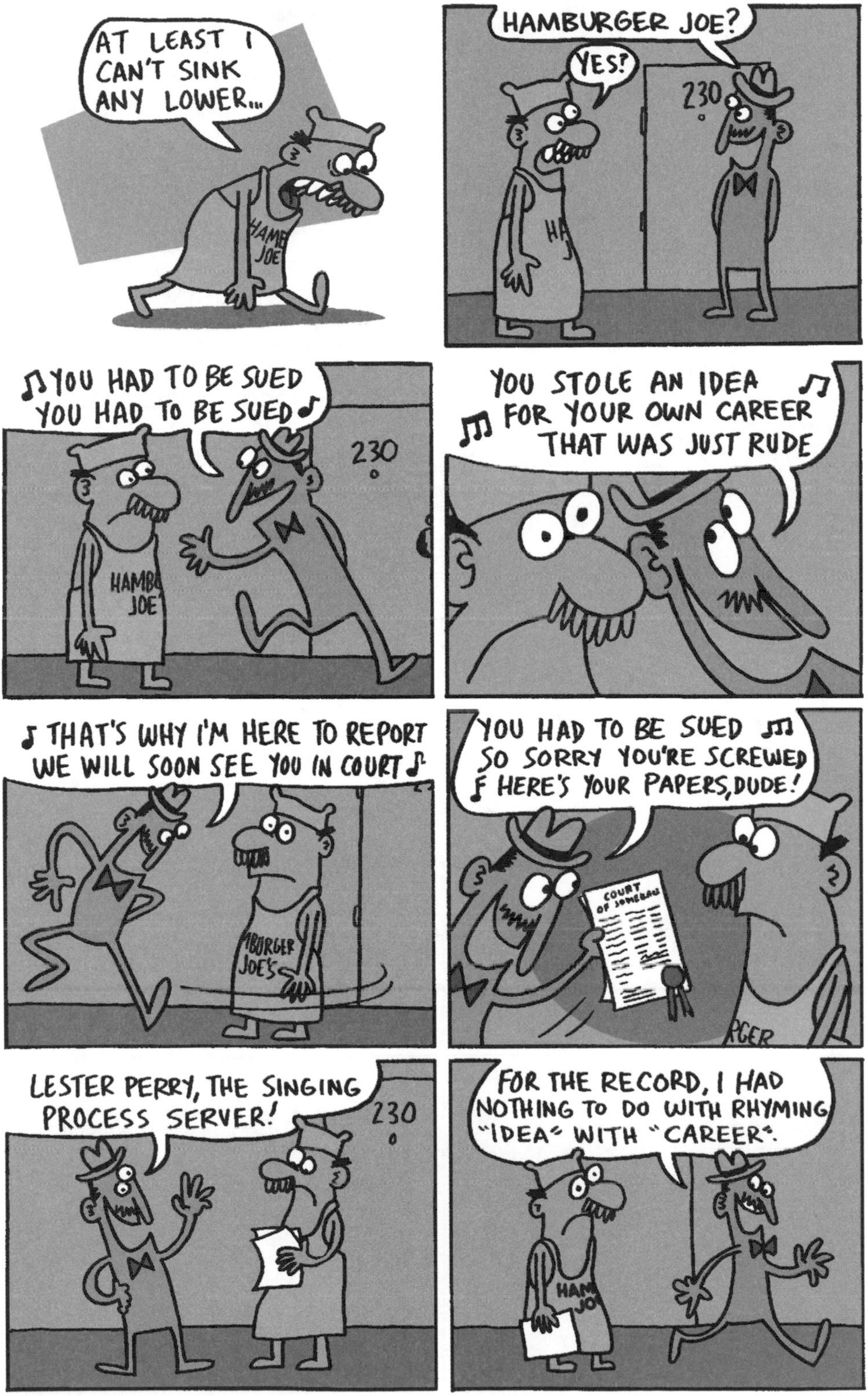
AT LEAST I CAN'T SINK ANY LOWER...
HAMBURGER JOE?
YES?
230
HAMB JOE
♫ YOU HAD TO BE SUED YOU HAD TO BE SUED ♪
230
HAMB JOE
YOU STOLE AN IDEA ♫ ♫ FOR YOUR OWN CAREER THAT WAS JUST RUDE
♪ THAT'S WHY I'M HERE TO REPORT WE WILL SOON SEE YOU IN COURT ♪
BURGER JOE'S
YOU HAD TO BE SUED ♫ SO SORRY YOU'RE SCREWED ♪ HERE'S YOUR PAPERS, DUDE!
COURT
LESTER PERRY, THE SINGING PROCESS SERVER!
230
FOR THE RECORD, I HAD NOTHING TO DO WITH RHYMING "IDEA" WITH "CAREER".

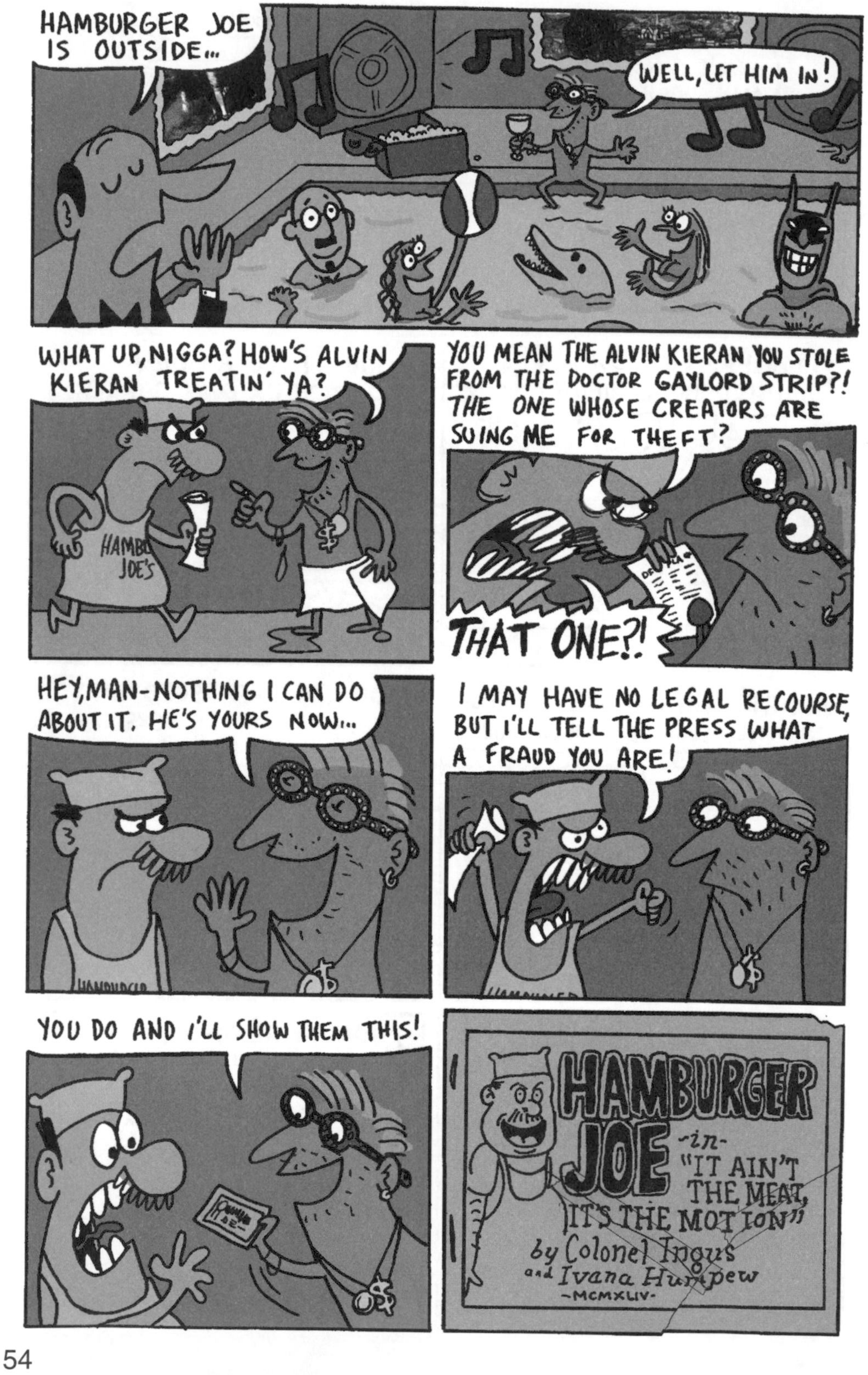
HAMBURGER JOE IS OUTSIDE...
WELL, LET HIM IN!
WHAT UP, NIGGA? HOW'S ALVIN KIERAN TREATIN' YA?
YOU MEAN THE ALVIN KIERAN YOU STOLE FROM THE DOCTOR GAYLORD STRIP?! THE ONE WHOSE CREATORS ARE SUING ME FOR THEFT?
THAT ONE?!
HEY, MAN- NOTHING I CAN DO ABOUT IT. HE'S YOURS NOW...
I MAY HAVE NO LEGAL RECOURSE, BUT I'LL TELL THE PRESS WHAT A FRAUD YOU ARE!
YOU DO AND I'LL SHOW THEM THIS!
HAMBURGER JOE -in- "IT AIN'T THE MEAT, IT'S THE MOTION"
by Colonel Ingus and Ivana Humpew
-MCMXLIV-

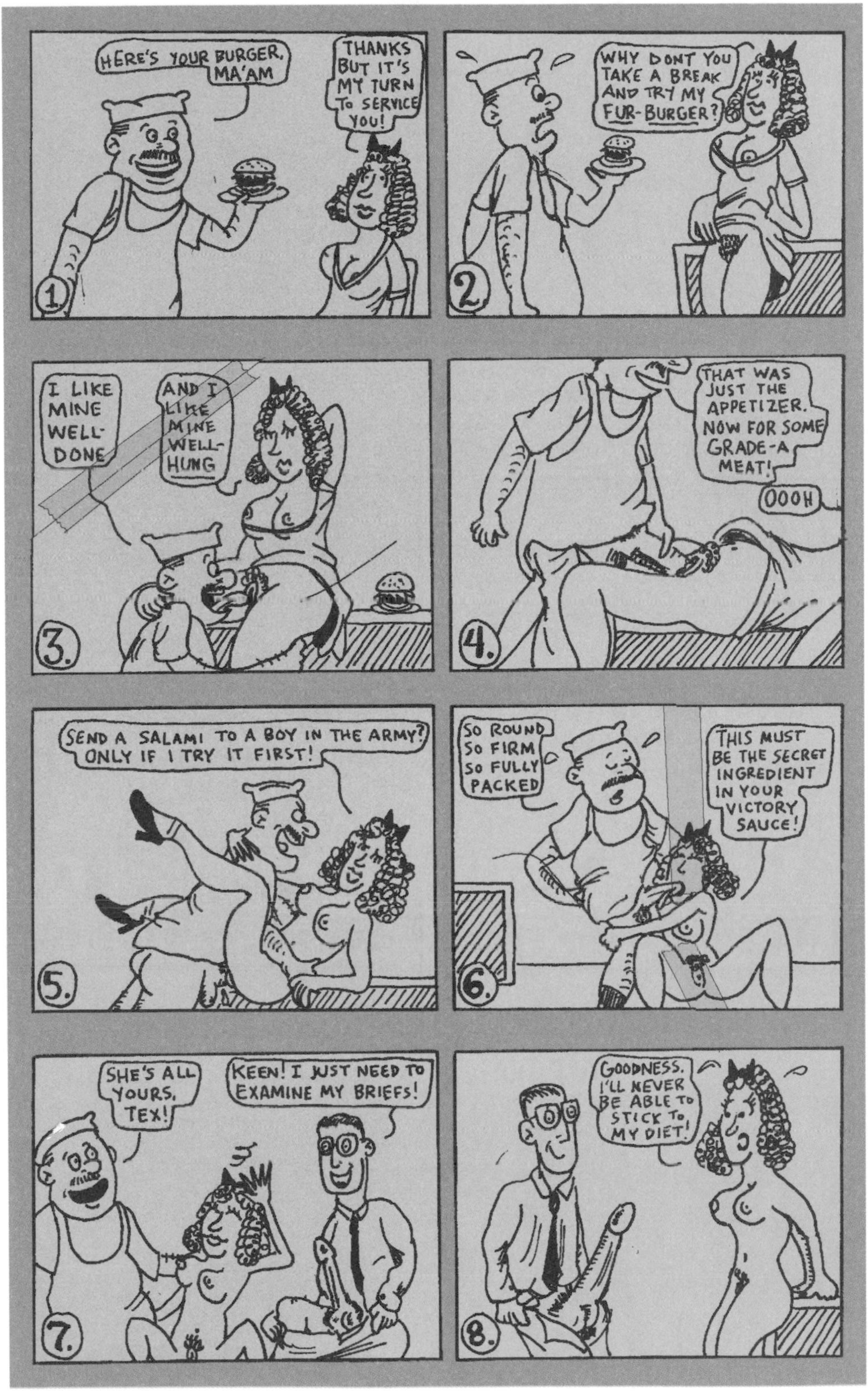
HERE'S YOUR BURGER, MA'AM
THANKS BUT IT'S MY TURN TO SERVICE YOU!
WHY DONT YOU TAKE A BREAK AND TRY MY FUR-BURGER?
I LIKE MINE WELL-DONE
AND I LIKE MINE WELL-HUNG
THAT WAS JUST THE APPETIZER. NOW FOR SOME GRADE-A MEAT!
OOOH
SEND A SALAMI TO A BOY IN THE ARMY? ONLY IF I TRY IT FIRST!
SO ROUND SO FIRM SO FULLY PACKED
THIS MUST BE THE SECRET INGREDIENT IN YOUR VICTORY SAUCE!
SHE'S ALL YOURS, TEX!
KEEN! I JUST NEED TO EXAMINE MY BRIEFS!
GOODNESS. I'LL NEVER BE ABLE TO STICK TO MY DIET!

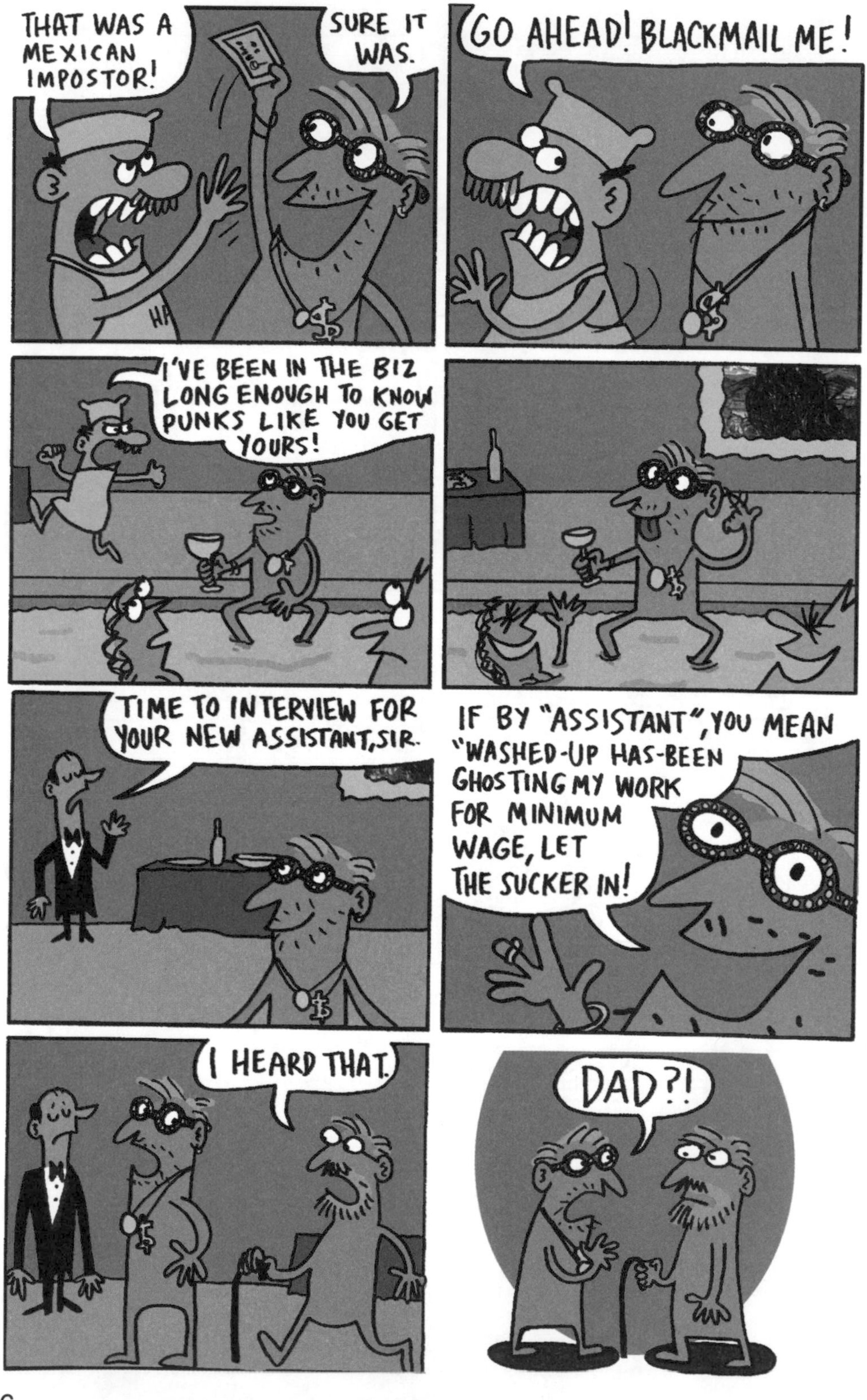
THAT WAS A MEXICAN IMPOSTOR!
SURE IT WAS.
GO AHEAD! BLACKMAIL ME!
I'VE BEEN IN THE BIZ LONG ENOUGH TO KNOW PUNKS LIKE YOU GET YOURS!
TIME TO INTERVIEW FOR YOUR NEW ASSISTANT, SIR.
IF BY "ASSISTANT", YOU MEAN "WASHED-UP HAS-BEEN GHOSTING MY WORK FOR MINIMUM WAGE, LET THE SUCKER IN!
I HEARD THAT.
DAD?!

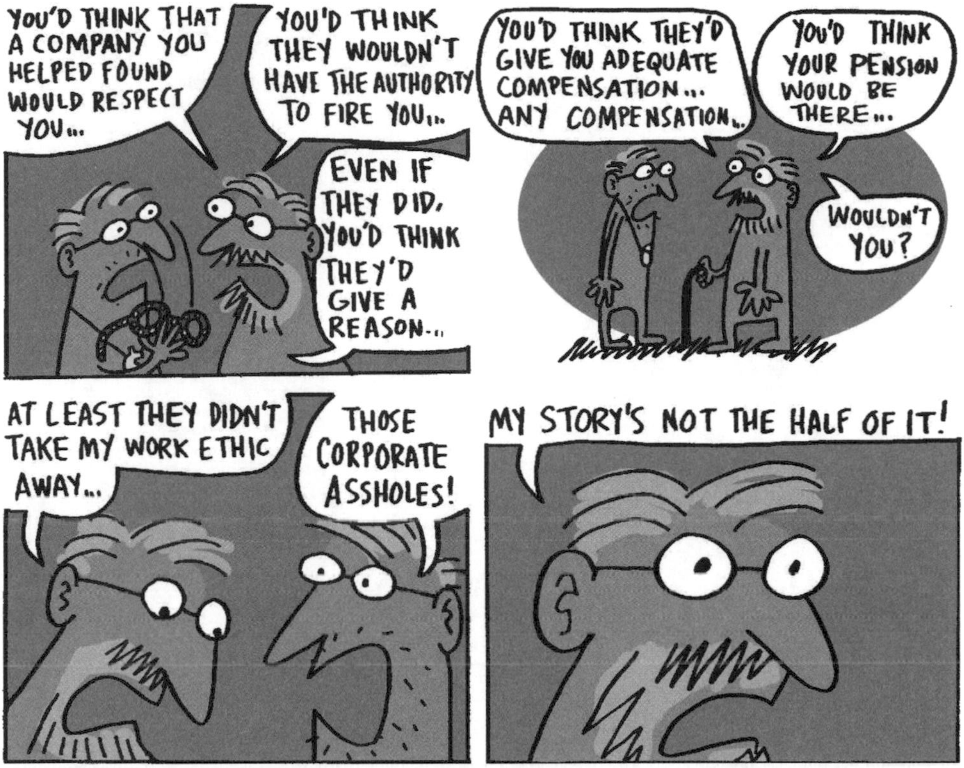
YOU'D THINK THAT A COMPANY YOU HELPED FOUND WOULD RESPECT YOU...
YOU'D THINK THEY WOULDN'T HAVE THE AUTHORITY TO FIRE YOU...
EVEN IF THEY DID, YOU'D THINK THEY'D GIVE A REASON...
YOU'D THINK THEY'D GIVE YOU ADEQUATE COMPENSATION... ANY COMPENSATION...
YOU'D THINK YOUR PENSION WOULD BE THERE...
WOULDN'T YOU?
AT LEAST THEY DIDN'T TAKE MY WORK ETHIC AWAY...
THOSE CORPORATE ASSHOLES!
MY STORY'S NOT THE HALF OF IT!

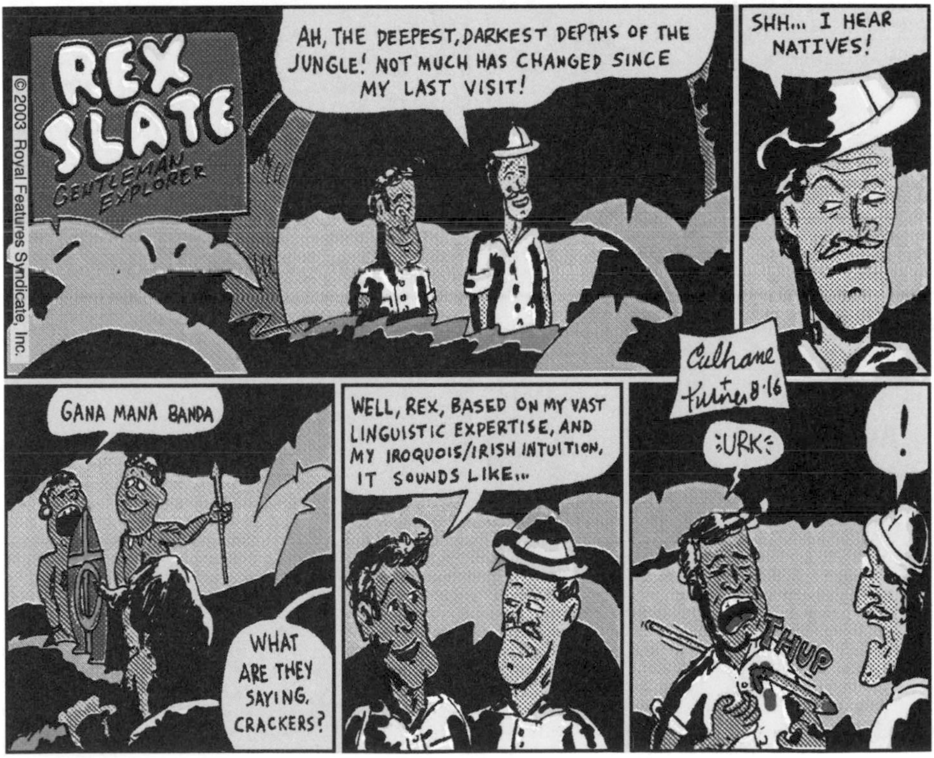
REX SLATE
GENTLEMAN EXPLORER
© 2003 Royal Features Syndicate, Inc.
AH, THE DEEPEST, DARKEST DEPTHS OF THE JUNGLE! NOT MUCH HAS CHANGED SINCE MY LAST VISIT!
SHH... I HEAR NATIVES!
Culhane + Turner 8·16
GANA MANA BANDA
WHAT ARE THEY SAYING, CRACKERS?
WELL, REX, BASED ON MY VAST LINGUISTIC EXPERTISE, AND MY IROQUOIS/IRISH INTUITION, IT SOUNDS LIKE...
URK
THUP
!

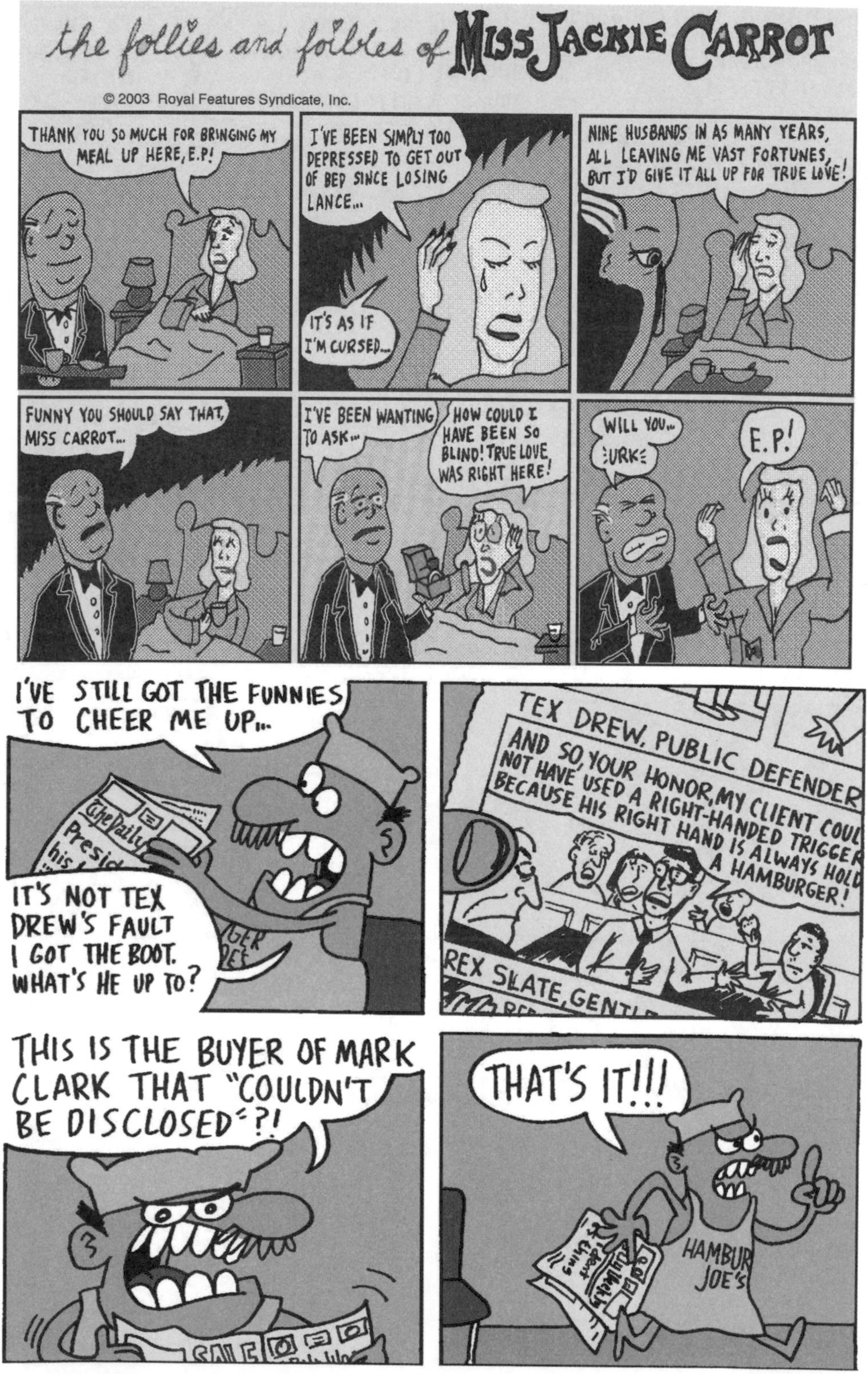
the follies and foibles of MISS JACKIE CARROT
© 2003 Royal Features Syndicate, Inc.
THANK YOU SO MUCH FOR BRINGING MY MEAL UP HERE, E.P.!
I'VE BEEN SIMPLY TOO DEPRESSED TO GET OUT OF BED SINCE LOSING LANCE...
IT'S AS IF I'M CURSED...
NINE HUSBANDS IN AS MANY YEARS, ALL LEAVING ME VAST FORTUNES, BUT I'D GIVE IT ALL UP FOR TRUE LOVE!
FUNNY YOU SHOULD SAY THAT, MISS CARROT...
I'VE BEEN WANTING TO ASK...
HOW COULD I HAVE BEEN SO BLIND! TRUE LOVE WAS RIGHT HERE!
WILL YOU...
URK
E.P.!
I'VE STILL GOT THE FUNNIES TO CHEER ME UP...
IT'S NOT TEX DREW'S FAULT I GOT THE BOOT. WHAT'S HE UP TO?
TEX DREW, PUBLIC DEFENDER
AND SO, YOUR HONOR, MY CLIENT COUL NOT HAVE USED A RIGHT-HANDED TRIGGER BECAUSE HIS RIGHT HAND IS ALWAYS HOLD A HAMBURGER!
REX SLATE, GENTL
THIS IS THE BUYER OF MARK CLARK THAT "COULDN'T BE DISCLOSED"?!
THAT'S IT!!!
HAMBUR JOE'S

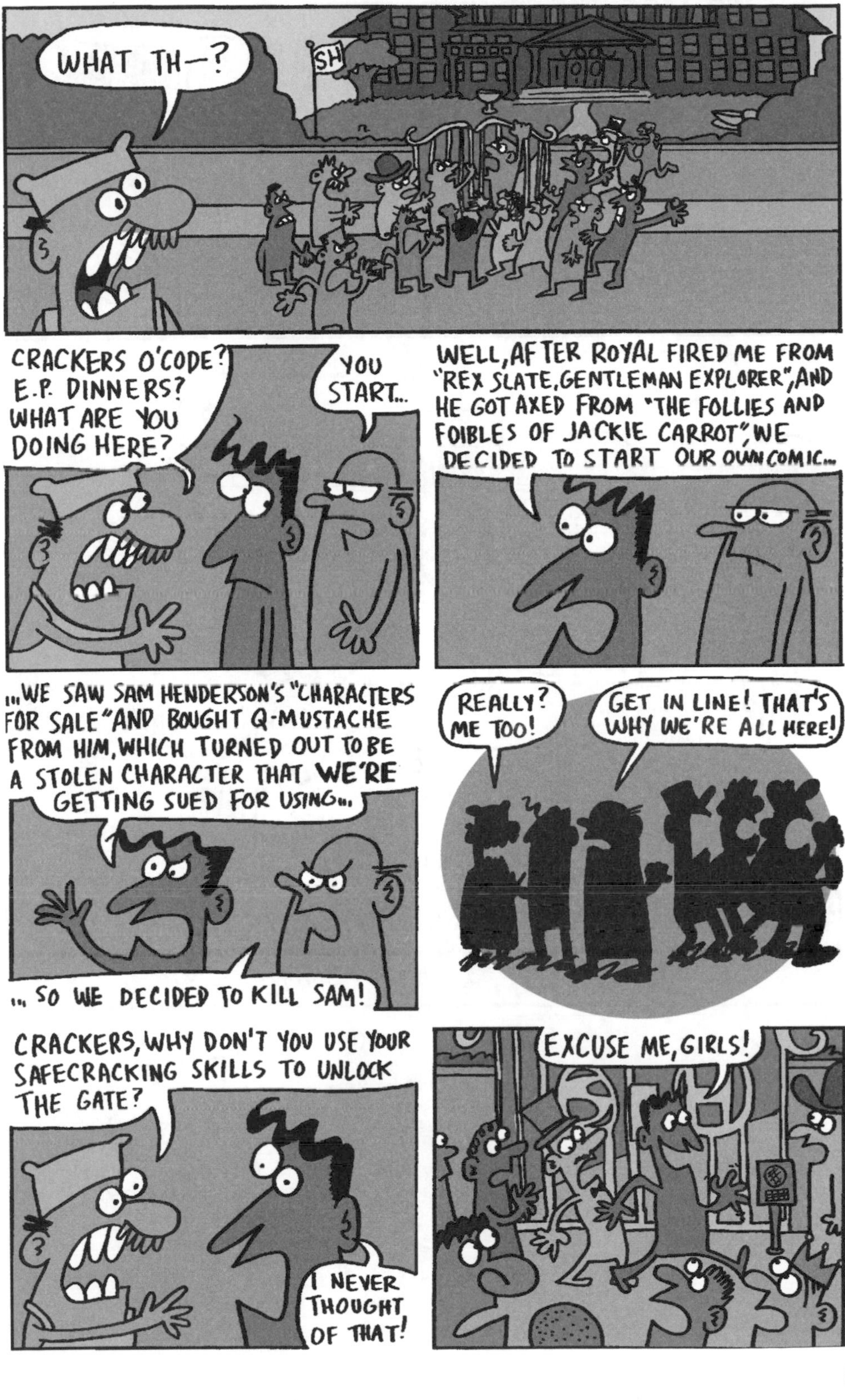
WHAT TH—?
SH
CRACKERS O'CODE? E.P. DINNERS? WHAT ARE YOU DOING HERE?
YOU START...
WELL, AFTER ROYAL FIRED ME FROM "REX SLATE, GENTLEMAN EXPLORER", AND HE GOT AXED FROM "THE FOLLIES AND FOIBLES OF JACKIE CARROT", WE DECIDED TO START OUR OWN COMIC...
...WE SAW SAM HENDERSON'S "CHARACTERS FOR SALE" AND BOUGHT Q-MUSTACHE FROM HIM, WHICH TURNED OUT TO BE A STOLEN CHARACTER THAT WE'RE GETTING SUED FOR USING...
... SO WE DECIDED TO KILL SAM!
REALLY? ME TOO!
GET IN LINE! THAT'S WHY WE'RE ALL HERE!
CRACKERS, WHY DON'T YOU USE YOUR SAFECRACKING SKILLS TO UNLOCK THE GATE?
I NEVER THOUGHT OF THAT!
EXCUSE ME, GIRLS!

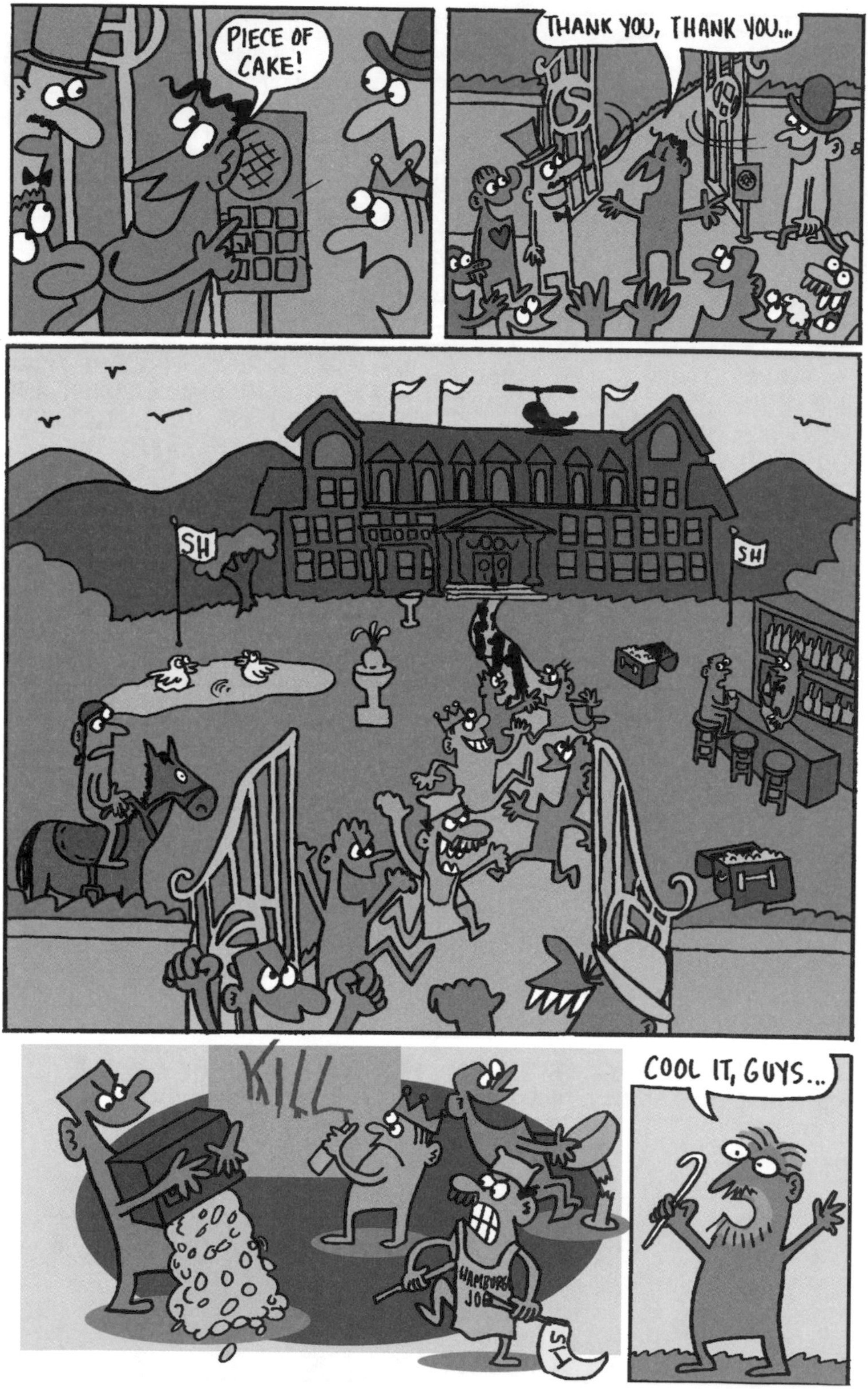
PIECE OF CAKE!
THANK YOU, THANK YOU...
SH
SH
KILL
COOL IT, GUYS...

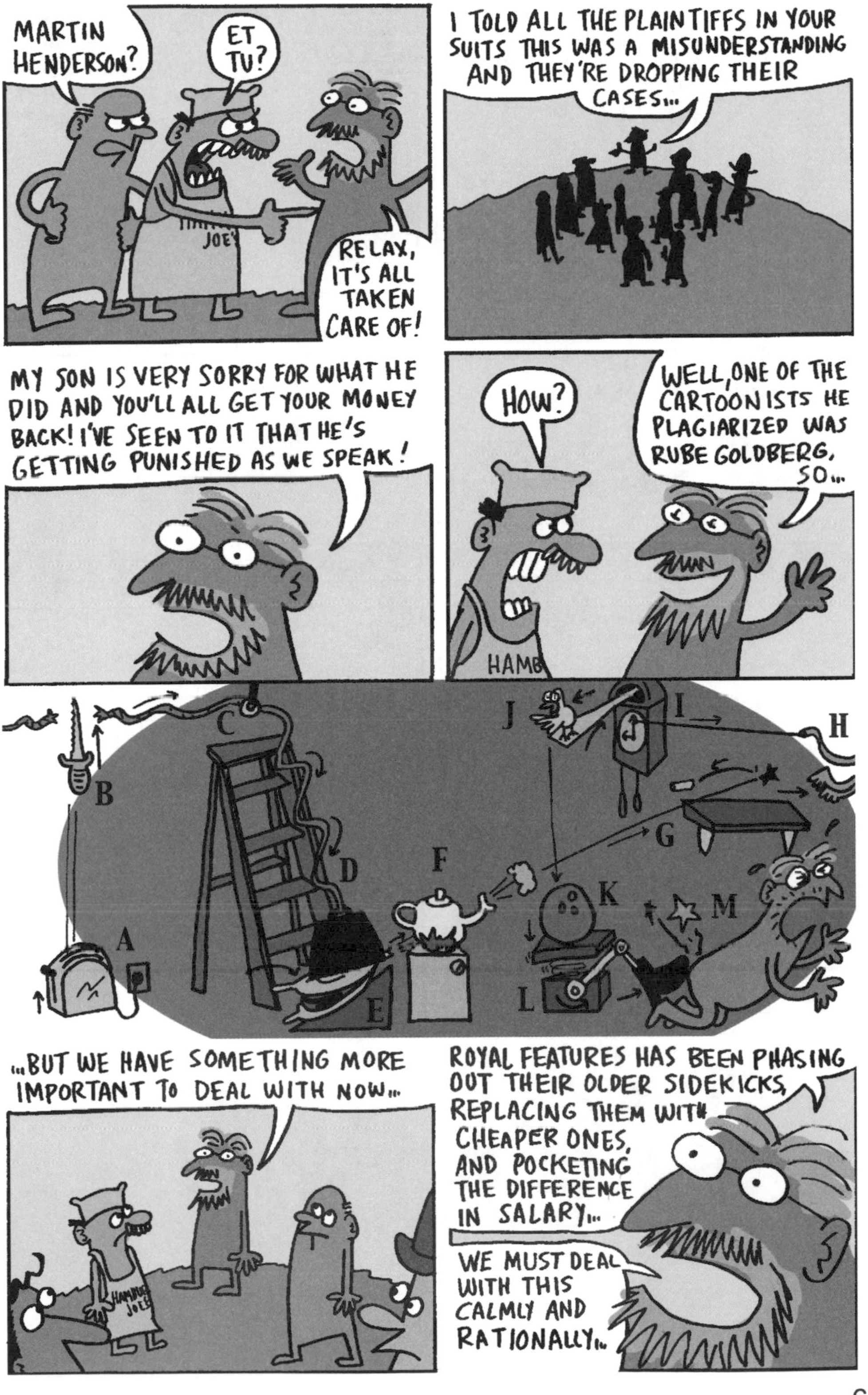
MARTIN HENDERSON?
ET TU?
JOE'S
RELAX, IT'S ALL TAKEN CARE OF!
I TOLD ALL THE PLAINTIFFS IN YOUR SUITS THIS WAS A MISUNDERSTANDING AND THEY'RE DROPPING THEIR CASES...
MY SON IS VERY SORRY FOR WHAT HE DID AND YOU'LL ALL GET YOUR MONEY BACK! I'VE SEEN TO IT THAT HE'S GETTING PUNISHED AS WE SPEAK!
HOW?
WELL, ONE OF THE CARTOONISTS HE PLAGIARIZED WAS RUBE GOLDBERG, SO...
HAMB
A
B
C
D
E
F
G
H
I
J
K
L
M
...BUT WE HAVE SOMETHING MORE IMPORTANT TO DEAL WITH NOW...
ROYAL FEATURES HAS BEEN PHASING OUT THEIR OLDER SIDEKICKS, REPLACING THEM WITH CHEAPER ONES, AND POCKETING THE DIFFERENCE IN SALARY...
WE MUST DEAL WITH THIS CALMLY AND RATIONALLY...

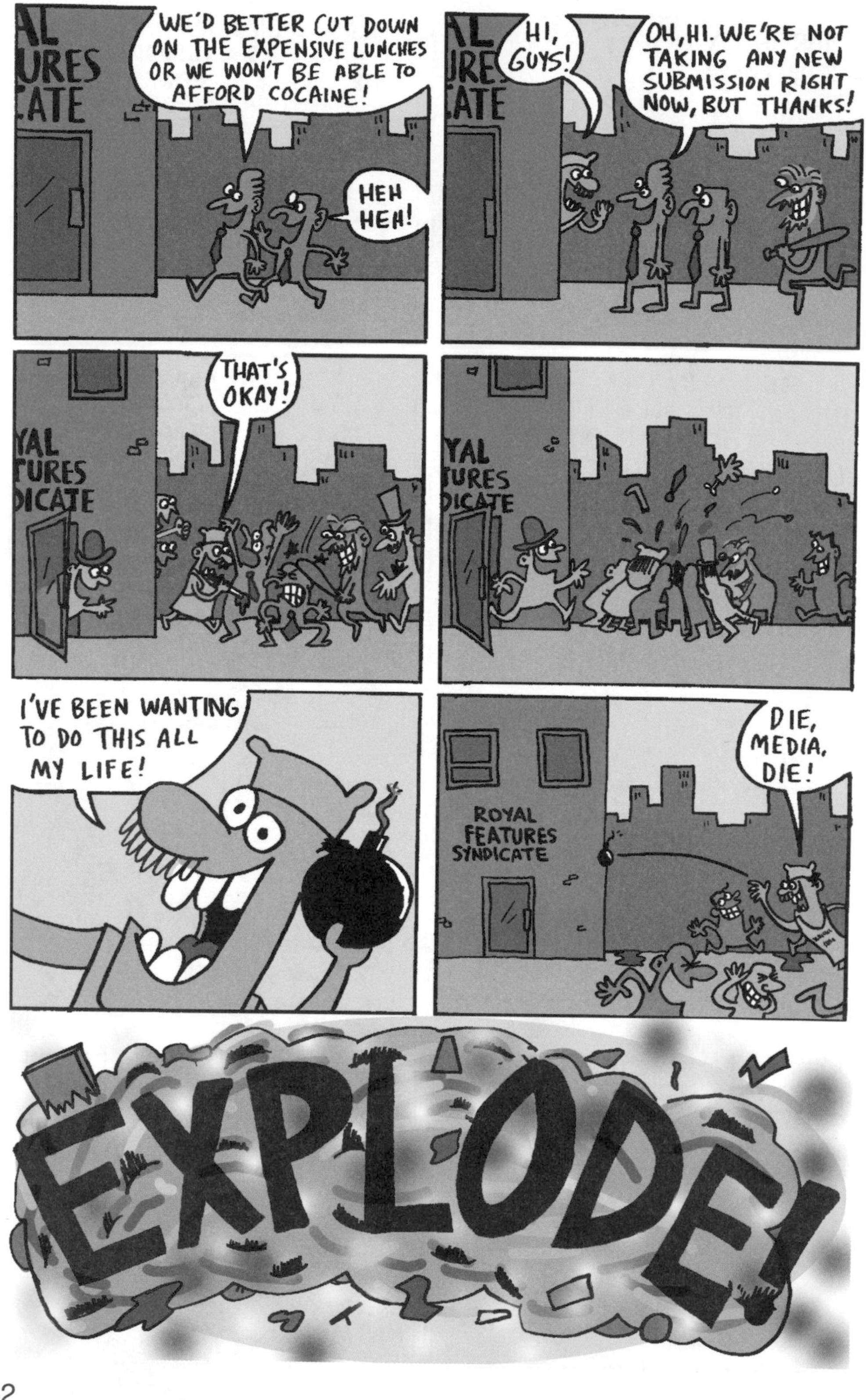
WE'D BETTER CUT DOWN ON THE EXPENSIVE LUNCHES OR WE WON'T BE ABLE TO AFFORD COCAINE!
HEH HEH!
HI, GUYS!
OH, HI. WE'RE NOT TAKING ANY NEW SUBMISSION RIGHT NOW, BUT THANKS!
THAT'S OKAY!
I'VE BEEN WANTING TO DO THIS ALL MY LIFE!
ROYAL FEATURES SYNDICATE
DIE, MEDIA, DIE!
EXPLODE!

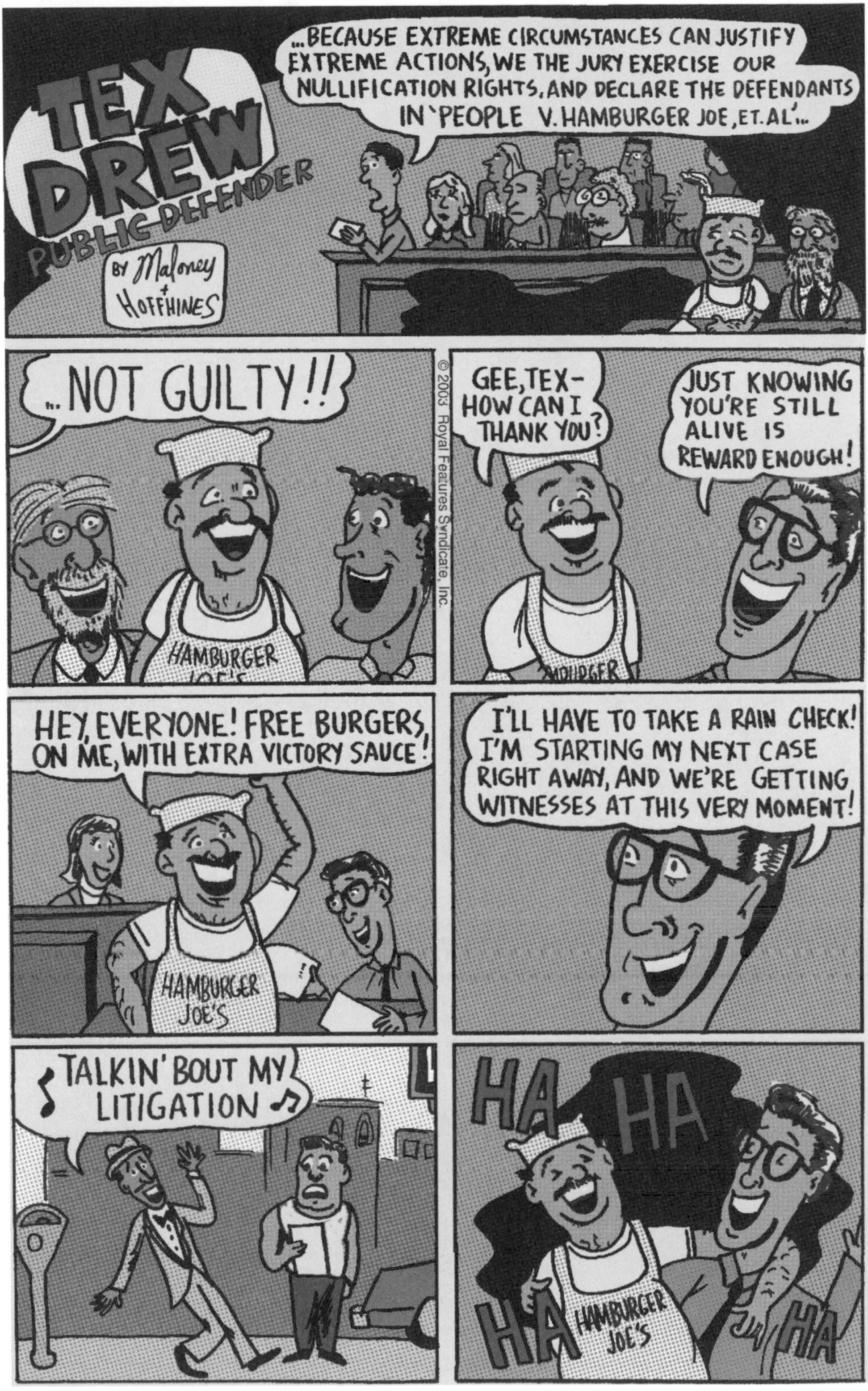
TEX DREW
PUBLIC DEFENDER
BY Maloney + HOFFHINES
...BECAUSE EXTREME CIRCUMSTANCES CAN JUSTIFY EXTREME ACTIONS, WE THE JURY EXERCISE OUR NULLIFICATION RIGHTS, AND DECLARE THE DEFENDANTS IN 'PEOPLE V. HAMBURGER JOE, ET. AL'...
...NOT GUILTY!!
© 2003 Royal Features Syndicate, Inc.
HAMBURGER JOE'S
GEE, TEX- HOW CAN I THANK YOU?
JUST KNOWING YOU'RE STILL ALIVE IS REWARD ENOUGH!
HEY, EVERYONE! FREE BURGERS, ON ME, WITH EXTRA VICTORY SAUCE!
HAMBURGER JOE'S
I'LL HAVE TO TAKE A RAIN CHECK! I'M STARTING MY NEXT CASE RIGHT AWAY, AND WE'RE GETTING WITNESSES AT THIS VERY MOMENT!
TALKIN' BOUT MY LITIGATION
HA HA
HAMBURGER JOE'S
HA HA

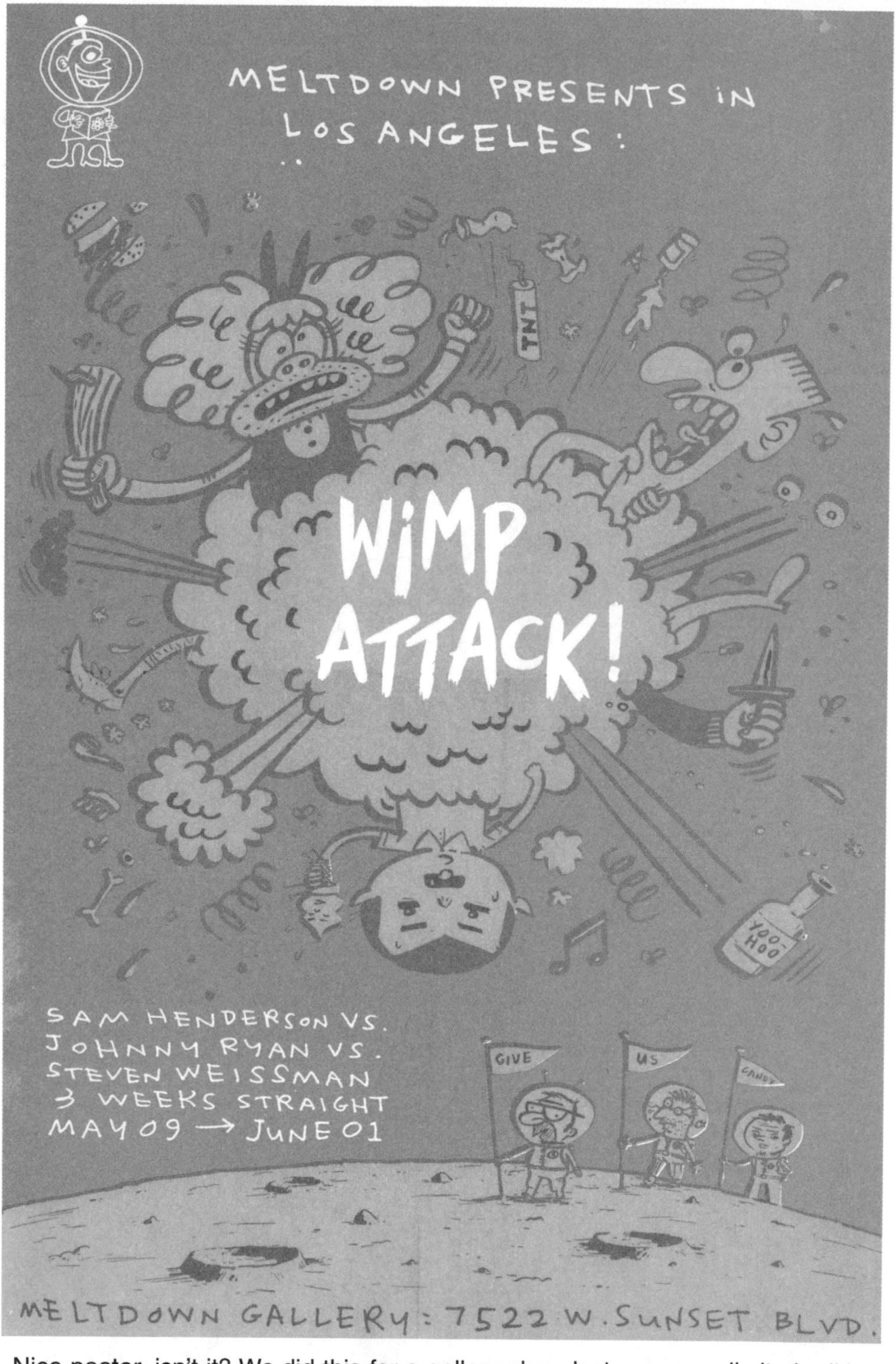
MELTDOWN PRESENTS IN LOS ANGELES:
WIMP ATTACK!
TNT
YOO-HOO
SAM HENDERSON VS.
JOHNNY RYAN VS.
STEVEN WEISSMAN
3 WEEKS STRAIGHT
MAY 09 → JUNE 01
GIVE
US
CANDY
MELTDOWN GALLERY: 7522 W. SUNSET BLVD.

Nice poster, isn't it? We did this for a gallery show last year as a limited edition 11" x 17" silkscreen printed by Jordan Crane. I may still have a few left for $25. E-mail me or check comicartcollective.com.

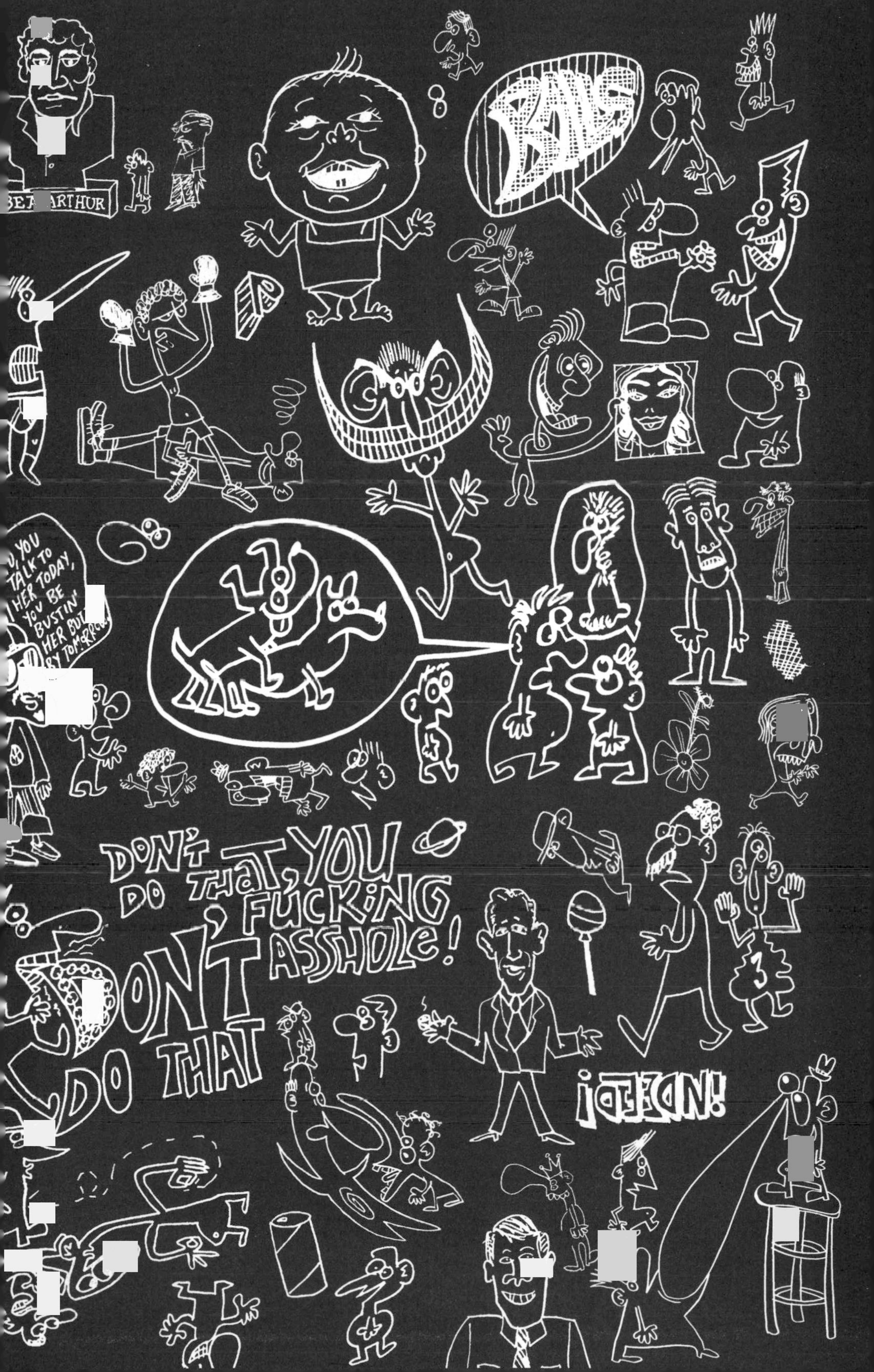
BEA ARTHUR
YOU TALK TO HER TODAY, YOU BE BUSTIN' HER BUT BY TOMORROW
DON'T DO THAT, YOU FUCKING ASSHOLE!
DON'T DO THAT

THE CONCEPT HAS BEEN USED BEFORE--TWO PEOPLE PLAYING SCRABBLE WITH THEIR INTERESTS, THOUGHTS, OR PERSONALITIES REFLECTED IN THE WORDS THEY'RE PUTTING ON THE BOARD. I CAN'T WIN WITH THIS ONE BECAUSE IF YOU'RE NOT FAMILIAR WITH THE GAME YOU WON'T GET IT, BUT IT SEEMS TO BE EVEN LESS FUNNY IF YOU ARE. FOR EXAMPLE, I WAS TRYING TO EXPLAIN THE CONCEPT TO MY GIRLFRIEND, AND THE FIRST THING SHE SAID WAS THAT 'CADILLAC' COULD NEVER BE USED IN A REAL GAME. NOW, SHE'S NOT ONE OF THOSE TYPES WHO DOESN'T GET MY SHTICK. IN FACT, HER BEING A FAN OF MY CARTOONS IS WHAT GOT US TOGETHER IN THE FIRST PLACE. I MEET CREATIVE PEOPLE ALL THE TIME AND OFTEN THEY'LL SAY, "MY WIFE/HUSBAND NEVER READS/SEES MY [CREATIVE WORK]. S/HE DOESN'T UNDERSTAND IT". NOT THAT EVERYONE SHOULD HAVE 100 PERCENT IN COMMON BUT SOMETHING LIKE THAT MAKES ME WONDER WHY THEY'RE TOGETHER. NOT ONLY COULD I NOT HANDLE THAT KIND OF ARRANGEMENT, I DON'T EVEN KNOW HOW IT'S POSSIBLE ANYONE COULD SEE ANYTHING IN ME OTHER THAN MY CREATIVITY. MAYBE THAT'S WHY I SPEND THREE YEARS SINGLE IN BETWEEN GIRL-FRIENDS. MY BASEBALL HAT THAT SAYS "MY CUM + YOUR LIPS = DESTINY" MAY HAVE SOMETHING TO DO WITH IT, TOO. BACK TO MY POINT, I NITPICK ALL THE TIME AND LET MY NOTICE OF FLAWS KEEP ME FROM APPRECIATING WORKS WHEN IT'S COMPLETELY IRRELEVANT TO THE ARTISTIC INTENT. LIKE WHEN I SEE A MOVIE MADE IN NEW YORK AND A SCENE SET IN THE EAST VILLAGE IS ACTUALLY SHOT ON NINTH AVENUE. THE ACTUAL LOCATION IS UNIMPORTANT AND WERE I NOT FROM NEW YORK I'D BE NONE THE WISER, YET I CAN'T TAKE THE LEAP OF FAITH. SAME WITH THE PEPE LEPEW CARTOONS. AFTER TAKING FRENCH IN HIGH SCHOOL, I COULDN'T WATCH THEM ANYMORE BECAUSE IT BOTHERED ME THAT HE ALWAYS SAID "MON CHERI" WHEN THE PROPER POSSESSIVE WOULD BE "MA" UNLESS HE WAS CHASING A MAN. WELL, SOMETIMES IT TURNED OUT TO BE A MAN AT HE END, BUT HE DIDN'T KNOW THAT. I COULDN'T STAND HOW A STOP SIGN WOULD READ "STOP-AY-VOO". IT'S NOT THE FAKE FRENCH THAT'S ANNOYING, I'D ACCEPT "STOPPEZ-VOUS". IT'S HOW FAR THEY STRAYED FROM THE RULES OF GRAMMAR WITHIN THAT CONTEXT, WHICH IS ESPECIALLY BUGS ME KNOWING HOW ERUDITE CHUCK JONES WAS. DON'T GET ME STARTED ON CHARACTERS USING "LE" IN FRONT OF WORDS THAT WEREN'T NOUNS (FOR SOME REASON INTERJECTIONS ARE OKAY) FOR THESE REASONS I SYMPATHIZE WITH SCRABBLE ENTHUSIASTS WHO MAY LET INACCURACIES GET IN THE WAY OF A JOKE. I PLAY THE GAME MYSELF, SO I'M AWARE THAT SOME OF THE WORDS WOULDN'T BE ALLOWED IN A REAL GAME. THERE ARE ALSO WORDS WITH TOO MANY LETTERS TO REALISTICALLY BE USED IN ONE TURN, AS WELL AS A DISPROPORTIONATE AMOUNT OF SOME SPECIFIC LETTERS. THIS PIMP AND POLLYANNA AREN'T PARTICULARLY GOOD PLAYERS EITHER, WASTING SO MANY OPPORTUNITIES TO INCREASE THEIR SCORES. THE GIRL TOTALLY BLEW IT BY USING THE "M" IN 'MOFO' TO MAKE 'SMILE', WHEN SHE COULD HAVE USED THOSE LETTERS TO PUT 'LIES' PERPENDICULAR TO 'CADILLAC', CREATING TWO WORDS AND SCORING A 51 INSTEAD OF AN 18. IT WAS CLEVER OF HER TO MAKE 'HO' INTO 'HORSIE', THOUGH SHE PROBABLY COULD HAVE TAKEN ADVANTAGE OF THE DOUBLE WORD SPACE. IN MY DEFENSE, I HAVE TO SAY THAT I WAS ACCURATE IN DRAWING THE RIGHT AMOUNT OF SQUARES AND SHADING THE DOUBLE AND TRIPLE AREAS IN THE RIGHT PLACES— EVEN IF THAT MEANS I NOW HAVE TO ACKNOWLEDGE THAT HASBRO IS THE OWNER OF THE REGISTERED SCRABBLE ® TRADEMARK IN THE UNITED STATES AND CANADA. THIS PARTICULAR WAY IN WHICH COLORS, LETTERS, AND NUMBERS ARE ARRANGED ON A 15X15 GRID IS © 2002 HASBRO. MAYBE IT WOULD HAVE WORKED IF I HAD A HIPPIE AND A PIRATE PLAYING. THAT WOULD BE BETTER AS A SEQUENTIAL NARRATIVE WITH THE PIRATE TRYING TO PICK UP THE TILES WITH HIS HOOK HANDS AND THE HIPPIE DISTRACTED BY THE GRAINS OF SAND IN THE TIMER OR THE FEEL OF THE INDENTATIONS IN THE TILES. WOULD THE HIPPIE CHALLENGE "AAHHRR" OR WOULD HE FEEL SOMETHING LIKE KEEPING SCORE WAS OPPRESSIVE? WOULD THE PIRATE, USING "AHHRR", TRY TO USE HIS BLANK TILE AS AN EXCLAMATION POINT BECAUSE SO HE COULD GET THE TRIPLE WORD SPACE? FUCK, FUCK, WHY DIDN'T I THINK OF THIS BEFORE?!

*After writing this, my girlfriend told me that there's no such thing as a timer in SCRABBLE, since there are officially no rules about how long a turn can take. I distinctly remember my family having one in the version they owned and she thought I might be mistaken. I went online and it seems we're both right.

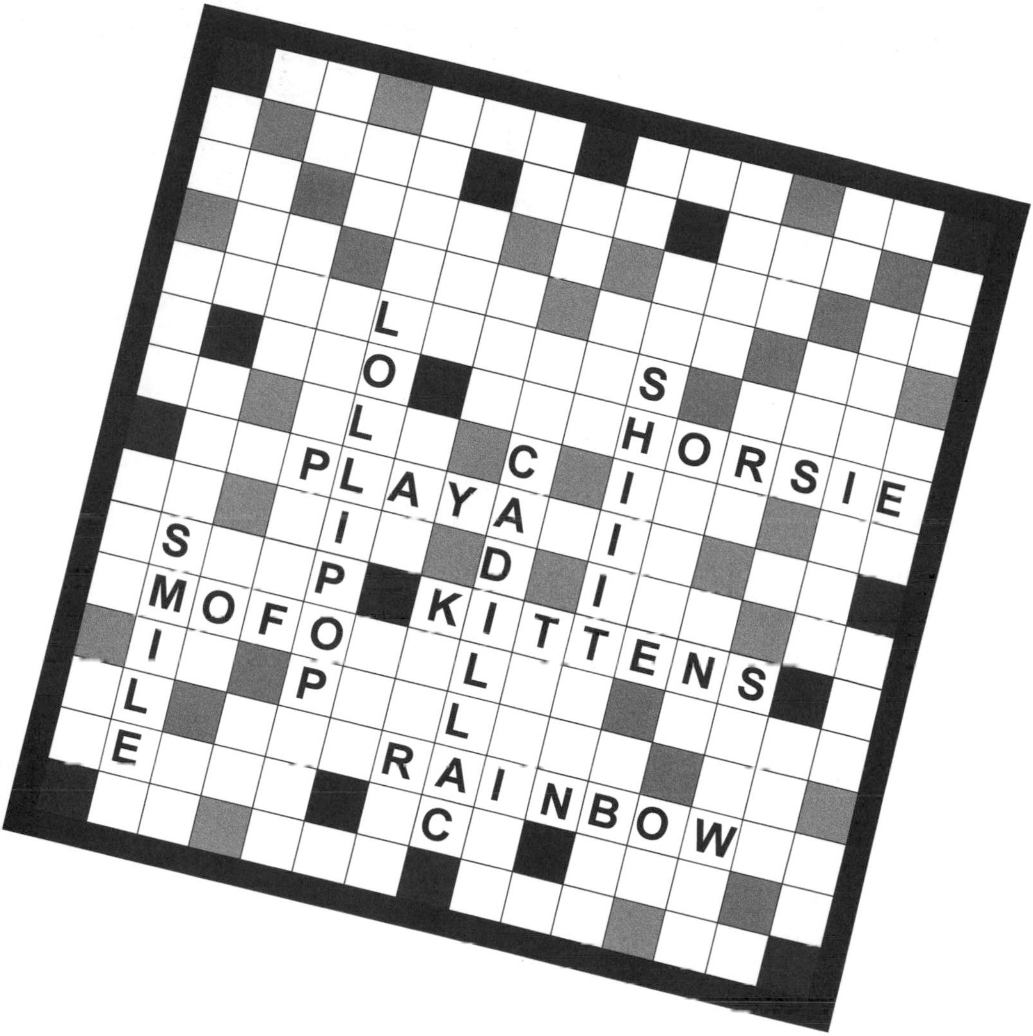
LOLLIPOP
SHIIIT
HORSIE
PLAYA
CADILLAC
SMILE
MOFO
KITTENS
RAINBOW

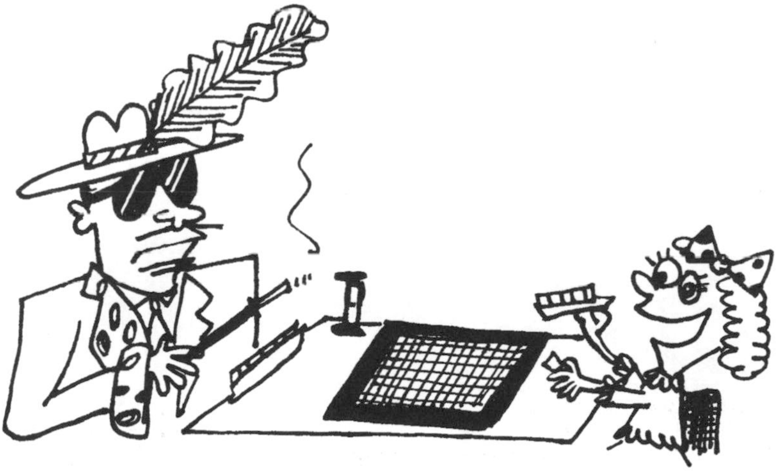

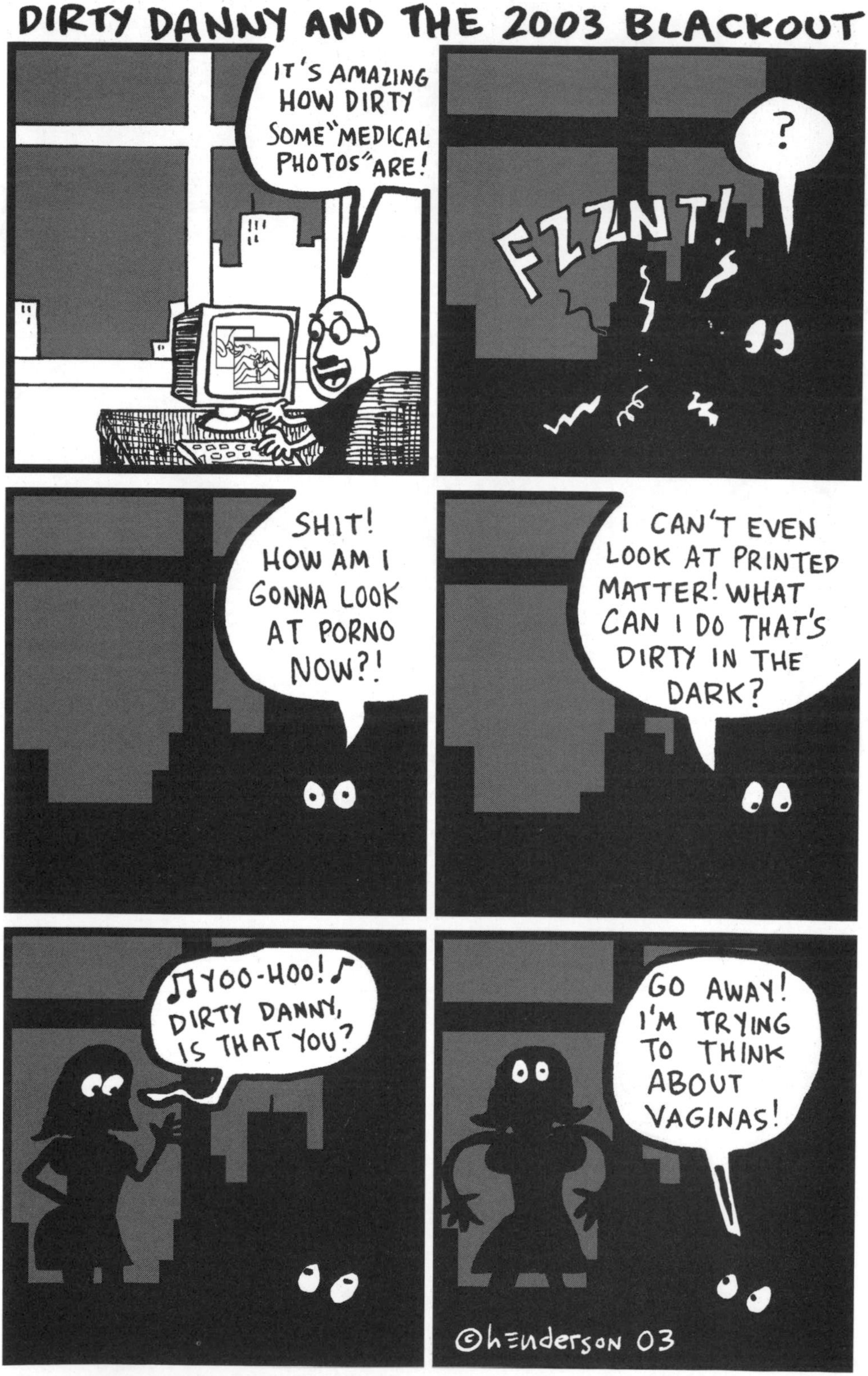
DIRTY DANNY AND THE 2003 BLACKOUT
IT'S AMAZING HOW DIRTY SOME "MEDICAL PHOTOS" ARE!
?
FZZNT!
SHIT! HOW AM I GONNA LOOK AT PORNO NOW?!
I CAN'T EVEN LOOK AT PRINTED MATTER! WHAT CAN I DO THAT'S DIRTY IN THE DARK?
♫YOO-HOO!♪ DIRTY DANNY, IS THAT YOU?
GO AWAY! I'M TRYING TO THINK ABOUT VAGINAS!
©henderson 03

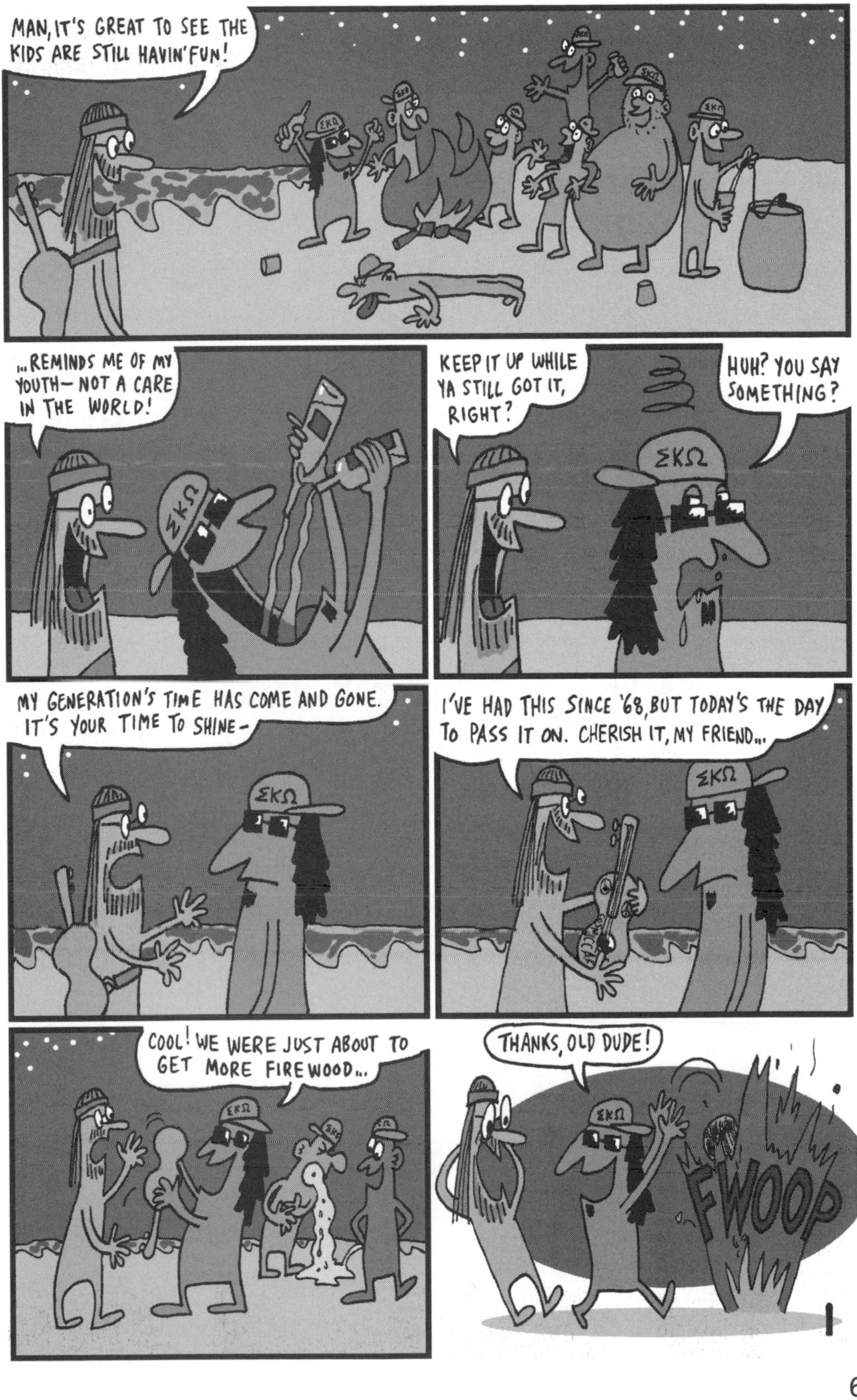
MAN, IT'S GREAT TO SEE THE KIDS ARE STILL HAVIN' FUN!
...REMINDS ME OF MY YOUTH— NOT A CARE IN THE WORLD!
KEEP IT UP WHILE YA STILL GOT IT, RIGHT?
HUH? YOU SAY SOMETHING?
MY GENERATION'S TIME HAS COME AND GONE. IT'S YOUR TIME TO SHINE-
I'VE HAD THIS SINCE '68, BUT TODAY'S THE DAY TO PASS IT ON. CHERISH IT, MY FRIEND...
COOL! WE WERE JUST ABOUT TO GET MORE FIREWOOD...
THANKS, OLD DUDE!
FWOOP

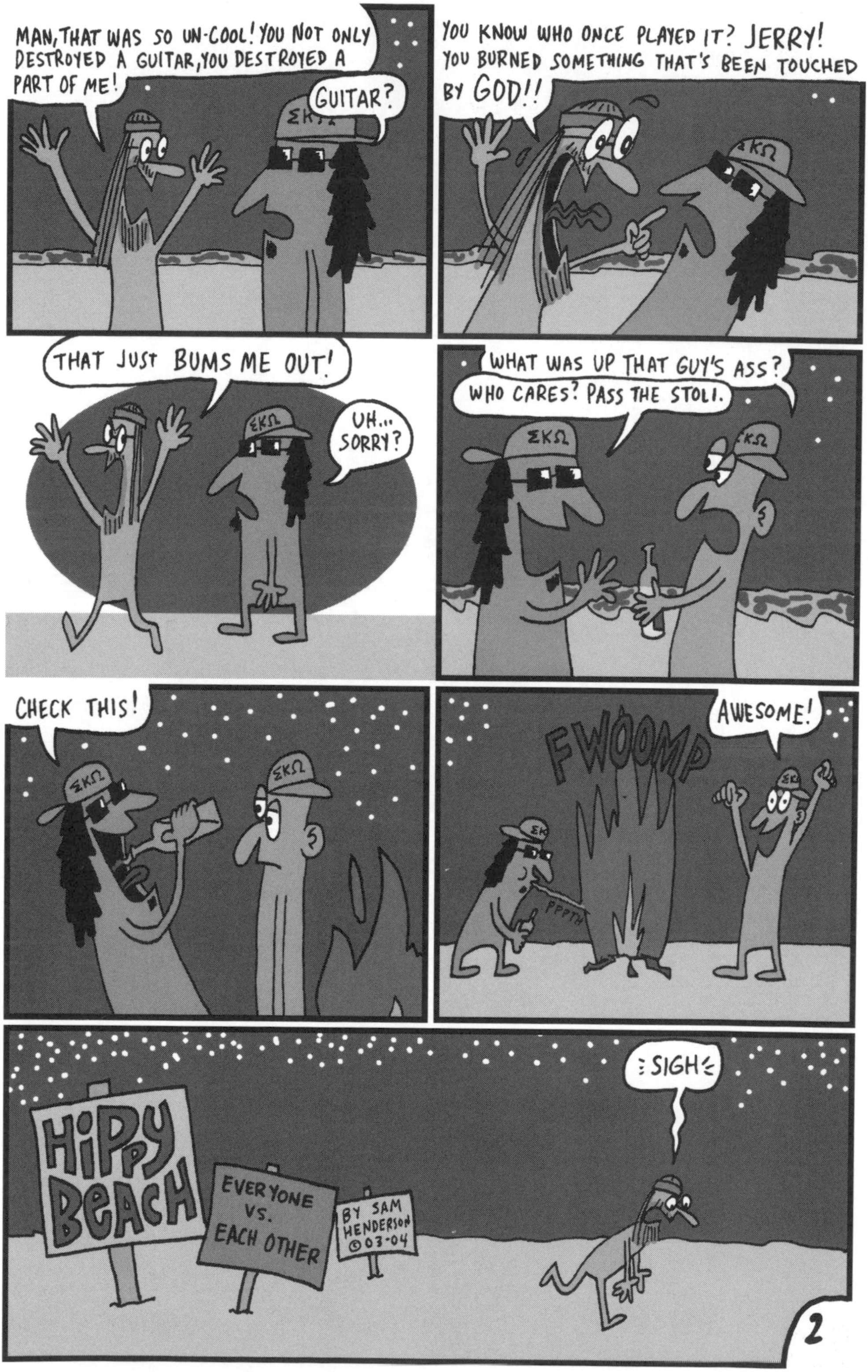
MAN, THAT WAS SO UN-COOL! YOU NOT ONLY DESTROYED A GUITAR, YOU DESTROYED A PART OF ME!
GUITAR?
YOU KNOW WHO ONCE PLAYED IT? JERRY! YOU BURNED SOMETHING THAT'S BEEN TOUCHED BY GOD!!
THAT JUST BUMS ME OUT!
UH... SORRY?
WHAT WAS UP THAT GUY'S ASS?
WHO CARES? PASS THE STOLI.
CHECK THIS!
FWOOMP
PPPTH
AWESOME!
SIGH
HIPPY BEACH
EVERYONE VS. EACH OTHER
BY SAM HENDERSON ©03-04
2

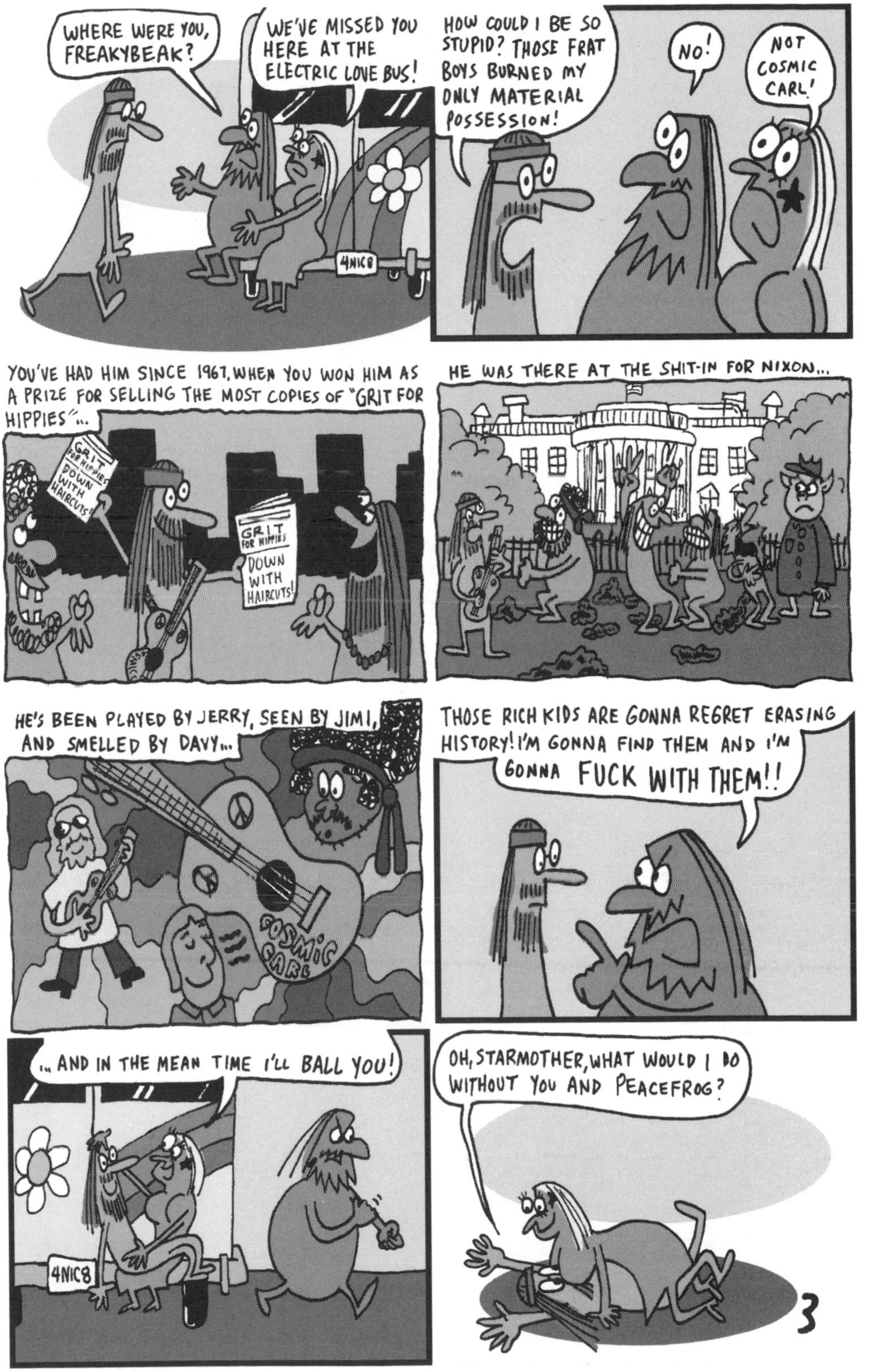
WHERE WERE YOU, FREAKYBEAK?
WE'VE MISSED YOU HERE AT THE ELECTRIC LOVE BUS!
4NIC8
HOW COULD I BE SO STUPID? THOSE FRAT BOYS BURNED MY ONLY MATERIAL POSSESSION!
NO!
NOT COSMIC CARL!
YOU'VE HAD HIM SINCE 1967, WHEN YOU WON HIM AS A PRIZE FOR SELLING THE MOST COPIES OF "GRIT FOR HIPPIES"...
GRIT FOR HIPPIES
DOWN WITH HAIRCUTS!
GRIT FOR HIPPIES
DOWN WITH HAIRCUTS!
HE WAS THERE AT THE SHIT-IN FOR NIXON...
HE'S BEEN PLAYED BY JERRY, SEEN BY JIMI, AND SMELLED BY DAVY...
COSMIC CARL
THOSE RICH KIDS ARE GONNA REGRET ERASING HISTORY! I'M GONNA FIND THEM AND I'M GONNA FUCK WITH THEM!!
... AND IN THE MEAN TIME I'LL BALL YOU!
4NIC8
OH, STARMOTHER, WHAT WOULD I DO WITHOUT YOU AND PEACEFROG?
3

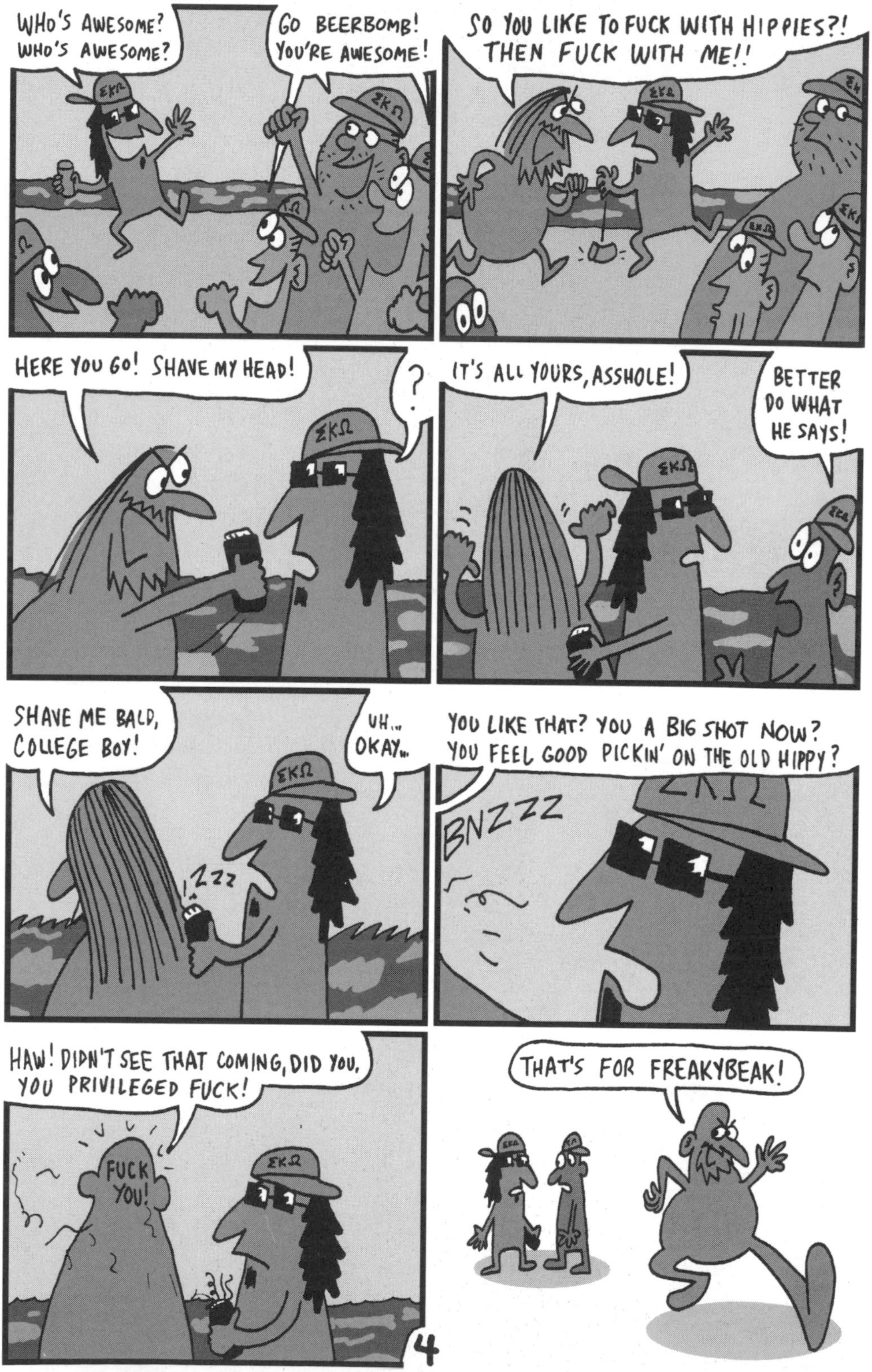
WHO'S AWESOME? WHO'S AWESOME?
GO BEERBOMB! YOU'RE AWESOME!
SO YOU LIKE TO FUCK WITH HIPPIES?! THEN FUCK WITH ME!!
HERE YOU GO! SHAVE MY HEAD!
?
IT'S ALL YOURS, ASSHOLE!
BETTER DO WHAT HE SAYS!
SHAVE ME BALD, COLLEGE BOY!
UH... OKAY...
ZZZ
YOU LIKE THAT? YOU A BIG SHOT NOW? YOU FEEL GOOD PICKIN' ON THE OLD HIPPY?
BNZZZ
HAW! DIDN'T SEE THAT COMING, DID YOU, YOU PRIVILEGED FUCK!
FUCK YOU!
4
THAT'S FOR FREAKYBEAK!

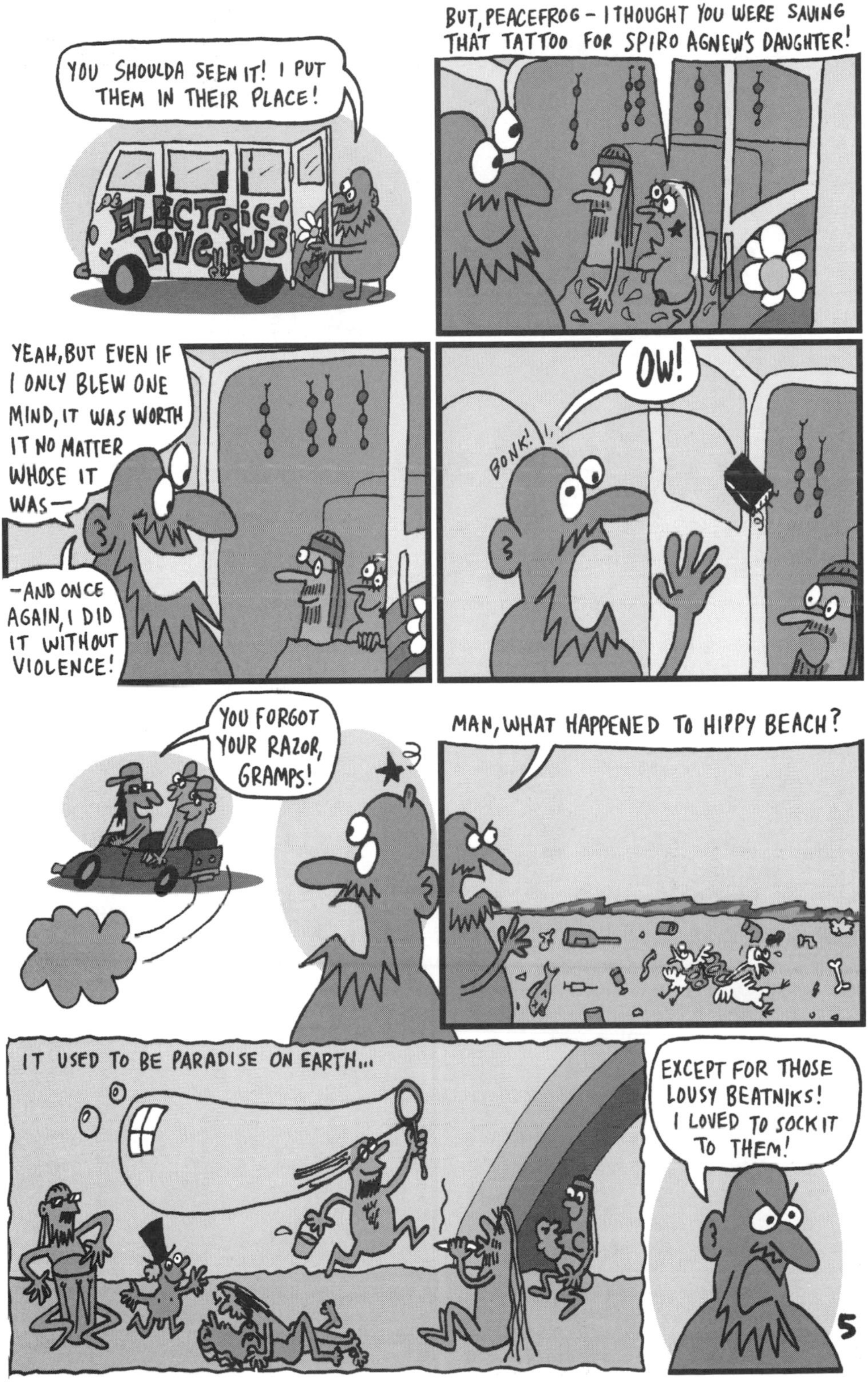

YOU SHOULDA SEEN IT! I PUT THEM IN THEIR PLACE!
ELECTRIC LOVE BUS
BUT, PEACEFROG - I THOUGHT YOU WERE SAVING THAT TATTOO FOR SPIRO AGNEW'S DAUGHTER!
YEAH, BUT EVEN IF I ONLY BLEW ONE MIND, IT WAS WORTH IT NO MATTER WHOSE IT WAS—
—AND ONCE AGAIN, I DID IT WITHOUT VIOLENCE!
BONK!
OW!
YOU FORGOT YOUR RAZOR, GRAMPS!
MAN, WHAT HAPPENED TO HIPPY BEACH?
IT USED TO BE PARADISE ON EARTH...
EXCEPT FOR THOSE LOUSY BEATNIKS! I LOVED TO SOCK IT TO THEM!
5

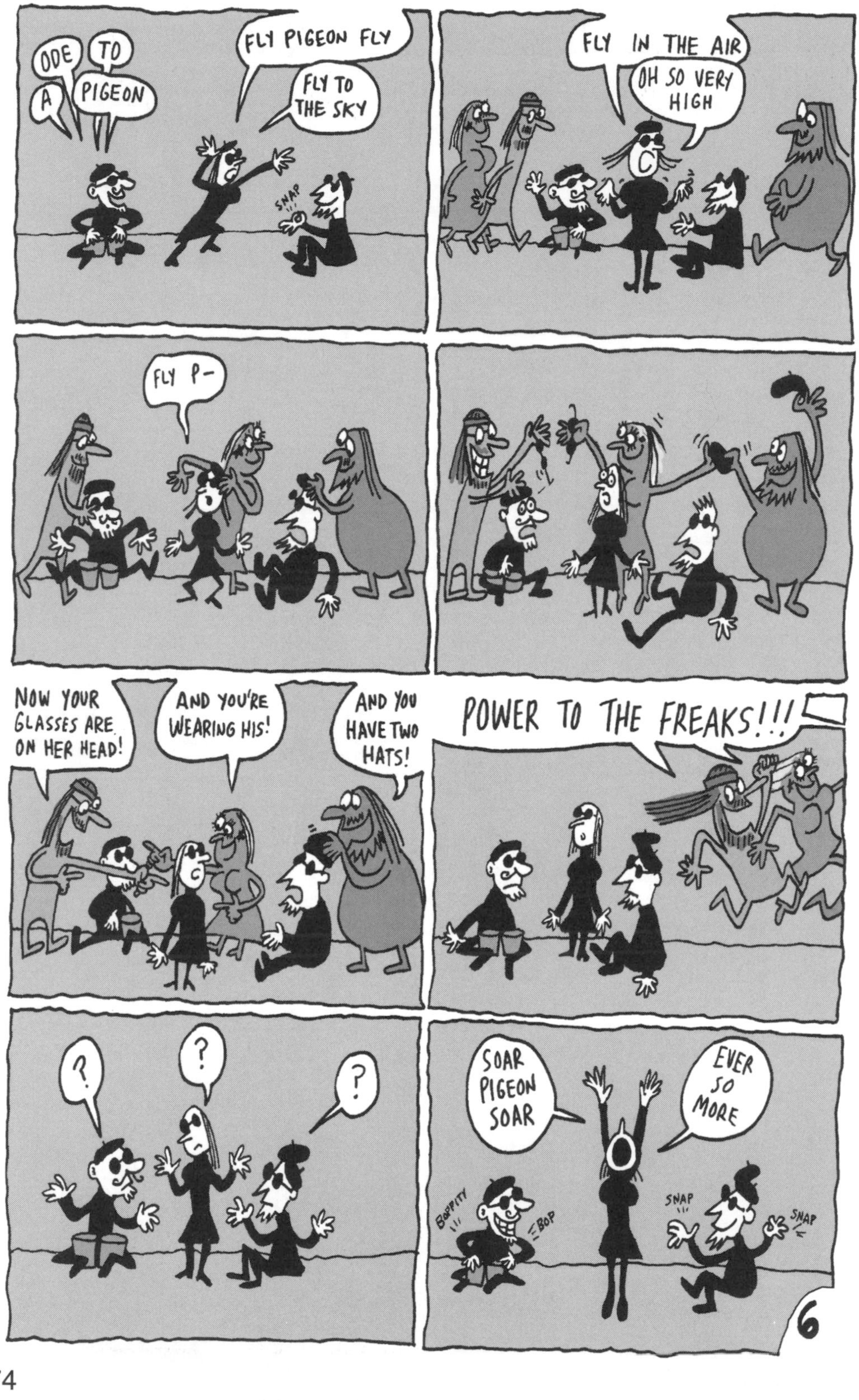
ODE TO A PIGEON
FLY PIGEON FLY
FLY TO THE SKY
SNAP
FLY IN THE AIR
OH SO VERY HIGH
FLY P-
NOW YOUR GLASSES ARE ON HER HEAD!
AND YOU'RE WEARING HIS!
AND YOU HAVE TWO HATS!
POWER TO THE FREAKS!!!
?
?
?
SOAR PIGEON SOAR
EVER SO MORE
BOPPITY
BOP
SNAP
SNAP
6

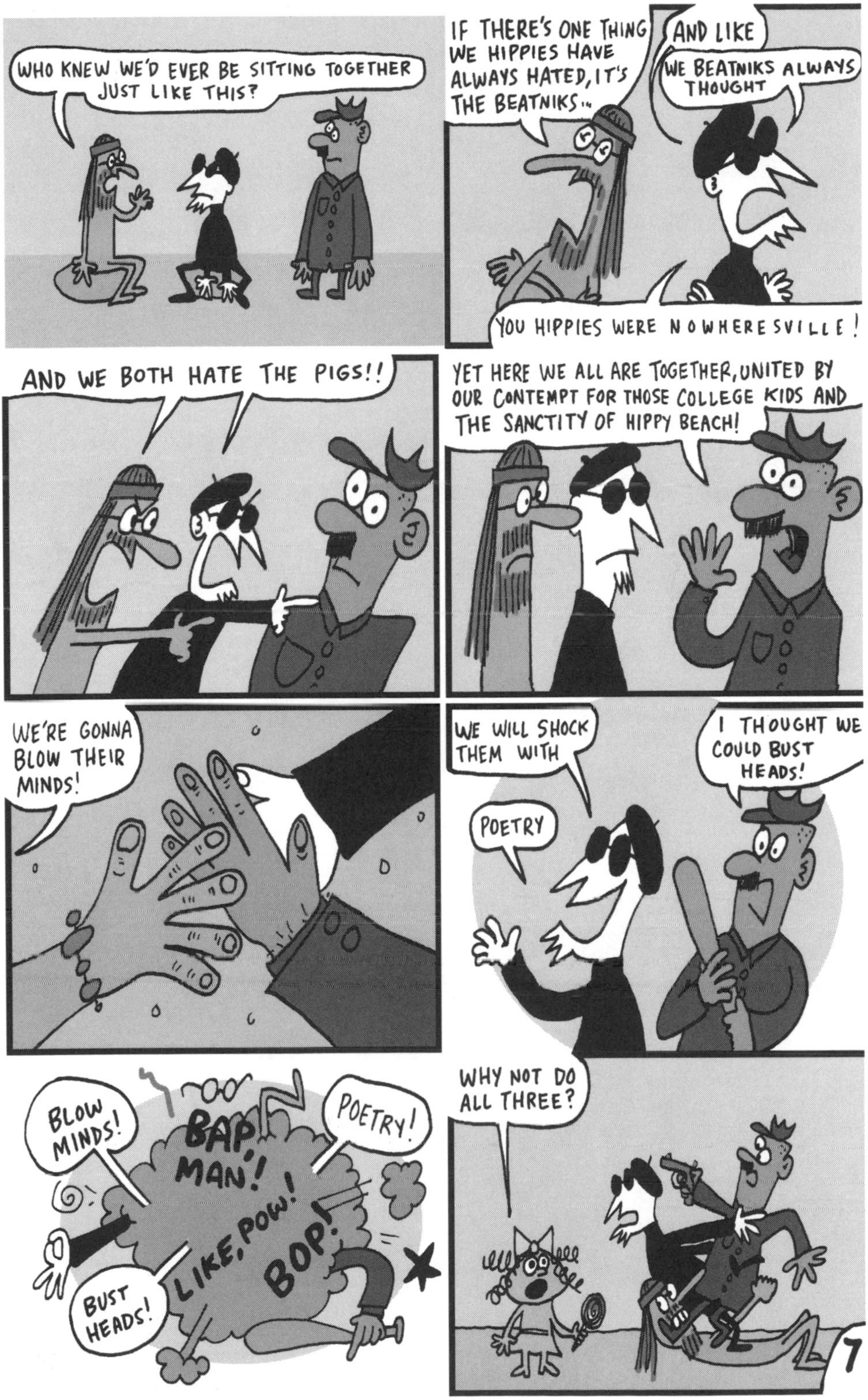
WHO KNEW WE'D EVER BE SITTING TOGETHER JUST LIKE THIS?
IF THERE'S ONE THING WE HIPPIES HAVE ALWAYS HATED, IT'S THE BEATNIKS...
AND LIKE
WE BEATNIKS ALWAYS THOUGHT
YOU HIPPIES WERE NOWHERESVILLE!
AND WE BOTH HATE THE PIGS!!
YET HERE WE ALL ARE TOGETHER, UNITED BY OUR CONTEMPT FOR THOSE COLLEGE KIDS AND THE SANCTITY OF HIPPY BEACH!
WE'RE GONNA BLOW THEIR MINDS!
WE WILL SHOCK THEM WITH
POETRY
I THOUGHT WE COULD BUST HEADS!
BLOW MINDS!
POETRY!
BAP, MAN!
LIKE, POW!
BOP!
BUST HEADS!
WHY NOT DO ALL THREE?

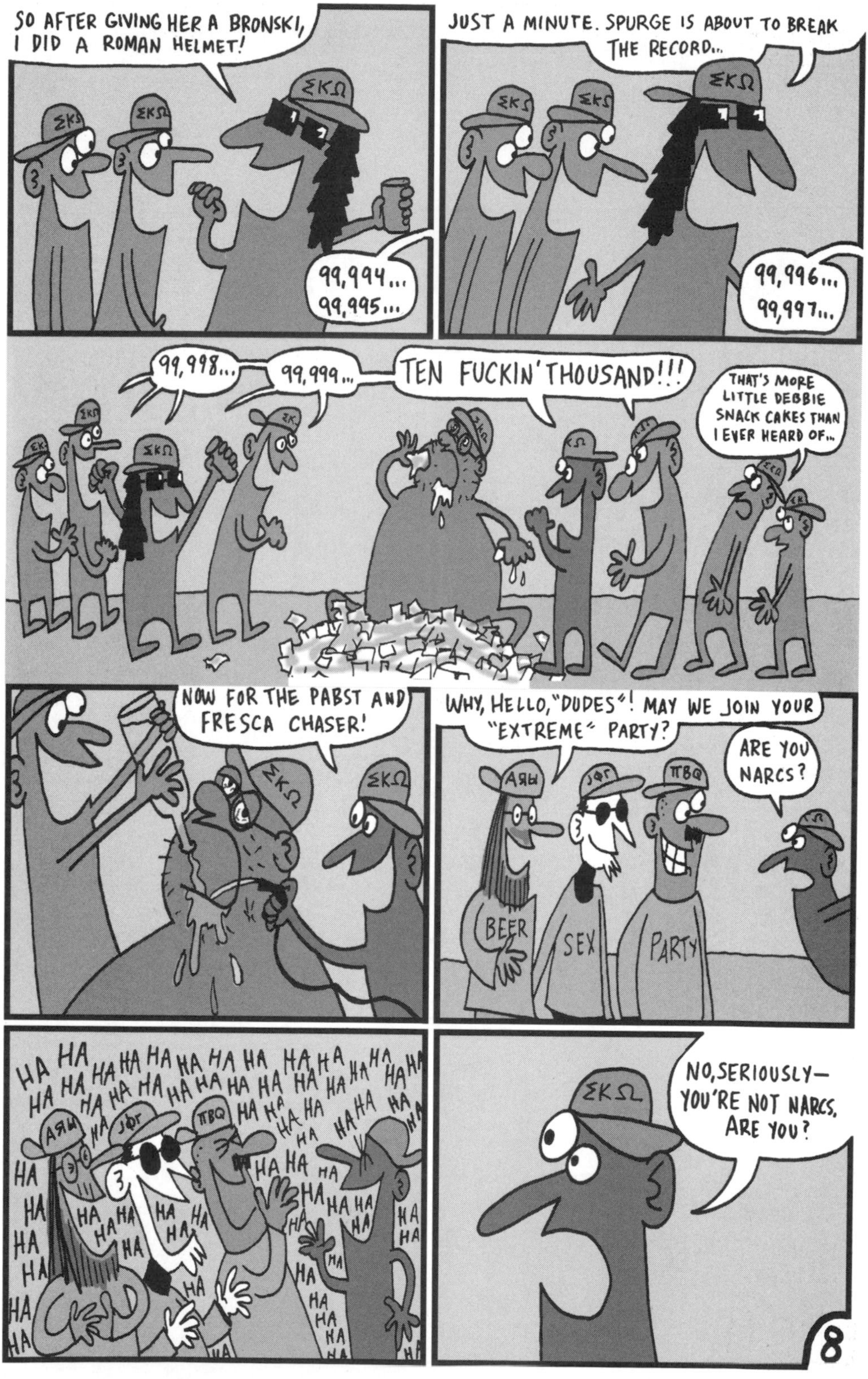
SO AFTER GIVING HER A BRONSKI, I DID A ROMAN HELMET!
99,994... 99,995...
JUST A MINUTE. SPURGE IS ABOUT TO BREAK THE RECORD...
99,996... 99,997...
99,998...
99,999...
TEN FUCKIN' THOUSAND!!!
THAT'S MORE LITTLE DEBBIE SNACK CAKES THAN I EVER HEARD OF...
NOW FOR THE PABST AND FRESCA CHASER!
WHY, HELLO, "DUDES"! MAY WE JOIN YOUR "EXTREME" PARTY?
ARE YOU NARCS?
BEER
SEX
PARTY
HA HA HA HA HA HA HA HA HA
NO, SERIOUSLY— YOU'RE NOT NARCS, ARE YOU?
8

HOLD ON — MY "BROS" AND I NEED TO "CHECK" SOMETHING...

FLIP FLIP FLIP

FLIP

FLIP FLIP!

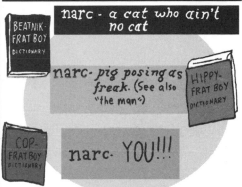

narc - a cat who ain't no cat

BEATNIK-FRAT BOY DICTIONARY

narc- pig posing as freak. (See also "the man")

HIPPY-FRAT BOY DICTIONARY

COP-FRAT BOY DICTIONARY

narc- YOU!!!

NOPE!

GOOD...

...'CUZ IF YOU WERE, BY LAW YOU'D HAVE TO SAY "YES"!

YEAH, WE'D NEVER VIOLATE MUNICIPAL CODE 912-B, ER... I ONLY KNOW THE NAME OF THE LAW BECAUSE...UH... I KEEP TRACK OF LAWS SO I KNOW TO BREAK...

HEY, I'M JUST FUCKIN' WITH YA! YOU GUYS ARE STONE COLD SHAZZIZ-BAZIZ-NIZIZZLE!

FLIP FLIP FLIP

9

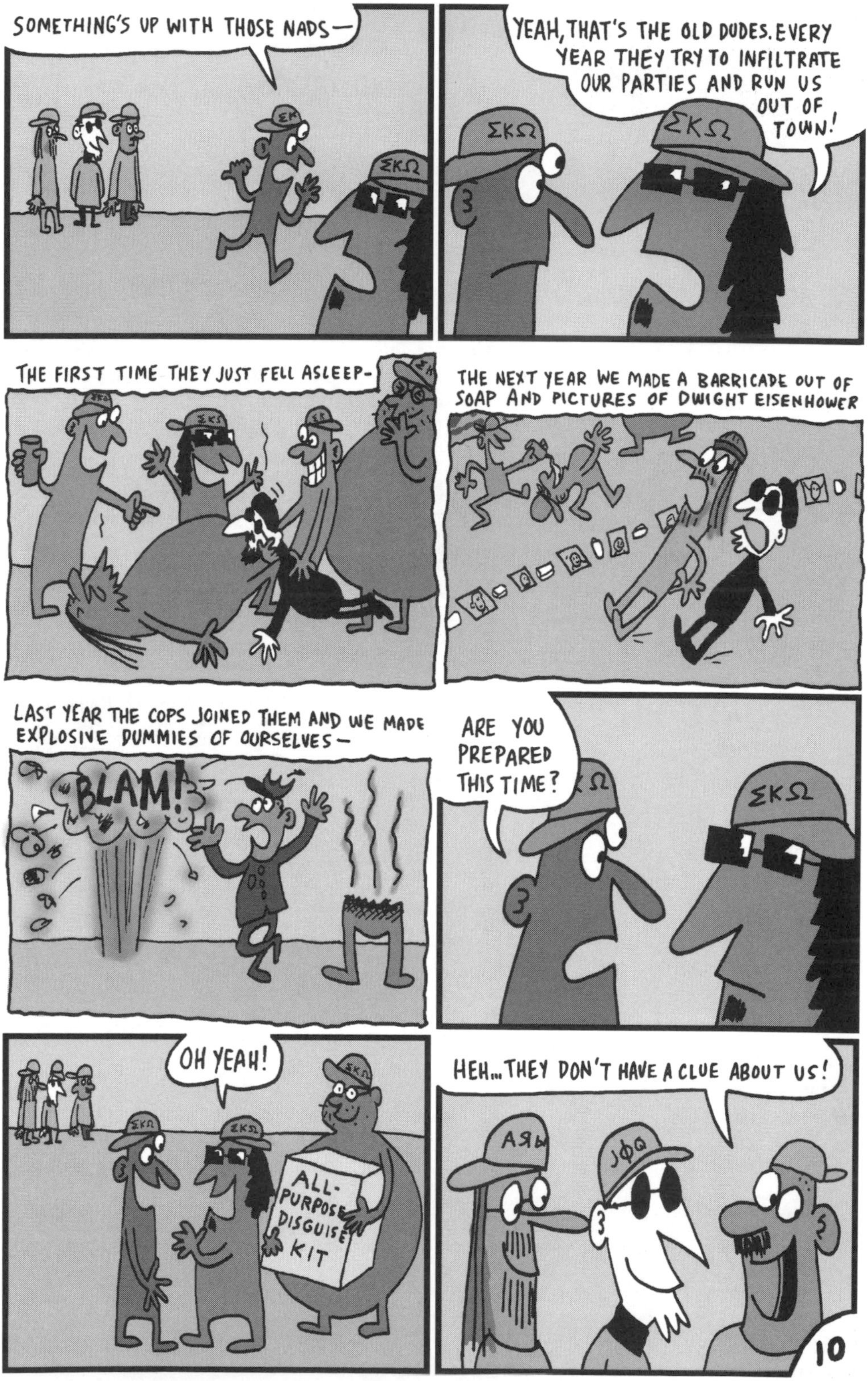
SOMETHING'S UP WITH THOSE NADS—
YEAH, THAT'S THE OLD DUDES. EVERY YEAR THEY TRY TO INFILTRATE OUR PARTIES AND RUN US OUT OF TOWN!
THE FIRST TIME THEY JUST FELL ASLEEP-
THE NEXT YEAR WE MADE A BARRICADE OUT OF SOAP AND PICTURES OF DWIGHT EISENHOWER
LAST YEAR THE COPS JOINED THEM AND WE MADE EXPLOSIVE DUMMIES OF OURSELVES—
BLAM!
ARE YOU PREPARED THIS TIME?
OH YEAH!
ALL-PURPOSE DISGUISE KIT
HEH... THEY DON'T HAVE A CLUE ABOUT US!
10

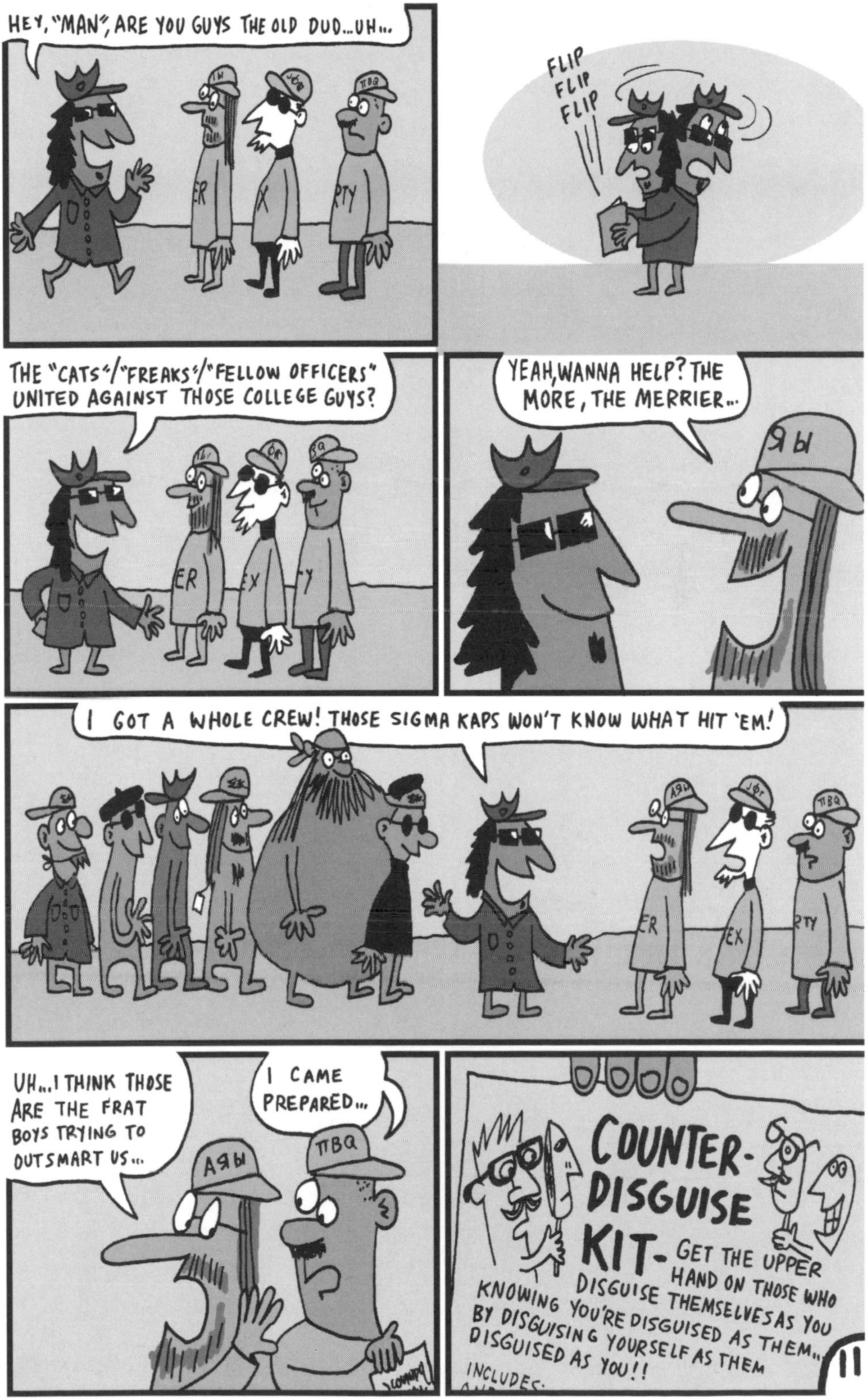

HEY, "MAN", ARE YOU GUYS THE OLD DUD...UH...
FLIP FLIP FLIP
THE "CATS"/"FREAKS"/"FELLOW OFFICERS" UNITED AGAINST THOSE COLLEGE GUYS?
YEAH, WANNA HELP? THE MORE, THE MERRIER...
I GOT A WHOLE CREW! THOSE SIGMA KAPS WON'T KNOW WHAT HIT 'EM!
UH...I THINK THOSE ARE THE FRAT BOYS TRYING TO OUTSMART US...
I CAME PREPARED...
COUNTER-DISGUISE KIT- GET THE UPPER HAND ON THOSE WHO DISGUISE THEMSELVES AS YOU KNOWING YOU'RE DISGUISED AS THEM... BY DISGUISING YOURSELF AS THEM DISGUISED AS YOU!!
INCLUDES:

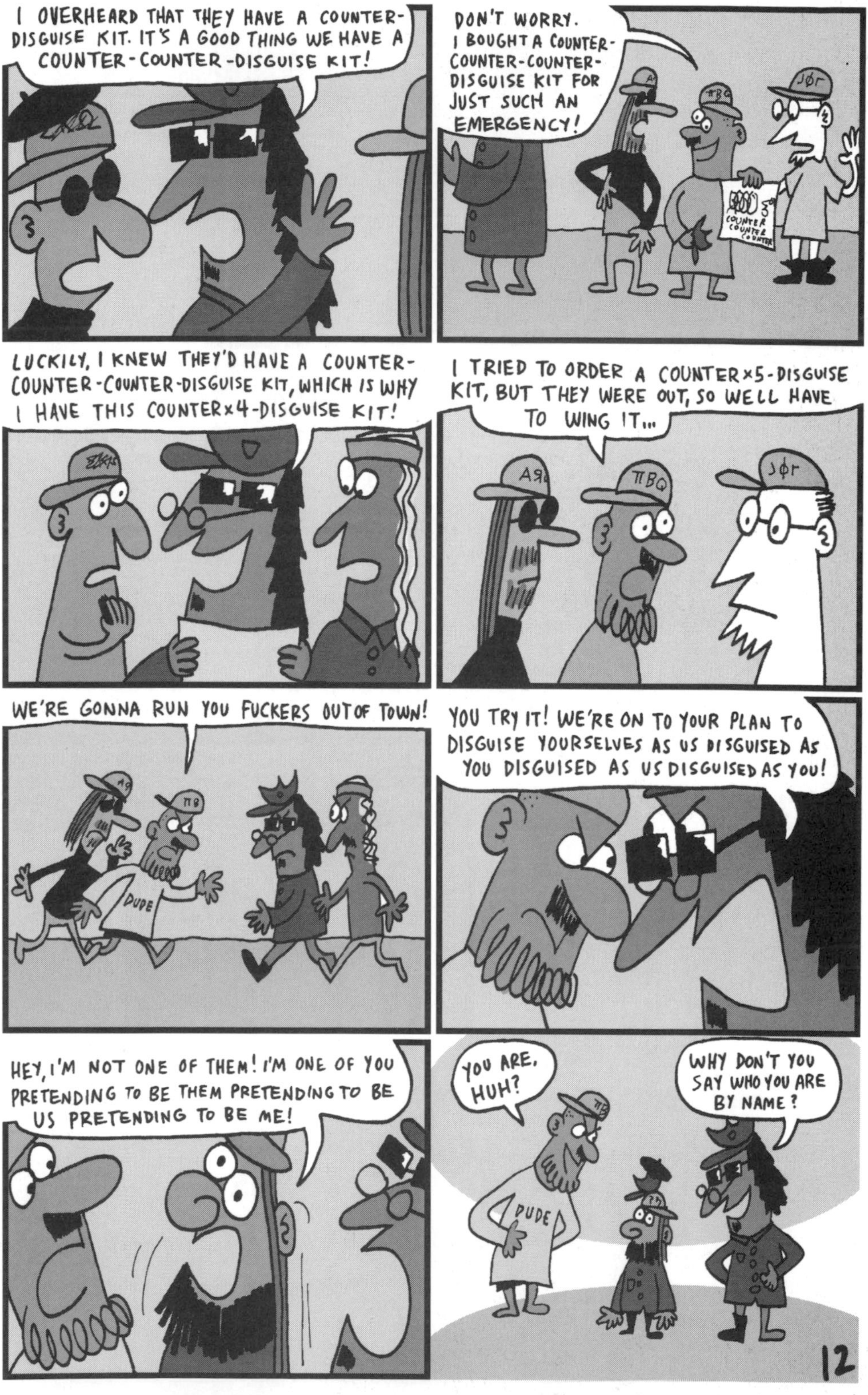
I OVERHEARD THAT THEY HAVE A COUNTER-DISGUISE KIT. IT'S A GOOD THING WE HAVE A COUNTER-COUNTER-DISGUISE KIT!
DON'T WORRY. I BOUGHT A COUNTER-COUNTER-COUNTER-DISGUISE KIT FOR JUST SUCH AN EMERGENCY!
COUNTER COUNTER COUNTER
LUCKILY, I KNEW THEY'D HAVE A COUNTER-COUNTER-COUNTER-DISGUISE KIT, WHICH IS WHY I HAVE THIS COUNTER×4-DISGUISE KIT!
I TRIED TO ORDER A COUNTER×5-DISGUISE KIT, BUT THEY WERE OUT, SO WE'LL HAVE TO WING IT...
WE'RE GONNA RUN YOU FUCKERS OUT OF TOWN!
DUDE
YOU TRY IT! WE'RE ON TO YOUR PLAN TO DISGUISE YOURSELVES AS US DISGUISED AS YOU DISGUISED AS US DISGUISED AS YOU!
HEY, I'M NOT ONE OF THEM! I'M ONE OF YOU PRETENDING TO BE THEM PRETENDING TO BE US PRETENDING TO BE ME!
YOU ARE, HUH?
WHY DON'T YOU SAY WHO YOU ARE BY NAME?
DUDE
12

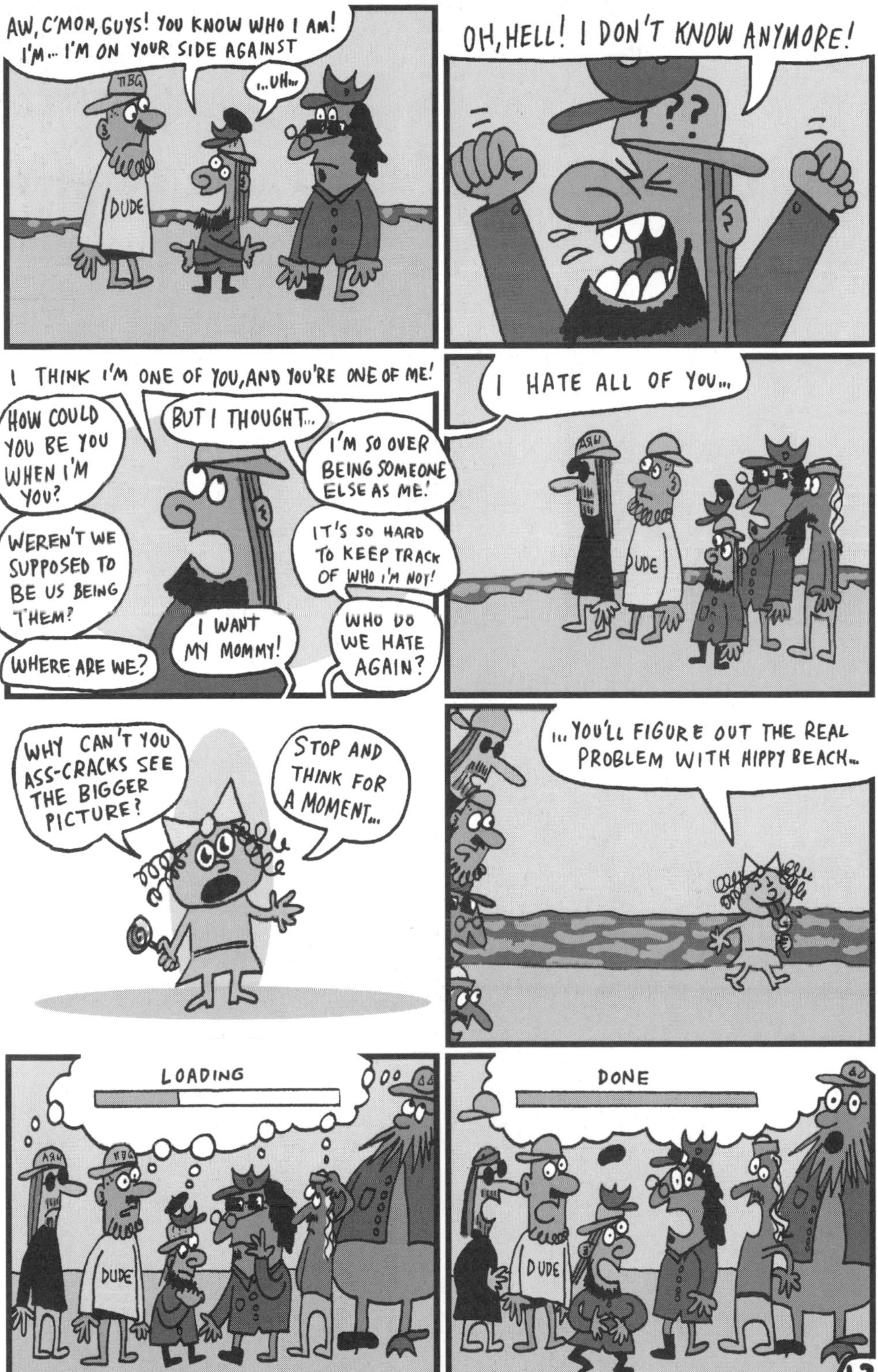

AW, C'MON, GUYS! YOU KNOW WHO I AM! I'M... I'M ON YOUR SIDE AGAINST
...UH...
TBG
DUDE
OH, HELL! I DON'T KNOW ANYMORE!
???
I THINK I'M ONE OF YOU, AND YOU'RE ONE OF ME!
HOW COULD YOU BE YOU WHEN I'M YOU?
BUT I THOUGHT...
I'M SO OVER BEING SOMEONE ELSE AS ME!
WEREN'T WE SUPPOSED TO BE US BEING THEM?
IT'S SO HARD TO KEEP TRACK OF WHO I'M NOT!
I WANT MY MOMMY!
WHO DO WE HATE AGAIN?
WHERE ARE WE?
I HATE ALL OF YOU...
DUDE
WHY CAN'T YOU ASS-CRACKS SEE THE BIGGER PICTURE?
STOP AND THINK FOR A MOMENT...
...YOU'LL FIGURE OUT THE REAL PROBLEM WITH HIPPY BEACH...
LOADING
DUDE
DONE
DUDE
13

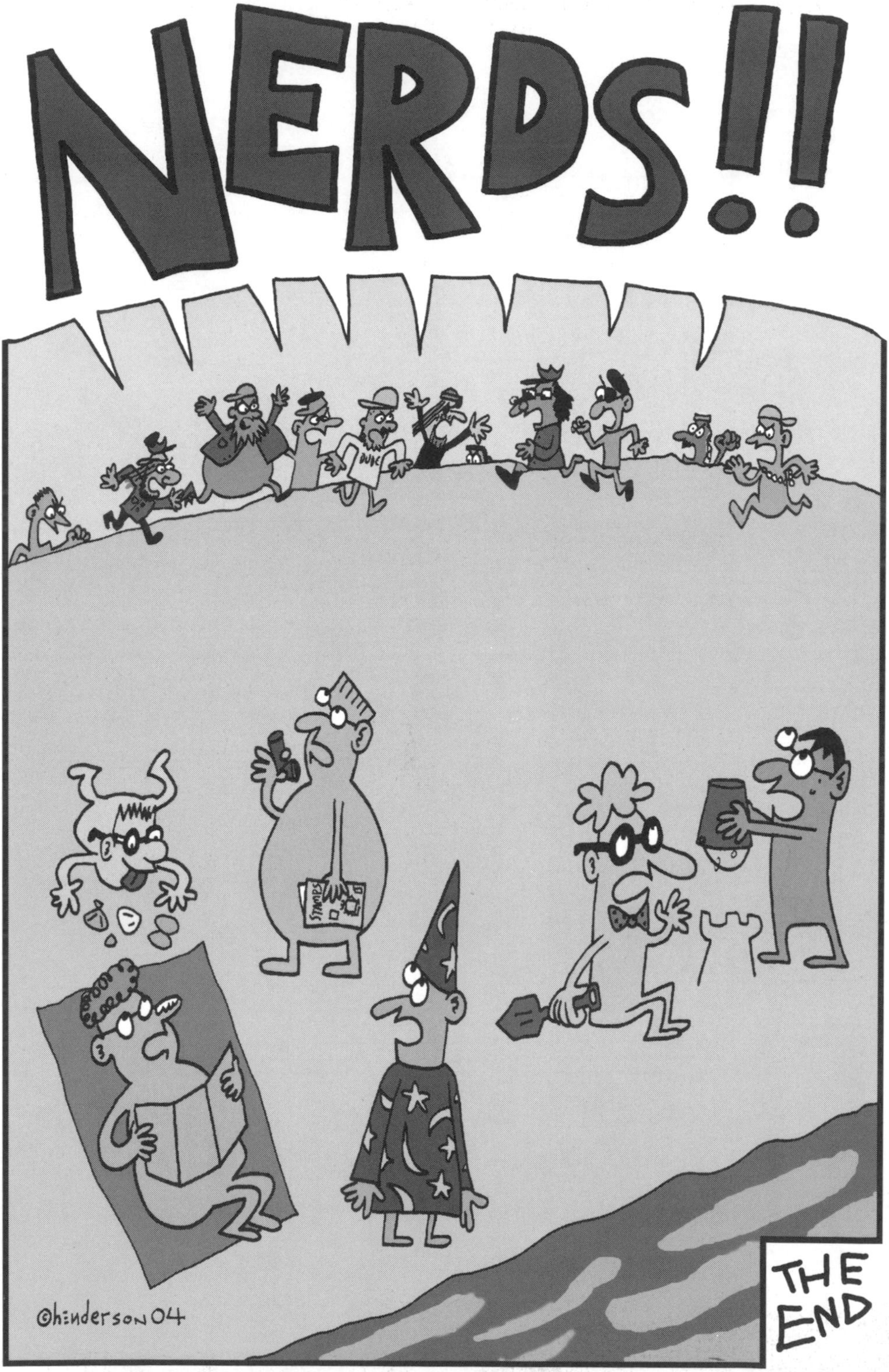
NERDS!!
DUDE
STARGATE
THE END
©h:nderson 04

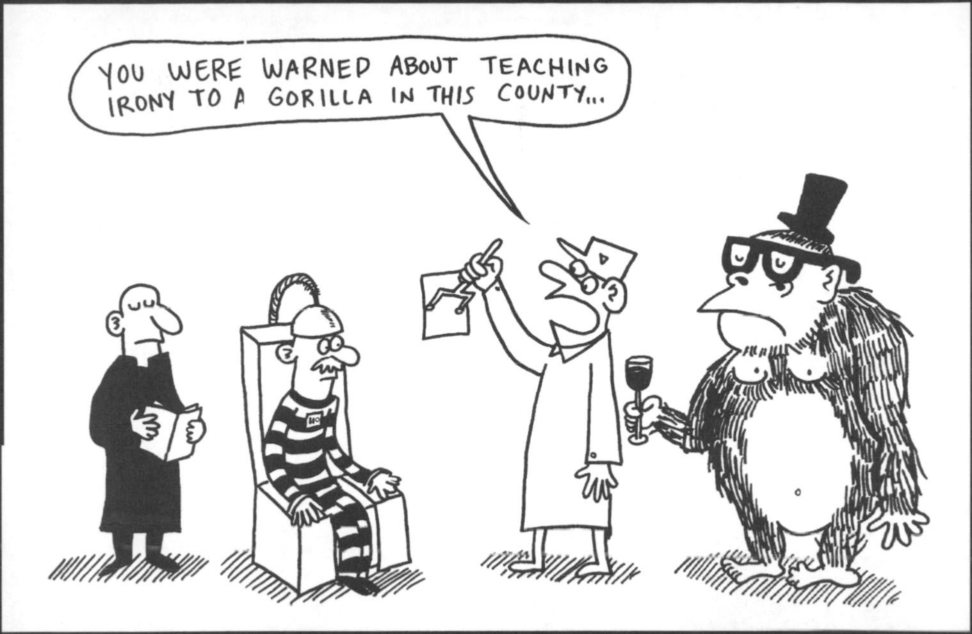
YOU WERE WARNED ABOUT TEACHING IRONY TO A GORILLA IN THIS COUNTY...

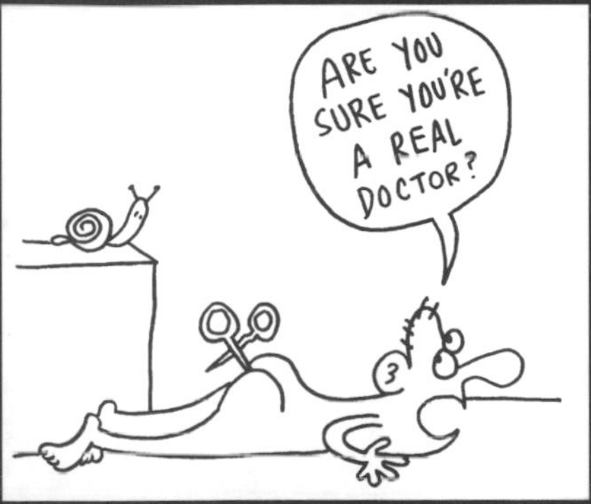
ARE YOU SURE YOU'RE A REAL DOCTOR?

WHAT DID I SAY ON PAGE 10?!

thank

you

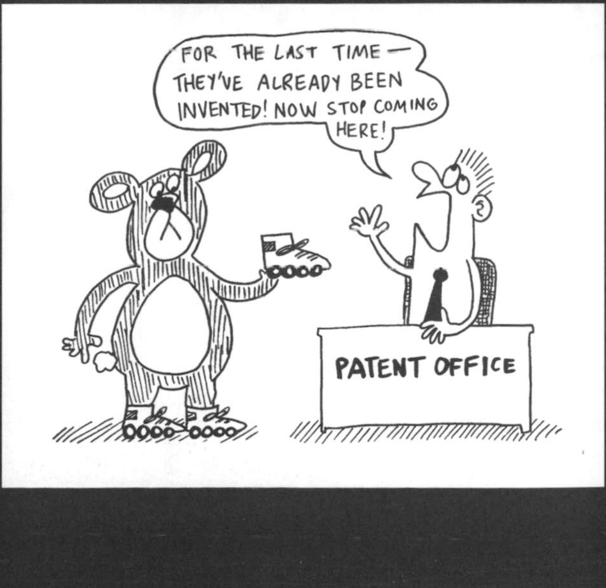
FOR THE LAST TIME — THEY'VE ALREADY BEEN INVENTED! NOW STOP COMING HERE!
PATENT OFFICE

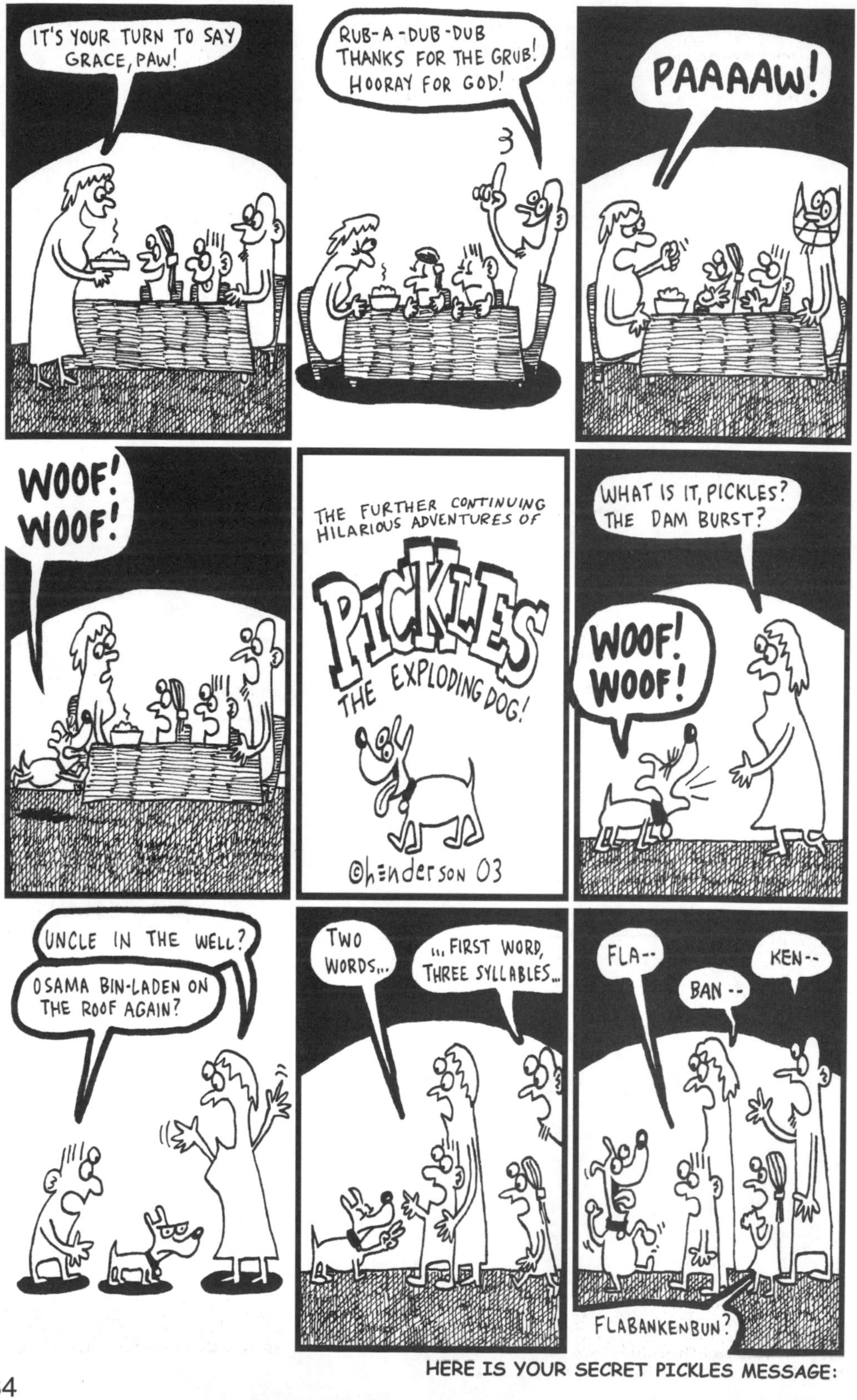
IT'S YOUR TURN TO SAY GRACE, PAW!
RUB-A-DUB-DUB THANKS FOR THE GRUB! HOORAY FOR GOD!
PAAAAW!
WOOF! WOOF!
THE FURTHER CONTINUING HILARIOUS ADVENTURES OF
PICKLES THE EXPLODING DOG!
©henderson 03
WHAT IS IT, PICKLES? THE DAM BURST?
WOOF! WOOF!
UNCLE IN THE WELL?
OSAMA BIN-LADEN ON THE ROOF AGAIN?
TWO WORDS...
... FIRST WORD, THREE SYLLABLES...
FLA--
BAN --
KEN--
FLABANKENBUN?

HERE IS YOUR SECRET PICKLES MESSAGE:

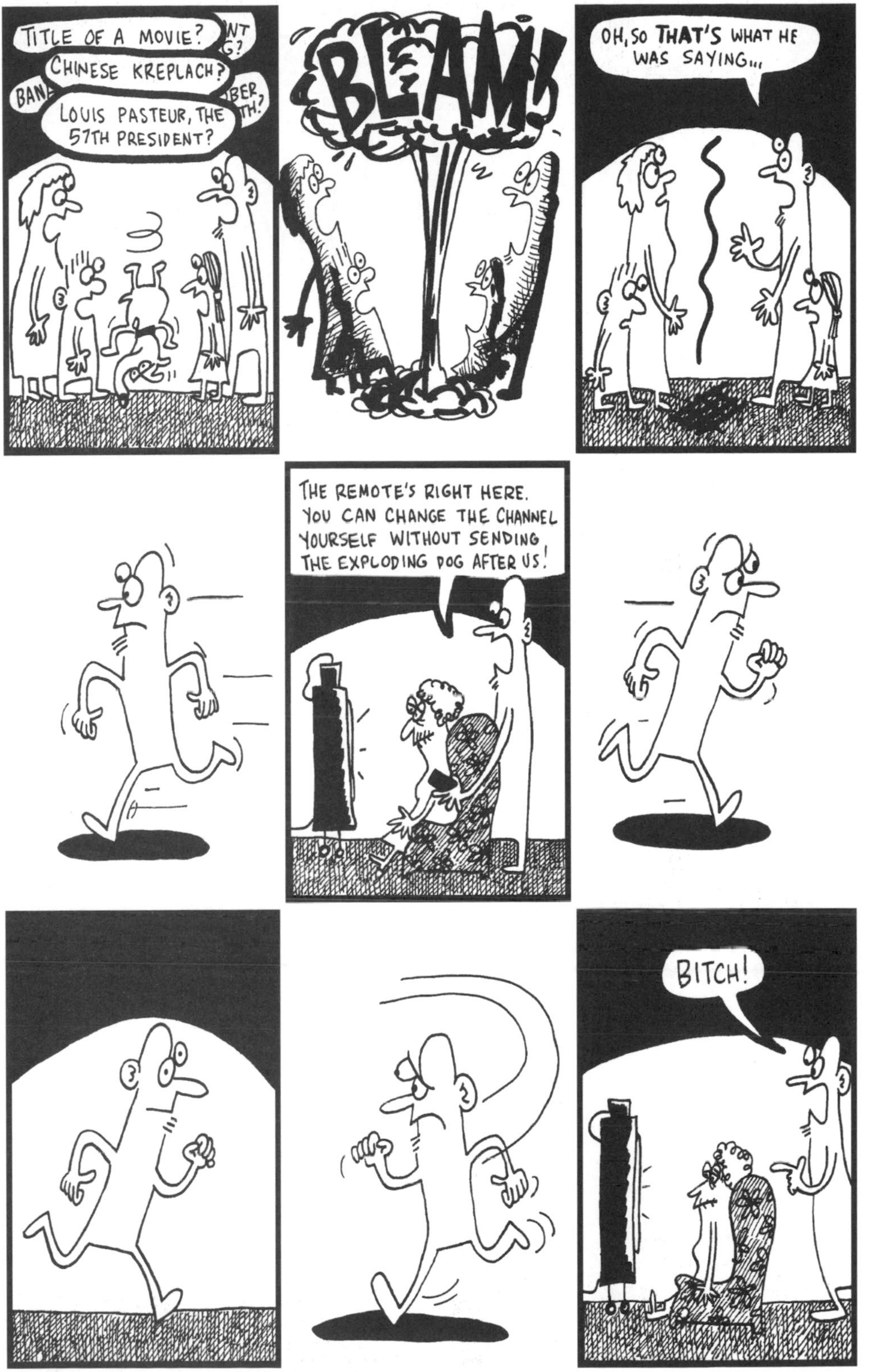
TITLE OF A MOVIE?
CHINESE KREPLACH?
LOUIS PASTEUR, THE 57TH PRESIDENT?
BLAM!
OH, SO THAT'S WHAT HE WAS SAYING...
THE REMOTE'S RIGHT HERE. YOU CAN CHANGE THE CHANNEL YOURSELF WITHOUT SENDING THE EXPLODING DOG AFTER US!
BITCH!

HP GIVL UOIT QPYJRT OM YJR SDD !

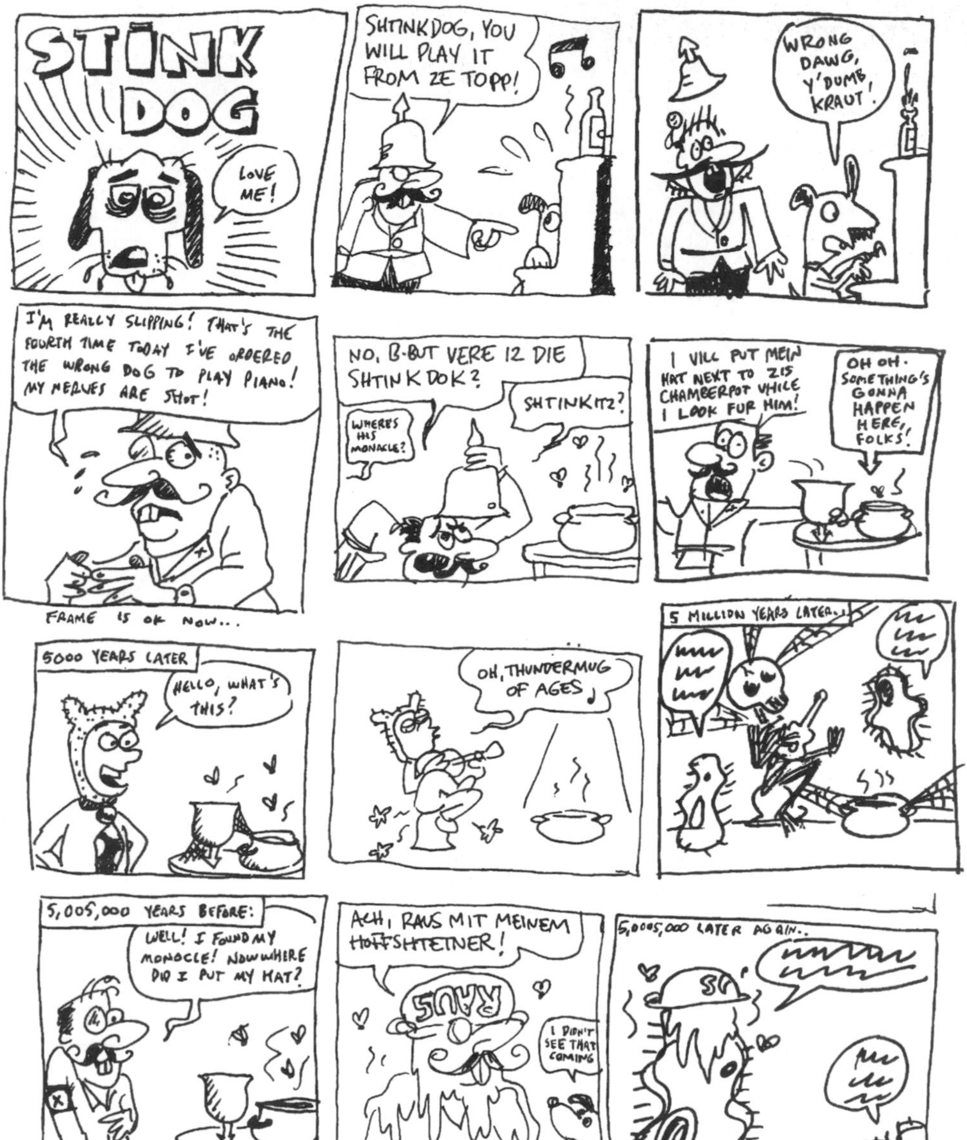
STINK DOG
LOVE ME!
SHTINKDOG, YOU WILL PLAY IT FROM ZE TOPP!
WRONG DAWG, Y'DUMB KRAUT!
I'M REALLY SLIPPING! THAT'S THE FOURTH TIME TODAY I'VE ORDERED THE WRONG DOG TO PLAY PIANO! MY NERVES ARE SHOT!
FRAME IS OK NOW...
NO, B-BUT VERE IZ DIE SHTINKDOK?
WHERE'S HIS MONACLE?
SHTINKITZ?
I VILL PUT MEIN HAT NEXT TO ZIS CHAMBERPOT VHILE I LOOK FUR HIM!
OH OH. SOMETHING'S GONNA HAPPEN HERE, FOLKS!
5000 YEARS LATER
HELLO, WHAT'S THIS?
OH, THUNDERMUG OF AGES
5 MILLION YEARS LATER..
5,005,000 YEARS BEFORE:
WELL! I FOUND MY MONOCLE! NOW WHERE DID I PUT MY HAT?
ACH, RAUS MIT MEINEM HOFFSHTEINER!
RAUS
I DIDN'T SEE THAT COMING
5,0005,000 LATER AGAIN..
the End

by Tim Maloney, Walt Holcombe, and Sam Henderson

March 9, 2002

cartoons i'm too lazy to send to

THE NEW YORKER

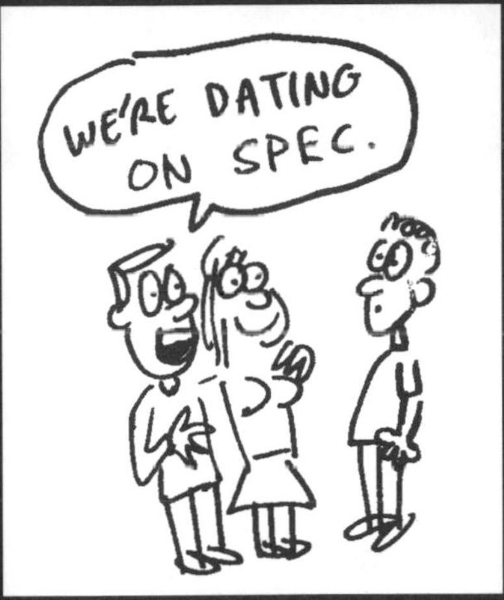
WE'RE DATING ON SPEC.

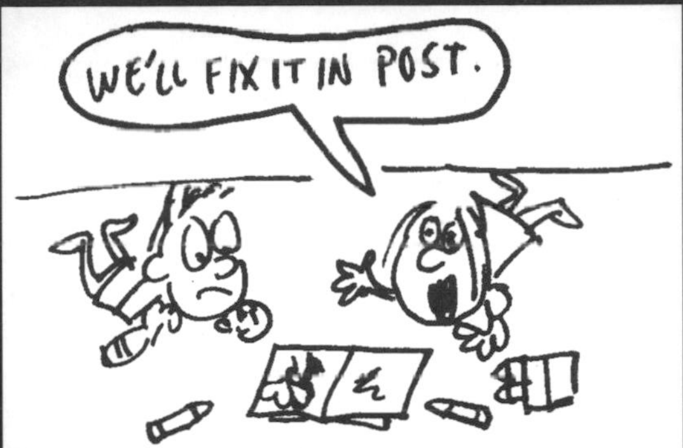
WE'LL FIX IT IN POST.

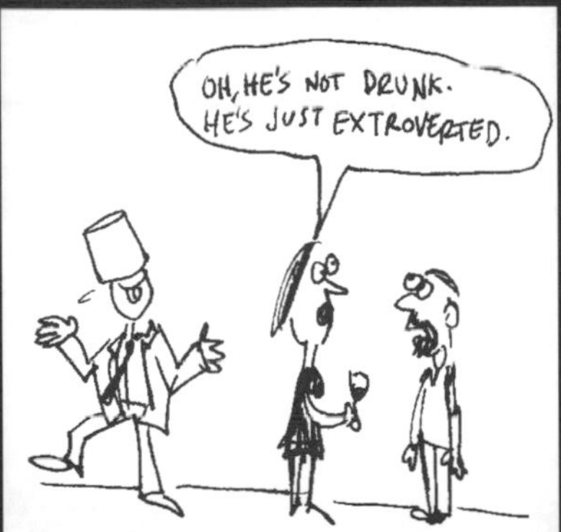
OH, HE'S NOT DRUNK. HE'S JUST EXTROVERTED.

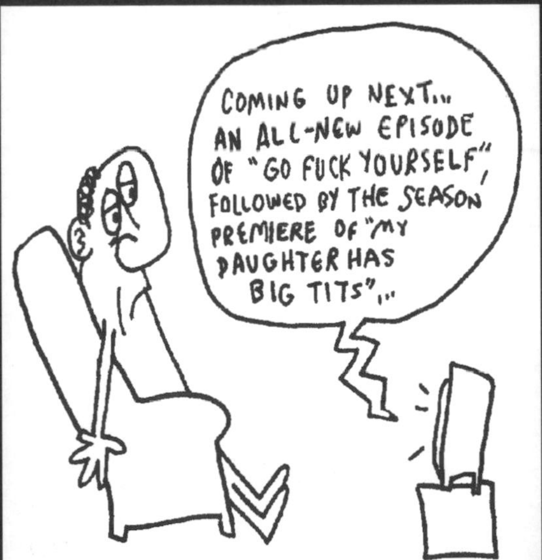
COMING UP NEXT... AN ALL-NEW EPISODE OF "GO FUCK YOURSELF", FOLLOWED BY THE SEASON PREMIERE OF "MY DAUGHTER HAS BIG TITS"...

WERE YOU ON DRUGS WHEN YOU DID THAT? *

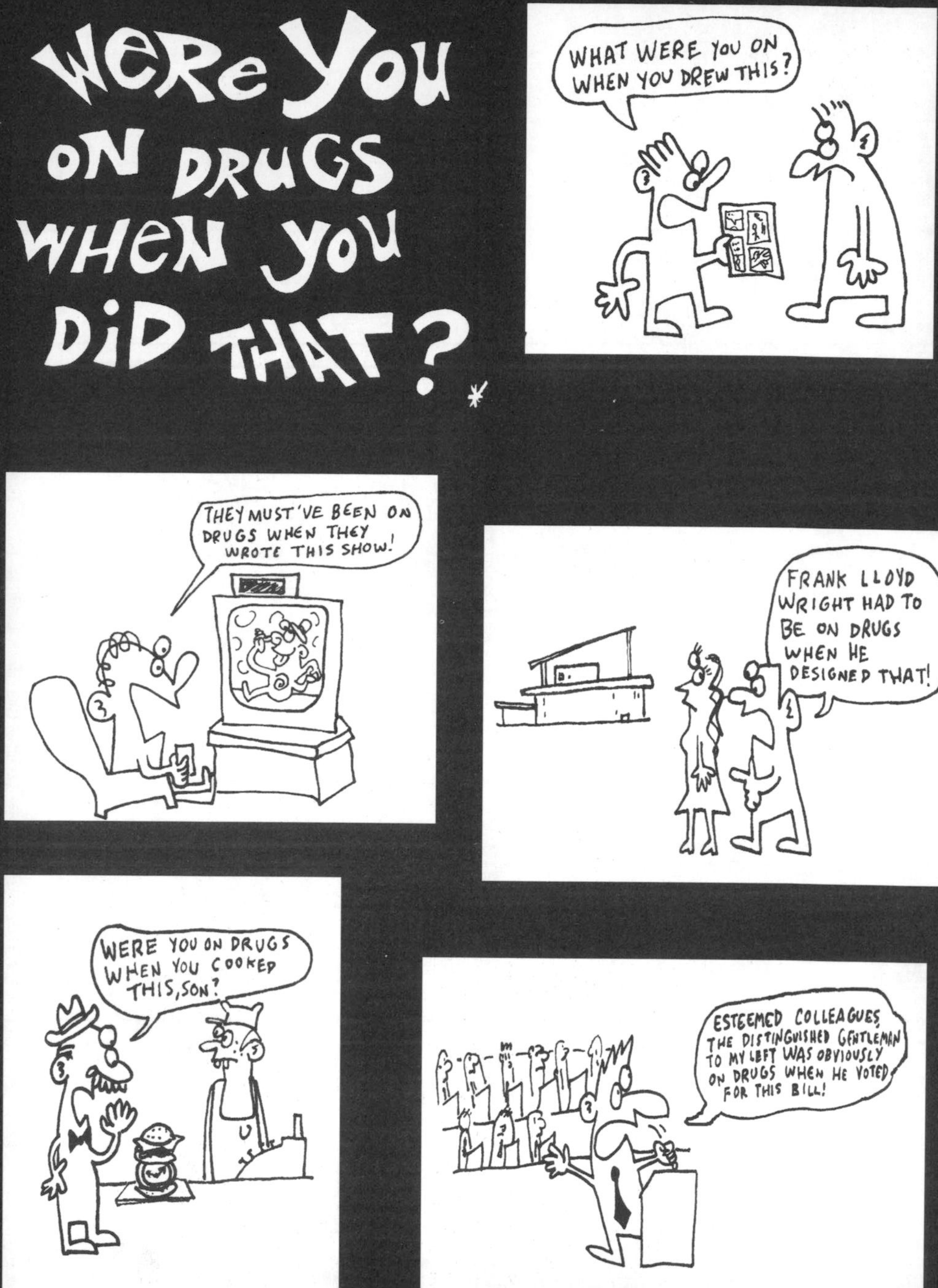

WHAT WERE YOU ON WHEN YOU DREW THIS?
THEY MUST'VE BEEN ON DRUGS WHEN THEY WROTE THIS SHOW!
FRANK LLOYD WRIGHT HAD TO BE ON DRUGS WHEN HE DESIGNED THAT!
WERE YOU ON DRUGS WHEN YOU COOKED THIS, SON?
ESTEEMED COLLEAGUES, THE DISTINGUISHED GENTLEMAN TO MY LEFT WAS OBVIOUSLY ON DRUGS WHEN HE VOTED FOR THIS BILL!

*AS A CREATIVE PERSON, I CAN VOUCH FOR THE FACT THAT THE HUMAN MIND IS INCAPABLE OF CONCEIVING IDEAS TOO OUT OF THE ORDINARY WITHOUT THE ASSISTANCE OF DANGEROUS CHEMICALS.

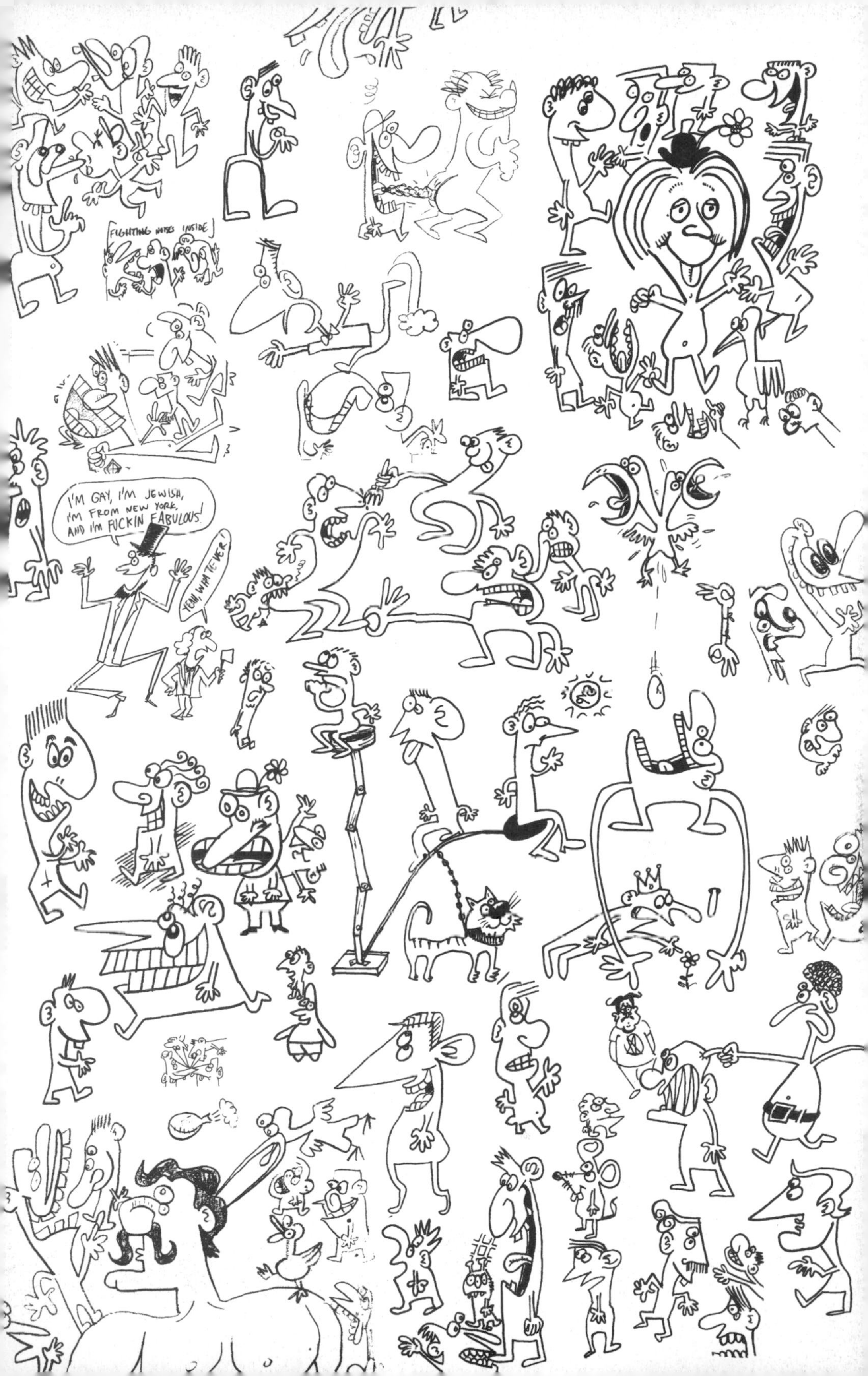
FIGHTING NOISES INSIDE!
I'M GAY, I'M JEWISH, I'M FROM NEW YORK, AND I'M FUCKIN FABULOUS!
YEAH, WHATEVER!

HERE'S WHERE I PUT THE LETTERS

Hallo Mwhistle,

Ist diese Homepage von Dir?
http://www.Mwhistles-world.com
Lädt zwar ein bischen lange, ist aber ganz hübsch geworden.

Gruss
Fabian Grela
Deutschland

* * * *

I learned a while back that while not all sociopaths are untenured comics academics, all untenured comics academics are sociopaths.

Name withheld

* * * *

I'm a friend of Mulvey's —you know him— that freaky hippie dude (in a good way) that lives next to your folks. I met them a couple weeks ago-naked in their sauna— what an icebreaker...

So anyway, I'm not exactly sure what I can do for you or why I was supposed to connect other than— hey I work in film and maybe could think of some peeps you should meet up with if you came back to NYC. I meant to give my card to your Pop.

Wendy Corn
Brooklyn, NY

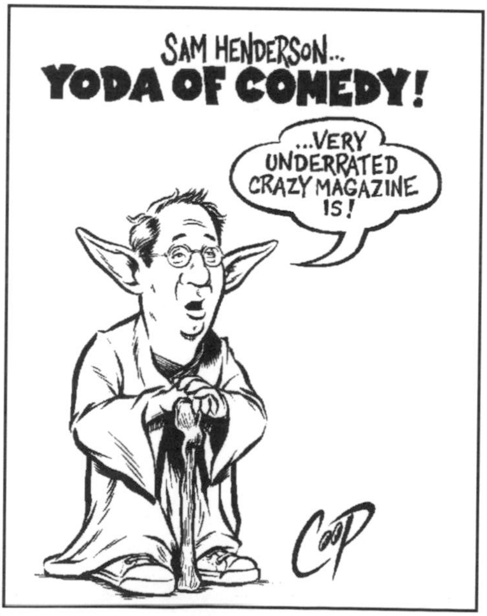
SAM HENDERSON...
YODA OF COMEDY!
...VERY UNDERRATED CRAZY MAGAZINE IS!
COOP

* * * *

I don't think I've ever written you before, but now's the time.

The best pick-up from the Alternative table was the new Magic Whistle. Boy howdy, can you make a guy snort selections from the complimentary beverage service featuring juice, soft drinks, and coffee with beer and wine for a $3 charge, cocktails at $4 out his nose.

I fear I made a public spectacle of myself on the last (St. Louis-to-Detroit) leg of my flight.

Which is just fine. I mean, it's St. Louis and Detroit, right?

Thanks for making such good comics.

Jim Ottaviani
St. Louis, MO

* * * *

Sorry to hear about you losing your gig at the Spongebob show. I've never actually seen the show, but my Mom says it's the stupidest show ever made. She actually gets mad when she sees Spongebob stuff in the store.

Mike Dixon
Chicago, IL

* * * *

There's an auto garage on my way to the subway. Yesterday there was this kitten playing in front. It was right on the shadow line, hopping in and out. The guy comes out and says to no one in particular "Ay, el gato es muy loco!"

I thought you'd appreciate that.

Mr. Richard J. O'Connor
Brooklyn, NY

* * * *

Are jokes about people or things being "on crack" still funny? I'm turning to you as the authority, since you called (and were right) the moratorium on the humor in the descriptor "from Hell". I wonder because I was watching the movie "Piñata Survival Island", which is about some kids on an island in a contest to collect as may pairs of underpants as possible, and then a piñata possessed by evil spirits starts killing them all. The piñata changes shape a few times, and

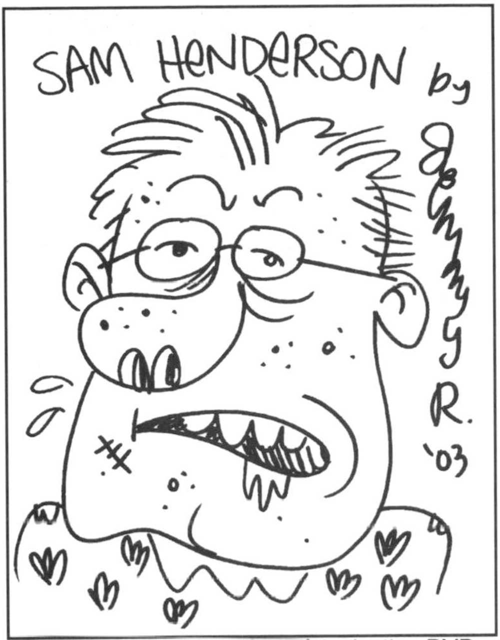
SAM HENDERSON by
'03

one of its forms is referred to in the DVD commentary from the writer/producer/director as "the Chimp on Crack" form. I did not think this was funny. But then, I wrote an email to someone and used the phrase "on crack" in that e-mail and asked if that was still funny. I was told that it was, as long as I wasn't actually on crack. But I think it might be funnier if the person/thing/piñata actually is on crack. What do you think?

Robert Newsome
Athens, GA

*

I am thinking of getting a tattoo on my inner lower lip and I wanted your input. I am torn between the following--"Fuck You", "Surly", "Go Die", and "Kill". What do YOU think? Do you remember my "fuck you" tattoo that I showed you few years back? Well it got removed. Yeah it's a LONG story.

Thanks for your input.

Nancy Langhofer
San Francisco, CA

* * * *

Jesse Fuchs introduced me to Ted Rall last night, who at one point told a story I had heard before, from your POV, about your writing a letter to the president, allegedly from someone else (can't remember who), that got you both "interviewed" by the Secret Service. It was one of those difficult social situations where someone's telling you a story in outrage that makes you want to laugh and you end up siding with the person in the story whom you're supposed to deplore. Very irresponsible of course, but very funny. Certainly the story didn't lower my opinion of you at all. Would that my own youthful indiscretions were as funny. Bravo, old man.

Tim Kreider
Charlestown, MD

* * * *

Heya Sam - for mothers' day I have decided to erase my porno video collection.

Jeff Mason
Gainesville, FL

* * * *

Henderson! Who are you to cast doubts on someone's sanity? If you're not crazy, answer me this: why would the Brube write a story about Batman masturbating when the two were on good terms and the Brube himself finds describing someone as a masturbator to be offensive? Coo-coo!

TK Enright
Internet

* * * *

Hi, Sam-

I came to the Comicon in San Diego with Jeff Mason last year and had the pleasure of hanging out with you, James Kochalka, Tim Hall and Dino for a few days... I had a blast, and I will never forget watching you in a restaurant, eating duck and drinking a piña colada, envying the hell out of you in that moment, thinking— "This guy just

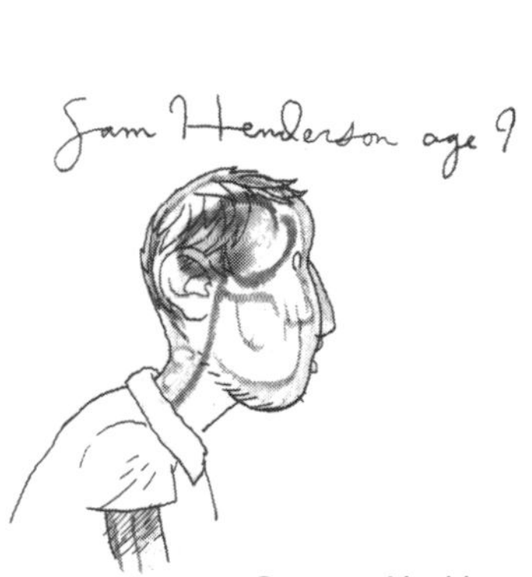
Sam Henderson age 9

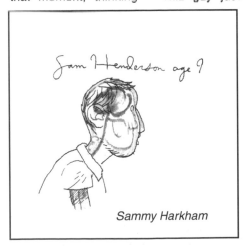

Sammy Harkham

doesn't give a fuck about fat calories, PC food choices, or any of that shit. He's my new guru."

Katie O'Donnell
Gainesville, FL

*   *   *   *

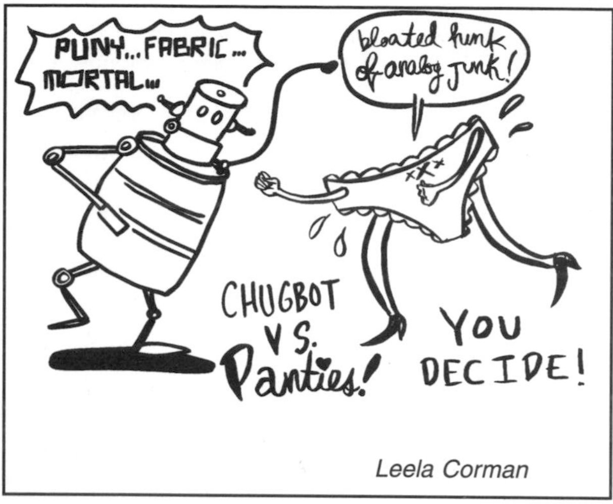
PUNY...FABRIC... MORTAL...
bloated hunk of analog junk!
CHUGBOT VS. Panties!
YOU DECIDE!

Leela Corman

derived from the old French word *materas*. But, more than likely, the mattress originated in Arabia where Al-Matrah was defined as "a place to throw out." People would lay out on large pillows on top of rugs as they traveled through the desert. The Egyptians would place these on raised pallets, the poorer ones slept on palms heaped in a corner. Later, in the 16th and 17th Centuries, these mattresses were stuffed with straw or down and placed atop ropes that criss-crossed on a frame. The expression "sleep tight" comes from the concept that one had to tighten the ropes of the bed that held the mattress. The first coil-spring construction mattress was patented in 1865. The queen-sized mattress is the most popular of our time, far surpassing the once popular twin.

Mark Curtis and Alvin
Atlanta, GA

Let's Clear The Air:
It's more your fault than mine that I was kissing you at my birthday, you dressing like you do; but as a gentleman, I should have been above such a common reaction, and for that I'm sorry. Steve says that you were giggling like a schoolgirl on the ride home, though.

Michael Daedalus Kenny
Los Angeles, CA

*   *   *   *

I have to fill out this grant application and for inspiration I turned to my 'Humor Can Be Funny' book- the one with your NEA application... and well I can't find the fucking book!!! Which means some chick ran off with it, and I am sure it's one I got nowhere with as well. I am very upset

1. where can I buy another one
2. do you have that thing in digital form and if you do could you send it to me?
3. can I be your friendster?

Benjamen Walker
Cambridge, MA

*   *   *   *

Thanks for the comics and Happy Halloween. It's funny that Spongebob should dress as a mattress. But what's more interesting is that the word mattress is

This was mailed anonymously to Eric Reynolds at Fantagraphics and postmarked here in LA. I'm impressed by the likeness of me.

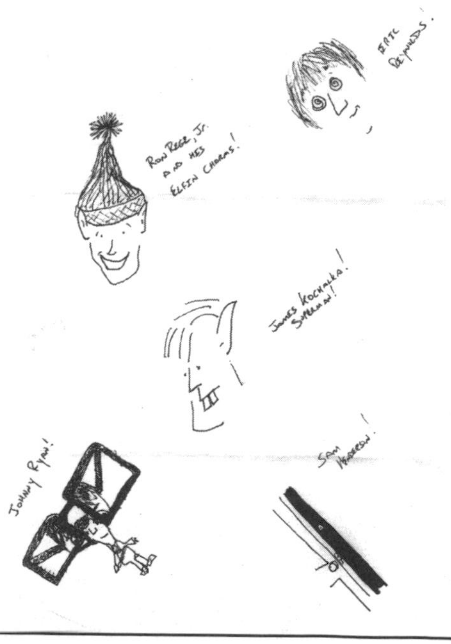
Johnny Ryan!

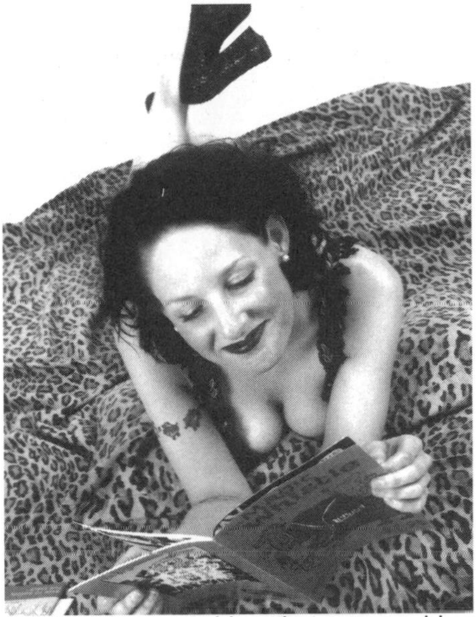

Had a character idea that you could run with... His name is Judge Fudge and he's a big fat judge that loves fudge. Everything revolves around fudge. For instance, he reprimands a criminal for stealing a car without fudge in it.

And then he questions a teenager about killing another teenager for his coat; "Was there fudge in the pockets?"

I don't know, it just seemed too silly not to do. It would kind of be like "He Aims to Please," but he likes fudge instead of sex.

Of course, he can be bribed with fudge, but that's an easy gag. And he gives out sentences like "20 years in a maximum security prison without fudge!"

Mike Rex
Queens, NY

* * * *

This is bound to surface any day now so I thought I'd come clean. Attached is a still from the tape.

Kaz
New York, NY

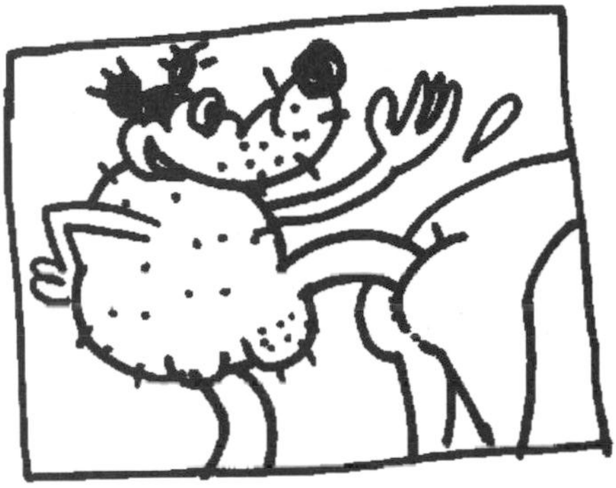

Advance readers were a bit squeamish about the ending to "The Newlyweds". While I agree these people may be weenies. I also agree that weenies are an important demographic. While Erica Merchant (top right, photo (c) Barry Tipping, used with permission) and I were co-writing the story, we were deciding on two different endings. Below is the second choice, which the aforementioned weenies can cut and paste.

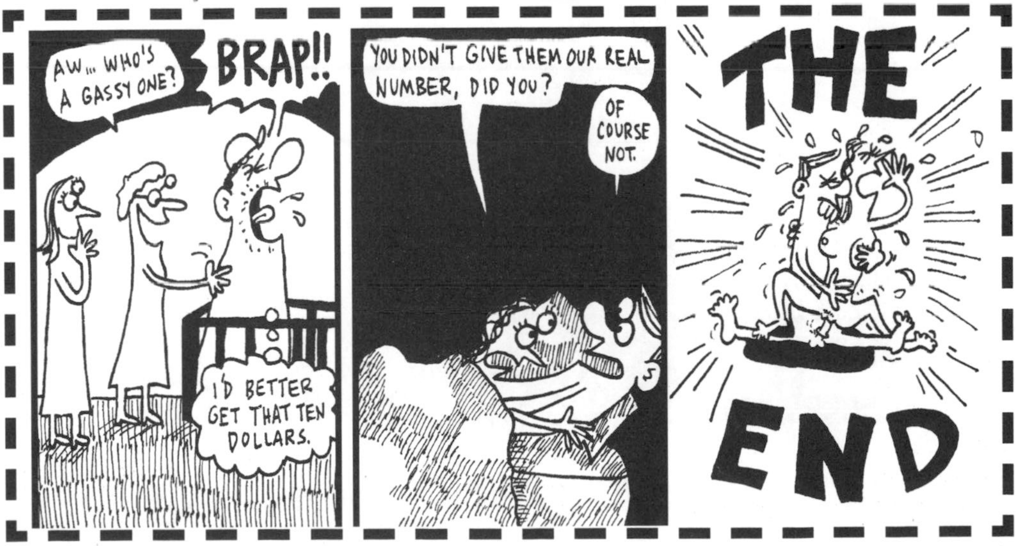
AW... WHO'S A GASSY ONE?
BRAP!!
I'D BETTER GET THAT TEN DOLLARS.
YOU DIDN'T GIVE THEM OUR REAL NUMBER, DID YOU?
OF COURSE NOT.
THE END

THE PUBLISHER WHO CARES SINCE 1993

MAGIC WHISTLE: BIGGER, LARGER AND BIGGER
(a/k/a MAGIC WHISTLE v.2 #9) is ostensibly published annually by
Alternative Comics
503 NW 37th Ave.
Gainesville, FL 32609-2204

Jeff Mason: proprietor

The author can be reached at mwhistle@aol.com.

The publisher can be reached at jmason@indyworld.com

Special thanks to Graham Annable, Ivan Brunetti, Charissa Chu, Michael Colton, Coop, Dave Cooper, Leela Corman, Jordan Crane, John Culhane, Patty DeFrank, Chris Duffy, Andrew Farago, Josh Frankel, Friendsters, Sammy Harkham, Tom Hart, Danny Hellman, John Hoffhines, Walt Holcombe, Jim Hanley's Universe, Kaz, Tom King, Michael Kupperman, Cecilia Lee, Jon Lewis, Tim Maloney, Joey Manley, Jeff Mason, Erica Merchant, Eric Millikin, Tony Millionaire, Meltdown Comics, Jeanette Moreno, Robert Newsome, Jenny Nixon, Pam Noles, Kevin Parrott, Rainbow of Hatred, Michael Rex, Eric Reynolds, David Roman, Johnny Ryan, Matthew Salata, Bill Smith, Spongebob Alumni, Jim Treacher, Ruth Waytz, Lauren Weinstein, Bobby Weiss, Steven Weissman, and Caleb Wright for their assistance-- whether technically, emotionally, financially, aesthetically, promotionally, altruistically; or any combination thereof.

First Printing: March, 2004

Printed in Canada

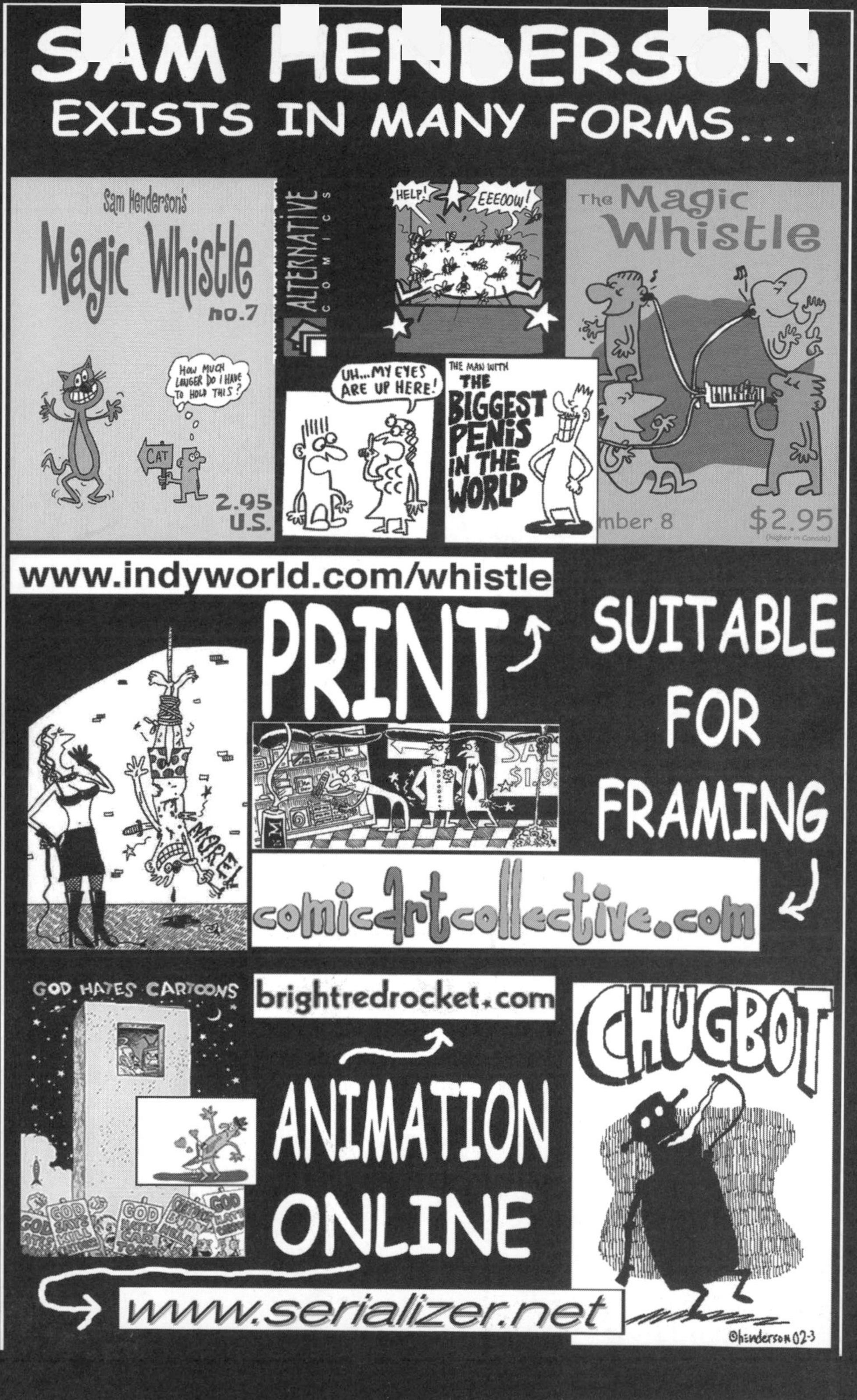
SAM HENDERSON
EXISTS IN MANY FORMS...
Sam Henderson's
Magic Whistle
no.7
HOW MUCH LONGER DO I HAVE TO HOLD THIS?
CAT
2.95 U.S.
ALTERNATIVE COMICS
HELP!
EEEOOW!
UH...MY EYES ARE UP HERE!
THE MAN WITH THE BIGGEST PENIS IN THE WORLD
The Magic Whistle
mber 8
$2.95
(higher in Canada)
www.indyworld.com/whistle
PRINT
SUITABLE FOR FRAMING
MORE!
SALE $1.99
comicartcollective.com
GOD HATES CARTOONS
brightredrocket.com
ANIMATION ONLINE
CHUGBOT
www.serializer.net
©henderson 02-3